McDougal's

HONOLULU
MYSTERIES

**Case Studies from the
Life of a Honolulu Detective**

Books by Glen Grant

Obake: Ghost Stories in Hawai'i

From the Skies of Paradise: Oahu

From the Skies of Paradise:
The Big Island of Hawaii

Hawaii The Big Island:
A Visit to a Realm of Beauty, History and Fire

Ellison Onizuka:
A Remembrance (co-author)

Memoirs of a Blue-nose Sea Captain (editor)

Kodomo no tame nii
(For the Sake of the Children):
The Japanese-American Experience in Hawaii
(co-author)

McDougal's

HONOLULU
MYSTERIES

Case Studies from the
Life of a Honolulu Detective

Edited by

GLEN GRANT

Illustrated by

ROSS YAMANAKA

MUTUAL PUBLISHING

But down these mean streets a man must go who is not himself mean, who is neither tarnished nor afraid. The detective in this kind of story must be such a man. He is the hero; he is everything. He must be a complete man and a common man and yet an unusual man. He must be, to use a rather weathered phrase, a man of honor—by instinct, by inevitability, without thought of it, and certainly without saying it. He must be the best man in his world and a good enough man for any world. I do not care much about his private life; he is neither a eunuch nor a satyr; I think he might seduce a duchess and I am quite sure he would not spoil a virgin: if he is a man of honor in one thing, he is that in all things.

He is a relatively poor man, or he would not be a detective at all. He is a common man or he could not go among common people. He has a sense of character, or he would not know his job. He will take no man's money dishonestly and no man's insolence without a due and dispassionate revenge. He is a lonely man and his pride is that you will treat him as a proud man or be very sorry you ever saw him. He talks as the man of his age talks—that is, with rude wit, a lively sense of the grotesque, a disgust for sham, and a contempt for pettiness.

The story is this man's adventure in search of a hidden truth, and it would be no adventure if it did not happen to a man fit for adventure. He has a range of awareness that startles you, but it belongs to him by right, because it belongs to the world he lives in. If there were enough like him, the world would be a very safe place to live in, without becoming too dull to be worth living in.

The Simple Art of Murder—Raymond Chandler

Design by Angela Wu-Ki
Illustrations by Ross Yamanaka

First Printing, February 1999
Second Printing, December 2002
2 3 4 5 6 7 8 9

ISBN 1-56647-229-6

Mutual Publishing
1215 Center Street, Suite 210
Honolulu, Hawaii 96816
Ph: (808) 732-1709
Fax: (808) 734-4094
e-mail: mutual@lava.net
www.mutualpublishing.com

Printed in Australia

Table of Contents

Acknowledgments

There are many people to thank for the successful publication of *Honolulu Mysteries*. To Bennett Hymer of Mutual Publishing, once again thanks is due for taking a chance on a project unlike any other presented to a local publishing house. His earnest efforts to bring variety to Honolulu readers through reprints of Hawaiian history, provocative new publications and community heritage projects has greatly elevated the art of Hawai'i publishing. Gratitude is also owed to Arnold Hiura, my writing collaborator who continually encourages me to push the acceptable range of what has been traditionally defined as "local writing." Mike Gordon of the *Honolulu Star Bulletin* deserves credit for initiating the original series of stories, "Murder, He Wrote." Bill and Ludie Striker during our years of friendship provided me with the names of local saloons, the flavor of prewar Hawai'i nightlife and the "lingo" of a bygone generation. So, too, has Ross Yamanaka provided the creative energy to re-create the feeling of the era of the hard-boiled detective without falling into simple imitation. *Honolulu Mysteries* is enhanced by Ross' artistic genius. Angela Wu-Ki's graphic design sensitively helps enhance the genre quality of the final product.

For many years the staff of the Hawai'i State Archives has endured my endless requests for information, carting back and forth the boxes of photographs which I have used to enhance all of my various walking tours. Their cooperation in reproducing the historic photographs in this collection is greatly appreciated. The Bishop Museum photography archives was also extremely helpful. Thanks are also extended to Jeannette Costa, the widow of my predecessor Benet Costa, for providing information on her husband's life as a writer.

To Honolulu TimeWalks and its guiding force, Jill Staas, a sincere *mahalo* for allowing detective McDougal's dark vision of the past to be a monthly tour offering. Through walking the lonely streets of Honolulu, especially Merchant Street, which has in the last few months reawakened in the evening with the opening of the Aloha Tower Marketplace, the specific places, people and events have taken on a reality far beyond that possible through only the written word. On that note, *mahalo* to Yi Long, the original "China," who for 50 many years walked those mean streets on the crime tour. To the thousands of Honolulu residents who have joined us on those tours to seek out the real and supernatural mysteries of our city's past, we convey our most sincere appreciation. Through these stories shared with you, I have been able to connect to a Honolulu long gone, but not forgotten.

A Note from the Editor

During the collection of these oral histories of a Honolulu detective, I made every effort to verify the truth of the stories as related by Arthur McDougal. The great majority of the businesses, hotels, buildings, saloons and scenes where these events took place have been authenticated; a few have not. I have not bothered to fully document all of these specific particulars in the story, but the reader should be warned that there are a few discrepancies in the chronology of events as narrated by McDougal. For example, the local burlesque queen "Orchid," who danced at the Blue Note club as described in "A Scratching Ghost at the Pali," was a very real person. However, her career as a striptease artist was NOT in the early 1930's. Obviously McDougal's penchant for shapely young women has clouded his memory, projecting Orchid through time to 1932. This is only one example of such jumbled sequences of truth, mingled with McDougal's own skill as a storyteller.

Many of the central events or characters in the stories seem to have a basis in fact, although I've not always verified McDougal's involvement in those events or entanglements with the historic people. At the end of each story I will try to briefly indicate those central aspects of the story that can be confirmed by either historical record or authentic folklore.

— Glen Grant

McDougal's

HONOLULU
MYSTERIES

When Merchant Street Wasn't for Sissies

W hen dusk comes to Merchant Street today, the sidewalks slowly die until only the still shadows of Honolulu's oldest ghosts cast their eerie shapes across the lonely pavement. The yellowish glow of the streetlights are a fitting adornment for this lonely sepulcher that only half a century ago teemed in the night with all variety of men and women who then comprised an island generation moving inexorably toward a great war. In those days, it was not uncommon to hear it said that "Merchant Street ain't for sissies." This narrow little avenue not only was home to the major counting houses, where all the kings' men and their accounts added up their saccharine wealth, but was where the Honolulu Police Station kept law and order and the toughest private "dicks" in the Territory hung out their shingles.

How empty this city street is tonight as you walk out of O'Toole's Pub on Nuuanu Avenue, at the head of Merchant Street. John Ferguson, O'Toole's genuinely Irish and genial innkeeper, wipes down the bar, taking care of the few remaining regulars who nurse down their last round. In the old days they used to call Nuuanu "Fid" Street, in reference to the sailor's term for "grog." While O'Toole's and Murphy's across the street keep a small portion of that tradition alive today, long gone are the saloons named the Royal, Union, Anchor, Beaver, Red Lion, Blonde, Ship and Whale, Rising Sun, White Swan or South Sea Taps, which for a century kept the reputation of Honolulu as a Port of Hell safe.

Merchant Street in the early days of horse and carriage. *(Hawai'i State Archives)*

Striding down empty Merchant Street to Bethel, on the left is the former Yokohama Species Bank building, where early Japanese immigrants nested whatever savings they could out of their meager wages from the back-breaking labor of the sugar plantations. This Japanese bank would close on December 7, 1941, when authorities turned its vault into a downtown bomb shelter and its offices into the headquarters of the provost marshal. Nearly two years later, in the early morning of October 19, 1943, Navy Lt. Peter Alport would leap up the front steps into the building with a hot .38, which he had just used to kill an MP across the street at Shore Patrol headquarters. Arrested for disorderly conduct at the Moana Hotel in Waikiki, Lt. Alport went berserk while being booked. Grabbing a .45 inside the provost marshal's office, he shot and wounded another MP before being pinned down in a barrage of gunfire a block away. War made some men do crazy things.

The Shore Patrol was located in the Honolulu Police Station, a 1931 ornate, terra cotta building, with huge Philippine mahogany doors at the *ewa-makai* corner of Merchant and Bethel Streets (it is now called the "Walter Murray Gibson" building). In 1886, an earlier police station had been built on this site, when the police were under the authority of the Marshal of the Kingdom of Hawai'i. In the early evening of January 17, 1893, the Hawaiian Kingdom took its last breath here, as Marshal Charles B. Wilson, who for hours had refused to turn over the police station to the revolutionaries, finally, at the written request of Queen Lili'uokalani, acquiesced authority to the Provisional Government.

Merchant Street with Police Station at right and Yokohama Species bank to the left.
(Hawai'i State Archives)

By 1930 the old building had fallen

The old 1888 Police Station. *(Hawai'i State Archives)*

into disrepair and was replaced by the beautiful "Hawaiian style" structure that one contemporary said looked more like a "gaily decorated hotel than an ordinary bastille." Changes came swiftly in the 1930's to law enforcement in Hawai'i. The control of the Honolulu police in 1905 came under an elected sheriff's office, which not only politicized the department, but weakened the professionalism of the police. The sensational Massie Case of 1931-32 revealed that poor organization, lack of training and sloppy investigation procedures plagued the department. Under federal scrutiny, the Honolulu Police Department was established under the supervision of a Chief of Police selected by a five-member Police Commission. This was to ensure professionalism, efficiency and honesty in Hawai'i's law enforcement agencies.

As elegant as the new police station was, the building quickly proved to be too small for the purposes of a police department protecting a quickly growing, postwar city. The police moved to the former Sears and

The "new" Police Station, 1930.
(Hawai'i State Archives)

Roebuck building on Beretania Street in 1959 as the older station was being converted into a district court. Recently a new Honolulu Police Station opened on Beretania near Alapai Street. The 1931 station was abandoned in the 1980's, the building being used for several years as a Halloween haunted house by the March of Dimes before undergoing renovation in 1987.

Sheriff Pat Gleason
(Hawai'i State Archives)

Serving on the police force in the early days was Honolulu's most famous detective, Chang Apana, renowned for his bravery and skill as a law enforcement officer. One of the most widely repeated exploits of this Chinese policeman was the arrest of a husband and wife who were suffering from *mai pake*, Hansen's disease, but refused to be exiled to the colony at Kalaupapa, Molokai. Armed "to the teeth" on the Dillingham Ranch at Mokuleia, they held off the police for hours, until Apana stealthily approached their cabin, pounced upon both of them, and disarmed them without firing a shot. In Chinatown, Chang Apana was also famous for his black whip, which would be vigorously applied to the *okole* of any disorderly person. While some historians question whether Apana was the inspiration for Earl Derr Biggers' detective hero Charlie Chan, there can be no doubt that this real-life police officer became a Honolulu legend.

There were other legends on the force whose names are less known. Crimefighters such as John Kellet, Charlie Rose, John Troche, Manuel "Hapai Mountain" Santos, Pat Gleason and Val Cederlof, all from this old station, walked the mean alleys of Hell's Half Acre,

The Bethel Police Station on King Street in 1886. *(Hawai'i State Archives)*

Blood Town, Mosquito Flats or Tin Can Alley— the rough, packed tenements on the *mauka* side of Beretania. Thanks to the colorful language of detective John Jardine, as recorded by Ed Rohrbough with the skillful editing of Bob Krauss, the stories of these police officers still live in *Detective Jardine: Crimes in Honolulu.* No slouch himself, Jardine's career on the Honolulu police force connected him to some of the biggest cases in the Territory's history, including the Boston Burglar case of 1930, the infamous Massie rape and murder trial of 1931-32, the 1936 Kaimuki murder of police Sgt. Henry A. Chillingworth, and the 1946 graft scandal involving Chief of Police William Gabrielson. A familiar figure at the corner of Hotel and Bishop Streets, Honolulu's busiest intersection, Jardine—in his familiar dark suit and fedora worn low across his eyes—would watch passersby as if they were suspects in a case. As one old-time reporter once explained, "Jardine had memorized every face on the 'wanted list' and figured that, since everyone passed Hotel and Bishop at least once a week, in time he would nab the 'wanted' man or woman."

Directly across the street from the Honolulu Police Station on the *makai*-Waikiki corner of Bethel and Merchant Streets is one of the oldest remaining commercial buildings in Honolulu—the Melchers Building, built in 1854. In 1923, a radio supply shop in this building mounted huge speakers on its roof, broadcasting the police court procedures of the investigation of graft charges against another legendary Honolulu detective, Arthur McDuffie. Crowds of Honolulu citizens who could not get into the police court located inside the station across the street, listened over the public speakers to the live KGU radio broadcast of the proceedings. According to the radio station owners, *The Honolulu Advertiser*, this was the first time in the United States that a courtroom proceeding was broadcast live! Radio history was made. The tradition of public media spectacles typified in the current O.J. Simpson murder trial had its beginnings in old Honolulu.

The interior of the 1930 Police Station. *(Hawai'i State Archives)*

Continuing a stroll down the empty evening sidewalks of Merchant Street, time seems to have stood still. The old Kamehameha V Post Office Building and the Bishop Bank building are little changed from the days in the 1880's, when this was the heart of town. Honolulu Hale, the government building, once stood on the site of the grassy park adjacent to the Post Office. The business of the Kingdom of Hawai'i was conducted here by such personages as Dr. Gerrit P. Judd and Robert C. Wylie, until the government buildings were moved away from old downtown with the construction in 1872 of Aliiolani Hale, the Judiciary Building behind the Kamehameha Statue on King Street. In 1866, Samuel "Mark Twain" Clemens visited the offices of the *Pacific Commercial Advertiser*, then located at this Merchant Street Honolulu Hale building, for the purposes of obtaining employment. At that time, the young journalist had only one published story to his name, "The Celebrated Jumping Frog of Calaveras County," and was serving as a correspondent for the *Sacramento Union*,

Detectives of the Honolulu Police, c. 1914.
(Hawai'i State Archives)

seeking, in his own words, stories with "local color." Hearing that the young writer had a reputation for laziness, editor Henry Whitney declined employment to the young Clemens, who went on to become one of the nation's most celebrated authors and humorists. Next door at the Union Saloon, entered through Cunha's Alley, another author named W. Somerset Maugham would be inspired to set his haunting tale "Honolulu" in this once-exclusive watering hole, now the site of the high-rise Pioneer Plaza building.

At the corner of Fort and Merchant Streets another small episode in the history of Honolulu took place in 1917, when the world's most famous movie star took center stage to direct traffic at this busy intersection. For several years Peter Hose, or the "Hula Cop," had become one of Honolulu's most beloved traffic control cops—guiding cars and pedestrians through this intersection. The first African-American officer in the Honolulu Police Department, Hose delighted Honolulu citizens with his graceful movements and always well-natured attitude. When Charlie Chaplin visited the islands in 1917, he donned his famous "Tramp" outfit and strolled up Fort Street from the harbor to watch the famous "Hula Cop." When Hose began to imitate Chaplin's famous walk, the delighted movie star reciprocated by taking over the "Hula Cop's" job. A huge crowd looked on in hilarity as the famous "Tramp" directed traffic at the intersection. When Peter Hose died in 1926, the people of Honolulu donated the funds for a memorial—a traffic signal located at the intersection where Emma, School, Magellan, Lusitana and Iolani Streets once all came together. "Dedicated to 'Pete Hose,'" a small plaque on its pedestal read, "Honolulu's Most Courteous Traffic Cop Who Smiled His Way into the Hearts of the People."

On the *makai* side of Merchant Street, between Fort and Bishop Streets, four old ghosts remain prominent and empty in the evening. The Judd Building, sometimes known as the Inter-Island Steamship Building, reputedly contains one of the first elevators in the islands, while next door the elegant Stangenwald Building is a reminder of the days when a law firm with this address had truly "arrived." At the former Honolulu Star-Bulletin Building—now in the evenings quiet and still—on the night of September 18, 1928, the presses ran their only midnight edition and thousands gathered in Merchant Street to get the sensational news that the young son of a *haole* executive of the Hawaiian Trust Company had been abducted that morning from exclusive Punahou School. Calling themselves the "Three Kings," the kidnappers later that night had obtained nearly $4,000 of the ransom money without turning over the boy before escaping through the detective nets at Thomas Square. The *Star-Bulletin* put out a midnight edition with the news of the kidnapping and a list of the ransom bills delivered over to the "Three Kings." Four days later, after the kidnapped victim was found dead near the Ala Wai Canal and the town was on the brink of a race riot, a lone,

Peter Hose, the "Hula Cop" directing traffic. *(Bishop Museum)*

mentally ill Japanese youth named Myles Y. Fukunaga was arrested for the crime. His confession confirmed he was the lone kidnapper/murderer who had created the ruse of the "Three Kings" so as to commit the "perfect" crime. At Oahu Prison on the morning of November 19, 1929, young Fukunaga was hanged.

In those days, the kidnapping of a *haole* boy by an Asian-American was an occasion to "pull out the stops" of law enforcement. While the police existed to maintain law and order, as in most American cities they were also there to maintain the racial status quo. Although most of the uniformed police in those days were Hawaiian, the Territory was under the tentacle control of the *haole* oligarchy that, through their economic domination of the islands, realized that they could ill afford racially motivated crimes against their small minority. The racial balances between the *haole* ruling elite and the non-*haole* majority were stretched nearly to breaking in cases such as the 1904 stabbing death of missionary scion Edward Damon at Moanalua by Puerto Rican immigrant Jose Miranda, the 1928 "Three Kings" kidnapping/murder case, and the 1931-32 alleged rape of Thalia Massie and subsequent murder of Joseph Kahahawai by her husband, Navy Lt. Thomas Massie. Through swift arrests, speedy trials and severe punishments, the law enforcement agencies made sure everyone knew their place in old Honolulu. Between 1897 and 1943, when capital punishment was abolished in Hawai'i, of the 47 men hanged at Oahu Prison, over 50 percent were Filipino; 21 percent were Japanese; 12 percent, Korean; 6 percent, Puerto Rican; and 6 percent, Hawaiian. Only one *haole* had ever been executed.

The once all-powerful *haole* oligarchy is today best symbolized by the elegant Alexander & Baldwin Building at the corner of Merchant and Bishop Streets. The massive, neoclassical Damon Building, which was home to the First Hawaiian Bank, formerly the Bishop Bank, has recently been razed, another victim of the craze for glass and steel monstrosities that has destroyed the unique architectural style of Honolulu, turning the town into a nondescript replica of an alien, continental city. While representing the days of the "Big Five" oligarchy, the Alexander & Baldwin Building, which was completed in 1929, also typifies the "Hawaiian" architecture made popular in the prewar years by C.W. Dickey and Hart Wood. Known for his high-pitched "Dickey roof," C.W. Dickey designed the Alexander & Baldwin Building with Hart Wood, who was the first architect to introduce Oriental styles into island buildings. The mixture of Chinese features in its motif and Mediterranean, Italian Renaissance and Hawaiian aspects in its design, the building is a melancholy reminder of what Honolulu could have looked like if the concept of architectural integrity had been a hallmark of city planners.

So much history is packed into four blocks along Merchant Street that it is no wonder that at nighttime the thoroughfare is densely haunted by old Honolulu ghosts. According to William Drake Westervelt, the famed folk tale collector at the turn of the century, the intersection of Alakea and Merchant Streets was rarely entered into by old Hawaiians for fear of restless ghosts called *lapu*. This intersection was the place to where those who had died without land, family or loved ones wandered, materializing in the early mornings in spirit forms, dancing and playing pranks on the foolish mortals who passed through this haunted ground.

There is no doubt that if the street is indeed haunted today, some of the spirits keeping guard would be three of Honolulu's toughest private "dicks," all of whom in 1936 had Merchant Street addresses. At 184 Merchant Street, Eddie Ross was for hire. A former police lieutenant with the Honolulu Police Department, Ross had spent 17 years on the force in the days of A.K. Vieira, Henry Silva, Charlie Rose and David Trask. As a member of the so-called Black Whip unit, he used the billy club and black snakewhip to break up the tough street-corner gangs that in the 1920's had dominated downtown. As a private operative, he established the night Patrol System, a Personal Evidence Bureau and a Domestic Investigations Department.

At 82 Merchant Street, on the third floor of the Judd or Inter-Island Steamship Building, C.W. Gibbs had established in 1924 the Honolulu International Detective Agency. In 1932, Gibbs was appointed by Governor Lawrence McCully Judd as a Special Investigator following the police department shake-up as a result of the Massie case. The Honolulu International Detective Agency ("No Case Too Small—None Too Large") specialized in "Shadowing, Tracing and Locating," with branch offices in San Francisco, Los Angeles, New York and Chicago. Advertising their motto that "Crime Does Not Pay," the agency also produced an original detective magazine with fiction and nonfiction tales of crimes set in Honolulu. The Honolulu Detective Journal under the editorship of Benet Costa was a short-lived organ of the Honolulu International Detective Agency that provided readers with hard-boiled thrillers such as "River of Death," described as "Two Men Came Down Aala Park's River—Headless!" "Night Murder in Kaimuki," the story of Sgt. Henry Chillingworth's murder in 1936, and "Horror in the Hilo Hills!"

Benet Costa was Honolulu's earliest detective genre writer, who struggled most of his life to establish himself as a national author. Born in Honolulu of Portuguese immigrant parents, Costa at the age of 15 moved to San Francisco, where he survived as a doorman at various hotels until he entered the University of California. After a few terms, he left college to travel throughout South America with a wealthy friend he had met at school. Returning to Hawai'i, he entered the real estate business for a brief time before moving to New York to pursue his dream of a writing career. In the big city, he worked on several little magazine projects and, by the age of 21, had published his first and only novel *At War with Passion*, set in the seamy side of Honolulu. Eager to establish his own magazine, he returned to Hawai'i and published the *Honolulu Detective Journal*. Friendly with all the old-time detectives, he tried to capture their lives and adventures in the "hard-boiled prose" being made popular by journals such as *The Black Mask*, which published authors such as Dashiell Hammett and Raymond Chandler. He also became friendly with a young police officer named John Burns, who was later to become the Governor of Hawai'i. Costa's stint as a detective journal editor was short-lived and he returned to New York, always hopeful that his writing career would take off. Restless and unable to stay in one place for long, he finally helped one of his brothers establish a Honolulu chemical company before passing away in 1954.

One of the "dicks" working at the Honolulu International Detective Agency in 1936 which Costa helped to popularize was former Chief of Detectives Arthur McDuffie, who had been the subject of the graft investigations broadcast over radio in 1923. A citizen of San Francisco who served in the United States Army during the Spanish-American War, McDuffie had settled in the islands as a dredge operator. Working on the fill of the harbor for Piers 8 and 15, as well as the Oahu Railway and Land Co. freight yards, he joined the Honolulu Police Force in 1905. "I was pretty dusky from all that outdoors work," he later told a reporter, "so friends of mine got me to join the Honolulu police."

Police Chief Charles F. Weeber (left) with Chang "Charlie Chan" Apana. *(Hawai'i State Archives)*

Promoted to Chief of Detectives, McDuffie was often the source of praise, as well as controversy. When a young Chinese storeowner and his wife were found butchered at their Fort Shafter store in May 1913, McDuffie busted the case wide open with a controversial confession from one of the suspects. The Chief of Detectives locked up suspect Hilao Bautista in a room with the bloody clothes of the victims and blown-up photographs of the "Bloody Store." By morning, a terrified Bautista confessed and named his two accomplices. On June 14, 1913, a triple hanging took place at Oahu Prison. For his efforts to bring in the murderers, a Chinese merchant association awarded McDuffie a special gold badge with a diamond inset which many years later was found missing from the police museum. McDuffie also "starred" in one of Hawai'i's first crime thriller films, the 1914 production *The Nation's Peril* that featured an automobile chase over the Pali.

Arthur McDuffie was also occasionally the target of police corruption charges. During the closing down of the Iwilei brothels in 1916, the Chief of Detectives was roundly criticized for having forewarned the red-light district that the raid was coming. He denied having taken graft from the operators of the houses of ill repute, defending his actions by stressing that there was no good purpose in arresting the prostitutes. During one of McDuffie's trials by fire on corruption charges, the local press vilified his abilities and integrity. To defend his honor, he had himself placed in a circus cage and pulled through the streets of Honolulu with a sign, "Am I a Detective? Ask the Advertiser."

His final fall from public grace came in 1923, when Chief of Detectives McDuffie was accused by John Austin of bribery and extortion. An embezzler out of Los Angeles, Austin had moved to Hawai'i and set up a jewelry store inside the fashionable Alexander Young

Hotel. Wanted by federal agents in California, he later claimed that he had given McDuffie a $10,000 diamond bracelet so that the Honolulu detective would conceal Austin's identity to the federal agents. Admitting that he had Austin's jewelry in his possession, McDuffie claimed that he had actually purchased the bracelet, but Austin had never sent him the invoice! Publicly ridiculed by the press and by Austin, who gave well-attended public lectures throughout town on the detective's corrupt actions, McDuffie was thoroughly investigated by a civil service commission. Though none of the charges were upheld against him, McDuffie retired as Chief of Detectives in December 1923 and joined the Honolulu International Detective Agency.

As a private operator, McDuffie still enjoyed the respect of the Honolulu Police Department, which frequently sought his assistance in their investigations. During the "Three Kings" kidnapping case of 1928, the Honolulu International Detective Agency was an active partner in the apprehension of the murderer. Indeed, during the trial of Myles Fukunaga, Arthur McDuffie was handcuffed to the defendant's wrist, escorting the young man back and forth to court from his cell. When the verdict of guilty was read in the courtroom, Fukunaga rested his head on the tall shoulders of Art McDuffie. During the Massie case three years later, McDuffie again was involved in the initial investigation that led to the arrest of the so-called "Ala Moana boys," the five local men falsely accused of having raped

Thalia Massie at the Ala Moana Animal Quarantine Station near Kewalo Basin. Active as a private investigator to his final days, Arthur McDuffie died at his 11th Avenue home in Kaimuki on October 3, 1954.

As Benet Costa wrote in his first issue of the *Honolulu Detective Journal* in March 1936, with men like Apana, Jardine, Ross, Gibbs and McDuffie all located on Merchant Street, it was "the street of a thousand thrills." With big money, stocks, newspapers, merchants, police and private detectives, Merchant Street was "no place for sissies."

Arthur McDuffie in his cage.
(Hawai'i State Archives)

The Gumshoe in the Gray Fedora

Though the thousand thrills are all long gone and the days of toughness are now only memories, several years ago I went looking for some remnant of the ghosts of Merchant Street. Ross, Gibbs and McDuffie were each buried in their graves, but I was hoping that someone would still be alive who had walked with these private "dicks" in the days when "hard-boiled" meant men, not eggs.

I had just initiated a walking tour entitled "Honolulu: The Crime Beat," which would later be expanded with another program, "The Infamous Massie Case," into the "Mystery Tours" of Honolulu TimeWalks, a private walking tour venture. While ghost hunting had been my familiar territory, I knew that crime, murder, extortion and greed always seemed to be intertwined with supernatural mysteries. Without any experience in crime-fighting—nor any desire to be even close to a crime as a victim, perpetrator or detective—I began to rummage through Honolulu's darker criminal past, stumbling upon forgotten historic crimes, little-known violent episodes in our city's past, and colorful characters who seemed to step right out of a Dashiell Hammett or Raymond Chandler novel. Seeking justification for this new personal fascination with the crime genre, I convinced myself that an historian is in essence a detective, sifting through endless archival facts, attempting to discern the truth of what happened and why.

Then I tripped upon a living, breathing relic—a ghost from old Merchant Street who had walked the mean streets, knew McDuffie well enough to call him "Mac" and could tell you tales of Chang Apana before he was celebrated as the prototype for Charlie Chan. This was a guy who not only knew where the Iwilei brothels were located, but could tell you where Cherry Malotte, a "soiled dove" from the Alaskan dance halls, had hidden a small heart tattoo on her posterior.

As is true with all of my Hawai'i supernatural investigations, I had come upon my "living crime treasure" through "sychronicity"—a "new age" concept defined as "meaningful coincidence." During the time that I was trying to research my crime tour, I had begun a project with a remarkable woman by the name of Jean Fowlds, who lived on the North Shore. Born in Hawai'i over 80 years ago, her white skin over the years had taken on an uncanny translucence, though her "baby blue eyes" had lost none of their youthful sparkle or enthusiasm for life. "Talking story" with Jean was a stroll through Hawai'i's past. One of her own private treasures was her father's diary, which he had kept when he served as a Nova Scotian sea captain before settling down in the islands as a sugar plantation mill supervisor. Jean showed me the contents of the diary, and I suggested that it be published. The result of our efforts was the small publication *Memoirs of a Blue-Nose Sea Captain*.

During the course of our work on that book, I had mentioned my interest in crime stories. Jean informed me that the remains of the old "Boys Industrial School" was still standing at the North Shore, near a convalescent home. I had long noticed this old, deserted two-story building, boarded up with miles of barbed wire at the remote north end of Oahu. It was out of place in an area better known for beach cottages and bungalows than massive concrete edifices. I had never heard any stories about the haunting of the old place, but in my imagination I figured that if any building was haunted in Hawai'i, this one seemed a prime candidate.

One afternoon, as Jean was reminiscing about how "naughty boys" used to be sent to the industrial school for smoking at school or for using bad words, her day nurse suddenly blurted out, "Oh, I know that place. Is that what it was used for? I work at the convalescent home nearby."

"Glen's doing some research on crime stories," Jean explained. "I was telling him about the reformatory."

"You ought to talk then to this old fellow that we have in the home," the nurse informed me. "He says he used to be a detective."

"Really? What's his name?"

"Art McSomething."

"What?" I said, somewhat astonished.

"McDuffie?"

"No, McDougal. Yeah, Art McDougal."

It was a very delicate matter getting to see this old man who claimed to have been a Honolulu detective in the days before the war. The privacy of each resident, I was sternly told by the convalescent home's authorities, could not be violated. They would neither confirm nor deny that a patient by the name of Arthur McDougal was residing in their retreat. The explanation that I was trying to collect true Honolulu crime stories from living participants in the cases fell entirely on deaf ears. I finally submitted a written request to the head physician to interview their elderly resident. While I waited for his response, I tried to flesh out the man who would be my link to the world of mysteries that so fascinated me.

From what I could discern from my exhaustive research at the State Archives, Art McDougal was at best a shadowy figure who had not distinguished himself either as a police officer, a detective or a private citizen. The historical record states only that he simply once existed, like many of the ordinary people of yesteryear—his name and address listed in various locations over the years in the city directory. I could find no references to him in the daily newspapers or city archives. As my curiosity concerning my "mystery man" increased, a letter from the convalescent home arrived at my office.

"After discussing your request with Mr. McDougal, he has agreed to meet with you. We believe that this oral history project may indeed have healthy benefits for him, since his health and spirits have been slipping of late."

I was totally unprepared for the Arthur McDougal whom I met on August 5, 1987. On the drive to the North Shore I had been picturing him to resemble the Dustin Hoffman character in *Little Big Man*, the lively western-theme film based on the Tom Berger novel concerning a withered-up "old Indian fighter." On his deathbed, the "ornery cuss" gives his life story to the scholarly researcher eager to know what the Old West was really like. I expected a shriveled old prune who would drool from the corners of his mouth while barking out orders to the nurses and uncontrollably spitting into the microphone during the taped interview. If he really knew and worked with Chang Apana, John Jardine and the Honolulu International Detective Agency operatives, then he must have been at least 90 years old.

The nurse who escorted me down the hall to his room spoke affectionately of "Arthur."

"He's really a sweetheart. Tough as nails on the outside, but inside he's a very kind man. And he's real sharp."

"How old is he? I couldn't figure that out from any of the records."

"He says he's 105 years old. By the way he looks, he seems more like 80."

"Does he have any family?"

She shook her head.

"If he does, he doesn't talk about it. He's been here at the home since I came in 1970. In all that time he's had no visitors. You're the first."

She knocked lightly on the door, opened it a crack and called in.

"Arthur, your visitor's here."

He sat up on his bed when I entered the room and stared me down like I had just asked his daughter out on a date. It was a hard stare that I knew he had used a thousand times to break a man down. I told myself not to flinch, but I was certain he noticed me swallow my heart.

"Are you Grant?"

His voice was as strong as his stare, with that Midwest *haole* twang that men like McDougal seemed born with and never lose no matter how long they live among islanders with their lyrical local dialect singsong. He probably could understand perfectly the old-fashioned pidgin that in his youth was so prevalent, but never once did I ever hear him dip into the lingo which in his day probably set him apart from non-*haole* locals.

The nurse was right. The old fellow looked much younger than 105 years old. His frame, probably once large and stocky, had been greatly reduced, but he was far from the shriveled *Little Big Man* character I had anticipated. His skin was as tight as a drum on his bones, his hands large and still muscular. That fist could crush my soft, unblistered hands like a steel vise and I wisely skipped shaking hands. The hefty growth of snow-white hair on his scalp was closely trimmed at the side and combed straight back into place with a light dose of witch hazel that I could smell from across the room. For my visit he had even spruced himself up, slipping a jacket over his aloha print pajama top. An old, faded gray fedora was pulled down over his brow.

"I said, are you Grant? What's wrong with you, deaf?"

"No, I hear fine, sir. Yes, I'm Grant. It's a pleasure to meet you, Mr. McDougal."

"Is it? Well, let's get started. Did you bring your recording machine?"

"Arthur," the nurse chimed in, "you forgot your carnation."

"I didn't forget it. I just thought I'd let you have the honors this morning."

She walked over to a bunch of red carnations in a vase on his desk, selected the biggest and clipped it a few inches on its stalk.

"In his heyday," she explained to me, "he was known as the Gumshoe in the Gray Fedora with the Red Carnation in His Lapel, isn't that true, Arthur?"

As she placed the flower in the lapel of his jacket, a small, wry smile came across his face.

"If you say so, honey." His language was peppered with all the racist and sexist remarks that seemed endemic to his generation. While she bent over fixing the flower in place, he looked my way and gave me a knowing wink. Which B-movie was this scene from? I thought. The flower in the lapel seemed a bit on the foppish side for a tough guy detective out of a hard-boiled novel.

"She's a sweet kid," he intimated to me as the nurse left the room. "I told her that about the fedora and carnation to make me seem more romantic, like Alan Ladd or Humphrey Bogart. So don't get any wrong ideas about who or what I am. Turn the damn machine on, and let's get started. It's my story you want, right?"

I had come with a long list of questions that now seemed totally irrelevant. As far as he was concerned, I hadn't come to interview him—I was there simply to record his life story, as he wanted to tell it. His small, private quarters were filled with photographs and bric-a-brac of his life—first as a homicide detective with the Honolulu Police Department and then as an operative for a firm he called the International Detective Agency. He spoke for hours that day, transporting me back to a Honolulu that had long ago met the bulldozer. All the ghosts of Merchant Street were resurrected, the gumshoes and grifters, the "soft drink parlors" and opium dens, crooked cops and mysterious damsels, bloody shoot-outs and sentimental romances. An old portable phonograph played his last few remaining 75 rpm records such as a scratchy rendition of the Tommy Dorsey trademark, "I'm Getting Sentimental Over You," and Glen Miller's "A String of Pearls." Whenever a record finished, he'd stop the interview and ask me to turn it over or put on a new one. By the end of the first day I had 10 solid hours of interview on tape. A week later, a metal file cabinet in my office was filling with recordings I now collectively labeled "The McDougal Tapes."

Although I knew that the stories were invaluable for my Honolulu Crime Beat walking tour, I wasn't sure of their historical accuracy. McDougal seemed to know everything that was going on in town between the day he joined the police force in 1907 and the day he retired as a private investigator in 1959—the same day that the police station was moved to Beretania Street. Yet, when I researched the newspaper files, the places, people and events he mentioned in his interviews seemed all mixed up. There were real people in his stories doing things that, according to their biographers, they never did. When I pointed some of these inconsistencies out, he laughed and reminded me how the newspapers always got things wrong.

"Biographies?" he said. "They are the pack of lies we want other people to remember us by."

There was also a startling similarity in McDougal's life to that of Arthur McDuffie, a man whom he rarely mentioned in his own "talk story." Although in their youth McDuffie had been a harness-maker from San Francisco and McDougal a Silver Springs, Nevada, silverlode miner, both of them had been Spanish-American War veterans. They had even served together on Corregidor as Army nurses after Admiral Dewey captured Manila. In fact, the one full reminiscence that McDougal shared about McDuffie was how the latter had almost died on Corregidor. After contracting typhoid fever, McDuffie had dropped from his usual 270 pounds (he had been a very big man) to 140 pounds.

"When he got better, the Army doctor and I took him to a warehouse at Corregidor, where the only remaining wooden coffin in the area was stored. 'We were saving this one for you, McDuffie,' the doctor said. He used to get a big kick from telling that story over and over again."

After the war and the annexation of Hawai'i, McDuffie returned to San Francisco, where, according to McDougal, "he ate everything in sight. When he came back to the islands in '05 he must of weighed nearly 300 pounds. I was no panty-waist either, tipping the scales at 225."

McDougal took a liking to the islands during a brief visit on his way to the Philippines and decided after the war to make a go of it in Honolulu. "Silver mining was back-breaking labor that never got me rich, so I decided to try my hand at insurance." For a few years he sold life insurance, but the life of a salesman was too tame. "Plus I didn't like begging people to buy something they wouldn't really need until after they were dead." A saloon buddy of his, John Kellet, had just joined the police force and invited McDougal to do the same. "I never regretted that decision," he told me over 80 years later.

"It must at first have seemed pretty slow, didn't it?" I naively asked. "After all, how much crime could a small town like Honolulu have?"

"Are you kidding me?" he bellowed. "This town was created with crime in mind. Hell, the Hawaiians had it stolen from them, didn't they? The *haole* came in here, took over everything and even changed the name to Honolulu. It was something else before, right? You're the historian; look it up."

"The Hawaiian name for the village was Kou," I explained to the old detective, nodding in agreement to his interpretation of the town's past. "Tradition says that a Captain William Brown named it Honolulu or 'Fair Haven' in 1794, when his ship the *Jackal* sailed into the deep-draft harbor."

"They were all jackals, Grant. Look at your history and you'll see that when the *haole* came into these islands, it was for rum, whoring, brawling and stealing. First they took the women, giving them diseases and then they took the sandalwood and then the whales. The missionaries moved in to set the moral compass right, but what can you expect of hypocrites? In the long run, they only ended up adding to the greed."

His vision of the past, I gently suggested, seemed a bit overly cynical.

"Cynics is what you academic boys become. On the street, we call that attitude realistic. Listen, son, there was enough murder, larceny, back-stabbing and greed in Honolulu in those days to keep any big city police force busy. All I'm saying is, don't be fooled by anyone who tells you that 'the good old days' were any less or more evil than they are today.

"That goes for the good men and women, too," he added, his voice maybe a bit melancholy. "I knew many of them. They came in all shapes and colors. You could trust them with your life."

"Was McDuffie one of the 'good guys'? There was talk that he was, well, dirty."

A plastic bottle from which he was sucking his daily shot of liquid vitamins came suddenly hurling towards me, a guided missile that struck me almost directly between the eyes.

"You son of a bitch. You never say that about Mac, you hear me? That bastard Austin knocked down a giant with those false allegations. Hell, we all used to buy things in town without using cash. In those days when you bought a suit, the clothing store owner sent the invoice to your office and you paid it in your own good time. People trusted one another in those days. I don't think I ever paid anything up front in cash, not my clothes, cars, jewelry, furniture or utility bills. Mac said that Austin never sent him the invoice, and I believe him. He was set up to take a fall."

I was thanking my blessings that the convalescent home used plastic, not glass, as I went ahead and pushed the envelope. The only thing near at hand was his red carnation.

"So how did you fall from grace? I heard somebody set you up with a sailboat. Did they forget to give you the bill, too?" Maybe I sounded a bit sarcastic, but the McDuffie defense sounded like my interviewee was expecting me to swallow the whole hook, line and sinker.

I had never stared down the barrel of a Colt .45 before, which helped to explain why I messed my pants so freely. He whipped it out from under his pillow, where, I later learned, he regularly concealed his "rod." After his partner Naoaki Odachi had been killed in 1926, a murder he had never solved, McDougal never went to sleep without his own personal protection. He explained to me once how an old Hawaiian had told him years ago how the native people used to practice something called *unihipili*—keeping the bones of a loved one in their pillow for comfort. The Colt was McDougal's *unihipili* and it was leveled with its sights on my gut.

"Go to hell, mister. If you ever step into this room again, I commit my first homicide."

It took me 10 letters, two weeks and a box of macadamia chocolates for the nurse who acted as my agent to get me back into his good graces. I never mentioned the sailing boat again, but he volunteered once that he hated the ocean. "Sailing makes me seasick," he offhandedly mentioned. If he had taken a bribe for any purpose, I'll never know. I certainly never asked him that question again. All he would say was that, like McDuffie and Sheriff Charlie Rose a few years later, he left the force in 1919 under a cloud of suspicion that was never cleared.

While McDuffie joined the Honolulu International Detective Agency, according to McDougal he was hired by the International Detective Agency after his resignation from the police department. "Was this the same firm?" I often asked him during the interviews.

"Yes and no," he answered. "Mac and I often worked together. I knew Gibbs. Enough said about that."

Maybe there had been a falling out between the two private gumshoes. Although he never spoke ill of McDuffie, McDougal rarely mentioned his name unless I brought it up. In all of his cases, he never made one reference to working with or against the other famous detective. When McDuffie died in 1954, he once confessed, he toasted him with a single shot of *okolehao*. And that was that.

On another occasion, I asked him whatever happened to China, his secretary at the agency who seemed to enter into every one of his stories.

"Was China her real name?" I once queried.

"No, I could never say her real name, so I gave her the nickname 'China.'" In his typical, racially demeaning manner, he categorized her as he had done most everyone else in his life. In fact, from his varying and sometimes contradictory descriptions of her, there seemed to have been more than one China. Whether she was one person or several, the implication was that China was more than simply a secretary to McDougal.

When he spoke of her, his voice reflected true affection. Once when I asked if she had passed away, he answered that he imagined she had, but they had lost contact with one another when he moved into the home. It may have been the poor lighting, but I swear that I saw his eyes glisten, fighting back a floodgate of tears. The nurse was right. His tough veneer shielded a heart sometimes on the edge of breaking.

In September 1988, the first opportunity to publish the "McDougal Tapes," whether they be fiction or nonfiction, came when Mike Gordon, a reporter with the *Honolulu Star-Bulletin*, asked if I would write a mystery story for the Halloween edition of the Sunday paper. At that time the *Star-Bulletin* staff was responsible for the Sunday features section and Mike wanted to try something different. He had taken one of my American Studies classes at the University of Hawai'i in 1981, when I dressed up in historical costumes and re-created the lives of people from history. He had heard that I was now portraying a detective in the crime beat tour and asked if I would be willing to contribute the first part of a mystery story to the newspaper. The readership would be invited to write the ending of the story, with the best rendition winning a special prize.

"I don't write mystery stories, Mike," I said, declining the invitation.

"Come on, Glen, where do you get all those stories for the tour?"

"I'm not sure that my source will want to go public," I explained. At Mike's insistence, I broached the subject with McDougal, whose face lighted up like a Chinese firecracker at New Year's.

"Hell, yes!" he shot back at me. "I'd love to be able to tell my side of the story."

Thus was born the series, "Murder, He Wrote," a plagiarism freely borrowed by Mike Gordon from the television series starring Angela Lansbury. The reaction of the public to the tale was impressive. Nearly 100 new mystery authors tried to write the conclusion, some giving twists and turns even better than McDougal's more truthful ending. Mike asked for more stories to be delivered to the public in the same fashion—a Sunday edition setup and a Monday edition conclusion.

"Leave the solution open at the conclusion of the first installment," Mike explained, "so that the public can guess 'whodunit' before Monday." Several such stories were published commencing in January 1989, with a few letters to the editor thanking the newspaper for providing such an entertaining family project. The public was invited to try their own hand one more time in October 1989, when Mike had moved to the mainland and Betty Shimabukuro had the unenviable job of getting me to meet my deadlines. She and Mike never truly understood how ornery McDougal could be when sharing one of his cases. If he didn't feel like talking, then he'd clam up for a week. Then I'd get a call at 2 o'clock in the morning.

"Grant, get the hell out here. I remember the ending."

Then the criticisms started coming in as a reaction to the stories. The majority of readers no doubt enjoyed them as fictional tales of old Honolulu (and who knew their validity?), but one critic went so far as to write the provost of the community college that I was working for, demanding my instant termination of employment! Not only was the writing extremely poor for a college instructor, but it was filled with racial and sexist stereotypes demeaning to every race in Hawai'i. We had set race relations back 50 years, he ranted.

I showed the letter to McDougal, and he nearly slipped a gut laughing.

"What a horse's ass," he reassured me. "What does he mean, ethnic stereotypes?"

"The stories have one-dimensional characters, Mac," I explained to him. "They seem like caricatures—you know, cardboard cutouts."

"Sure, that's true, Grant. In those days, in public we were all like cardboard cutouts. Hell, how do you think I got this tough-guy exterior? That fellow doesn't understand how things worked back then. Every one of us had a reputation in this town. Everyone knew everyone else. The Chinese acted just like you would expect them to act, just like the Japanese did. And you acted back towards them exactly as they expected a *haole* to act. If you didn't act that way, then, hell, you couldn't trust them."

"You never got to know the real person, then. Take the case of China. You never even knew her real name."

"That didn't mean I ever loved her less. Sure we stuck to our own kind and sometimes treated each other pretty bad in this town. We made fun of each other to each other's faces and behind our backs. I never knew what my Japanese partner's life was like inside his home. We didn't invite each other into our private lives. But you sure in the hell trusted them, no matter what their race, when they were at your back with pistols blazing as you busted up some bootlegging racket in Kalihi.

"As far as the criminals were concerned, they came in all colors, too. So, sure, we were prejudiced back then. We spread it around equally to everybody, but put it aside with our friends when we needed to work together. I guess that's what made the islands different than other towns I visited like L.A., Chi or Frisco."

"How was that?" I asked.

"There, if you didn't like, let's say, the Chinese, you could ignore them. Here, you never had that luxury. We lived too close to one another, getting into each other's face all the time. You either learned to get along, or in some cases ended up dead. Especially in my line of business. Now don't tell me it's any different today—only maybe a little worse. These days people don't need each other like they did 50 years ago."

In addition to the criticism of his ethnic slurs, there was additional comments, I told McDougal, complaining that the writing was very poor.

"'Hackneyed,' one critic wrote," I said.

"Well, that was your department, wasn't it? So take the blame, Grant. Only, remember, I wasn't trying to win points as a writer." His voice always rose when he began to philosophize.

"Who do those writers write for anyway, but the handful of people who tell them they're great writers? Grant, when you have a good story to tell, you tell it to the people who count the most to you. You ain't writing these stories for a bunch of folks who are going to criticize you for not being a Hemingway or Fitzgerald, are you? These stories are for regular folks like you and me who want to know what happened. The mysteries in old Honolulu are damn good stories. In fact, if I had my way, I'd sell these books in Piggly-Wiggly. That's where your audience is."

I informed my literary collaborator that long ago I had given up trying to write a novel to be approved by the cultural guardians of good taste. These were his stories, and I wanted to tell them as cleanly and directly as possible. Also, I reminded him, Piggly-Wiggly shut their doors in Hawai'i years ago.

"Is that true?" he muttered. "It was a damn good store."

The "Murder, He Wrote" series ended at the close of 1989, when I went to live in Japan for six months. Before I left, I had mentioned to McDougal that I was considering compiling all of the stories into one volume, creating an original Honolulu-based detective character. During that time, I would receive a letter written by the nurse and dictated by McDougal. The question was always the same: "When is the book coming out, damn it? Quit messing around with those geisha girls and get home so we can finish the book!"

When I did see him again, his health had greatly deteriorated. I hardly recognized him—he was so frail, his spirit so pessimistic. He told me he gave up on the book idea. Publishing them in the newspaper was enough.

"Let it go, Grant," he would whisper in a hoarse voice. "We are all dead now. Who cares about a bunch of cardboard cutouts? Anyway, did they even keep Merchant Street? Or have they torn all that down?"

I went ahead with the project despite my colleague's pessimism. What follows is a small portion of the Arthur McDougal Tapes that first appeared in a greatly edited version in the *Honolulu Star-Bulletin*. There are boxes of many more hours of interviews, telling more stories of the lives of desperate men and women, climbing up and over each other's backs, pulling themseves lower into this black crab basket called Honolulu. Maybe one day, if anyone cares, we'll transcribe those stories for another anthology of McDougal tales. I included two such tales, "The Kasha of Kaimuki" and "The Calling Spirit of Kipapa" in last year's publication *OBAKE: Ghost Stories in Hawai'i*.

◆ ◆ ◆

On the evening of June 2, 1995, Arthur McDougal went into a coma from which he now rouses only periodically. The doctors have been amazed that without respirators he has survived on the basis of his own strong lungs. His medical bills are paid, I'm told, by an anonymous donor whose return address is San Francisco, California. They were given a power of attorney by McDougal when he moved into the convalescent home years ago. According to this anonymous person's orders, he is to be kept alive despite his weakened state. Every day a masseur comes to his room to keep his withering legs and arms from becoming atrophied. By my estimation, this year he celebrated his 115th birthday.

I have done my best to maintain McDougal's own words in this work, except where they were too "colorful" for family reading. While some of the tales are of gangster, hoodlums and molls, some have supernatural overtones. As McDougal once explained to me, when you start prowling into the tunnel of a human being's most foul deeds, it's sometimes surprising the sources of danger you end up facing that are far beyond what ordinary folks call "natural." The gumshoe probes the tunnel for the rest of us who cling to our tangible, concrete, mundane and, therefore, safe realities. He walks down those streets not for sissies, crawling into those dirty little corners of Honolulu where passion, greed and hatred leave forever their taint of mystery.

Transcripts of

the McDougal Tapes

CHAPTER ONE

A Scratching Ghost at the Pali

Do I believe in ghosts? No, I never did. Sure, the local boys in the squad room talked story all the time about such things. Chang Apana and Hapai Mountain could really spin a yarn about spooks. But being a *haole*, I guess I just could never buy it. I'd rather face off with a specter than some mean slob coming out of Chaplain Lane with his pistols blazing. So, when it comes to ghosts, hell, I used to shrug it off as too much *okolehao*. That is, except that time the British scientist was found dead at the bottom of the Pali, all scratched up. When you come up against ghost dogs, I reckon there are more things in heaven and hell than you can dream up in your philosophy. I think Shakespeare said that.

It was 10 a.m., July 28, 1932, when China, my secretary, took the call. "Mac, please hurry. New York is on line." At first I thought it was more reporters and gossip hounds calling about the Massie case. I had been hired by one of the local *haole* big-wigs to dig into that dirty little affair. When a *haole* lady got raped at Ala Moana by what she described as local boys, all hell broke loose with the military and Big Five jockeying to bring down indictments while saving their own necks. My client had wanted me to get all the information I could about the case even before the cops knew, so that his associates on the West Coast could be assured that the islands were sewn up real pretty. He couldn't let his powerful buddies in California think that white women weren't safe at Waikiki from sex-crazed beachboys. Since the sensational trial had been conducted with famed defense lawyer Clarence Darrow orating before the jury, every hackneyed newsman in the world was calling me for some inside scoop.

So I was ready for the tight-lipped routine when I heard an oh-so-proper British accent of a Sir Walter Crowe ask if this was the International Detective Agency and whether we were available for a little delicate inquiry into the death of Sir David Duncan, famed botanist with the Royal Society of Scientists.

"The Brit who fell off the cliff up at the Pali?"

"That is precisely what we want you to investigate, Mr. McDougal. The Royal Society members and I want to confirm that our colleague's death was accidental."

All I knew about Duncan's death was what I had read in the *Star-Bulletin*—some big shot scientist had fallen off the Pali cliff last Saturday night. Or maybe he jumped. There was no mention of foul play.

"Listen, lots of people fall off the Pali, most of them accidentally. We get a few attempted suicides, but usually those blow back up against the wall of the mountain, breaking an arm or leg. What makes you think that he was pushed?"

Dr. Crowe explained to me in a matter-of-fact tone that Sir Duncan was an excellent mountaineer who, in the estimation of all concerned, was too experienced to have fallen from some Hawaiian cliffs without unwelcome assistance.

"Did he have any enemies?" I asked.

"He made enemies, Mr. McDougal, wherever he went. Sir Duncan was a brash, arrogant and seductive gentleman, who had a knack for getting other men to hate him, especially jealous husbands. Despite these peccadilloes in his moral character, he was an excellent scientist. And because he was a member of our Society, we feel it is our obligation to make certain that his death was accidental."

"I think you seriously underestimate Hawaiian volcanoes, dead or alive," I answered. "Fool malihinis are getting lost or killed all the time hiking in paradise."

My town, Honolulu, in the years before the war. *(Hawai'i State Archives)*

"Mali . . ."

"Newcomers. Well, I get $25 a day, plus expenses."
I sure in the hell didn't mind getting paid to tell the
Brits what they already knew. Anyway, it was a slow,
kona summer that needed a little action.

Dr. Crowe seemed happy when I took the job, asking me to promise to keep the investigation on the
hush. They didn't know my reputation as "tight-lip"
McDougal.

"I'll get back to you in a few days," I assured him,
thinking this was going to be easy dough.

I dragged China with me as we left my office in the
Inter-Island Steamship Building at Merchant and Fort
Streets and walked over to the fancy new Police Station
at Bethel. I collared Sergeant Henry Chillingworth, a
big, friendly Hawaiian who made a name for himself
playing football at Kamehameha Schools. Henry and I
were friends from way back, when I was one of the
Honolulu Poi Dogs (HPD). Consequently, he didn't
need much prodding to bring me the file on Sir Duncan.

It was all there, pretty straightforward. Duncan
fell off the Pali sometime at around 8 p.m. last
Saturday. It was a pretty nasty fall and the coroner
determined the cause of death as a broken neck. The
autopsy photos were ugly. Sir Duncan's body and face
were covered with horrible, deep wounds like animal
scratches. The mutilation was so severe, his face
resembled a bowl of mush. My stomach turned as
China nearly lost her *won ton*.

A few things puzzled me. What was Duncan doing up there in the dark and how did he get those ugly cuts? The detectives conjectured he was at the Pali doing a little ille-

The Pali Lookout where Duncan took the plunge. *(Hawai'i State Archives)*

gal digging for Hawaiian sacred artifacts. Trying to find a burial cave up on the Koolau, he slipped and fell off the Pali. The scratches were probably caused by his face scraping down the side of the mountain, snagging on protruding rocks. There was no evidence of a struggle at the lookout area where Sir Duncan's car was found with the headlights still on.

I asked Chillingworth about the Hawaiian icon business. Evidently our British malihini had a little side hobby—not only was he one of the world's foremost tropical botanists, but he had a passion for stealing sacred objects. His rented cottage in Manoa was filled with rocks from ancient Hawaiian *heiau*, small idol images, scary masks from Micronesia and voodoo dolls from the West Indies. He picked them up or stole them wherever he went.

Well, this gave the boys in the squad room all kinds of unofficial theories. "He was killed by spirits at the Pali." "His face was all cut up by the ghost dog that protects the sacred, hidden *ki'i*."

"What do you mean, *ki'i*? And what ghost dog?" I chimed in.

"*Ki'i*, Mac. You know, images of gods like in the Bishop Museum."

"You never heard of Poki, the guardian dog of Nuuanu?"

Officer Hiram Kamaka was a good cop who knew legends behind every rock on Oahu. He had grown up in Kahaluu with his grandparents, who spoke only Hawaiian and filled his head with all those stories. In fact, it wasn't until all officers were required to take an English language exam back in 1911 that Kamaka even bothered to learn English. I thought I had heard all of his tales before, but this Poki was new to me.

"So you think he attacked Duncan?"

"I don't know, Mac, but when I was a child, my grandparents would take me on horseback to Honolulu once a month to visit their *ohana* in Kakaako. On the way home, we'd pass Kapena Falls and they'd tell me about Poki, who guarded the entrance to Nuuanu valley. He was *eepa*, supernatural, and could change his shape at will."

"I saw him. Once," Another Hawaiian officer by the name of Poaha jumped in.

"A couple of years ago, I was patrolling up by the graveyard by Kapena, Oahu cemetery. I saw this little dog running in the graves. It started to chase my car and, I swear, the closer the dog got to me, the bigger that bugger got!"

"That's Poki," added Kamaka. "He has the ability to change his shape. I've been told that he can stretch his neck like a giraffe."

"Well, of course," I explained to Poaha, "the dog was running up to you. That's why it got bigger."

"No, I mean big! Like the size of a horse!"

I let out a laugh that quickly got me a stink eye.

"I'm not kidding you, *haole*. Poki is real."

I took a second look at the autopsy photos and pushed out of my mind any thought that some scratching ghost dog murdered this British ransacker of sacred caves. It was a solution that my clients weren't going to pay no $25 a day, plus a tip, for a job well done. If Duncan fell from the Pali, it was human hands, not ethereal paws, that did the job.

According to the newspaper account of his death, Sir Duncan had been working temporarily at the University of Hawai'i, doing research on a variety of tropical plants found only in the islands. Green stuff was always out of my league, so all the technical information I learned from calling the college went in one ear and out the other. What I wanted was a name, someone who was working with the scientist, I told the department chairman. Someone who could tell me what Sir Duncan was doing the week before his death. He gave me the name of Mike Shigetani, a research assistant who had been Duncan's right hand since the distinguished scientist had set up shop at the college.

I say college, but the University of Hawai'i was like a big, overgrown farm with a bunch of snooty-nosed teenagers who thought they needed a degree to learn how to plant corn. I drove around the quad area to Hawai'i Hall and tracked Mike Shigetani down to the Tank. The mugginess of the kona weather had brought out the students like locusts to the Tank's cool water. I felt like stripping down right there and joining them, but instead asked around for Shigetani. A wiry, well-built young fellow about to dive into the pool from the top springboard was pointed out to me. He wasn't much of a diver, but who was I to talk? I couldn't even swim.

When I finally got him to come out of the Tank, he seemed nervous and edgy. After I assured him I wasn't just another cop, he relaxed at bit. It wasn't long before Shigetani was all animated, talking about how Sir Duncan was a world-famous expert in tropical agriculture who had come over to the islands for a year, got a nice, juicy contract with a few companies and was working his assistants like slaves, including Shigetani. I looked into the young man's steely black eyes but I couldn't read them. I pressed for more information. What about this going hunting for idols in the middle of the night? Did he do that often?

"Either ancient images or ladies," Shigetani answered. When I pressed him about the ladies, the kid suddenly clammed up. He wouldn't say much more, except that Sir Duncan could turn the heads of quite a few coeds. It had to be his British accent, I thought, trying to picture the face of mush as ever being handsome.

Shigetani was one of those nisei boys whose immigrant parents had sacrificed everything to send him to college so he could graduate and be an overeducated plantation worker. But he wasn't one of those "student types." You could see that he was a cool customer—tough and ambitious. He had an edge of bitterness whenever he talked about Sir Duncan's research. I was getting the idea that maybe the Brit had stolen the local boys' work and put his own name on it. I was getting to like Sir Duncan less and less.

"Where were you Saturday night about 8 o'clock?" I suddenly asked Shigetani.

"At Sans Souci, over by the Natatorium. My friends and I were fishing."

"And drinking?"

"A little swipe, that's all."

That fermented potato crap could kill you, but it was easy to brew. I took down the names of the boys with him, thanked him for his time and left the land of higher education for the silk stocking district of College Hills, where the professor had rented a cottage. This district became pretty fashionable about 30 years ago, when Punahou School started selling off some of their surplus lands for tract homes. A finer class of citizens, like the Athertons, Joneses and Schmidts lived in College Hills, which was served by the Manoa trolley. When the University of Hawai'i started to grow in the twenties, the nearby, easily accessible and heavily land-scaped homes became very popular with the faculty. Duncan found a nice place on Kamehameha Avenue, not far from the Tennis Court. Since the cops didn't have the courtesy to leave the front door of his cottage open for me, I crawled in through a back window.

I don't take pride in snooping around a dead man's house. What made it worse was the creepy faces and goblins looking down at me in stones, wooden sticks, and weird masks painted hideous colors with silly feathers all stuck in them. What kind of man makes a hobby out of collecting such things? Dabble in magical stuff, I reckon, and you either lose your mind or fall off the Pali.

It didn't take long before I turned up some interesting little tidbits. Since the police thought Duncan's death was an accident, they did a sloppy job looking through his things, for our friend seemed to have taken a liking to more than coeds. In one of the cubbyholes in his desk I found a short, frantic note—"I've got to see you. Please don't say no. I'll be at our special place. B." The message was written on stationery from the First United Christian Church on the Pali Road in Nuuanu. Between some books, there was also a photograph of one of those Polynesian beauties who had a mixture of Hawaiian, French, Chinese or some other exotic blood. She was the type that ends up in the school yearbook as Miss Melting Pot. In the lower right-hand corner was an inscription, "To My Favorite Professor, Love, Your

Merchant Street with the Inter-Island Steamship Building the second structure on the right. My office was on the third floor. *(Hawai'i State Archives)*

Favorite Student." For a moment, I felt a pang of jealousy. Then I remembered mush face and felt lucky.

His bedroom was as immaculate as his desk area. Sir Duncan was fastidiously clean, at least when compared to my own personal habits. Everything seemed pretty much in order, except for a dirty shirt and pants in the hamper. I routinely checked the pockets of both garments and found a wadded-up note which read "7:45. Meet Pali." There was no date and it was only an idle doodle. But it registered in my old gray matter.

The bathroom was spick-and-span, although I made an interesting discovery behind a tall bottle of witch hazel and talc. I had seen those small oriental glass jars when I used to walk the Chinatown beat down near River Street. A small amount of black, sticky opium still clung to the bottom of the glass. Sir Duncan had been an opium-eater.

Honolulu was filled with the dream smoke back in those days. Smugglers brought the living death in from Asia and it turned grown men into vegetables and ruined the morals of the ladies. Not only Chinese smoked it, but the idle rich who tired of jazz parties and wanted to spice up their lives by prowling Chinatown for the opium dens. Duncan must have picked up the habit in Hong Kong or Peking, I guessed. A real Jekyll and Hyde my boy was turning out to be. No wonder the Society asked for discretion. If opium was involved, I needed to talk to the Iceman.

I gathered up my little pieces of evidence and high-tailed it back downtown to find out what China had turned up on Duncan from the newspaper files. I stopped for a toot at the "soft drink parlor" in the basement of the old Hocking Hotel at King and Nuuanu Streets. While on the mainland these gin joints were called speakeasies, by any name the rotgut was my kind of poison. Reading through the material about Sir Duncan, there was nothing said about his life half as interesting as what I had turned up. However, there was a small item about some deal he was working on with McIntyre Plantation Co., a small agricultural company that had the silly idea that macadamia nuts could be a profitable cash crop. I made some calls and tracked the company man who had hired Duncan. His name was Charles Harrison III, as if I cared about the other two, who had his offices in Pier 7 near Aloha Tower. I took the short walk over from the Hocking in the final hours of what had been a sticky, hot day.

Mr. Harrison the Third was sweating like an *imu* pig behind his mahogany desk. A little fan was trying to cool him off and a light sea breeze blew in through the open windows. The heat spell had been going on all month and it was nice to know that even VIP's suffer. As his secretary introduced me, I made a quick survey of his office. Plenty of books, mostly about agriculture, plants and Hawai'i. The spread was nicely decorated with rattan, giving it a tropical flair, which everyone was emulating these days. I plopped myself into a cushy seat and stated my business. I wanted to know if Sir Duncan was in his employ, if he knew any reason why he'd be up at the Pali at that hour and had the Brit been depressed or maybe suicidal?

Harrison parted his hair straight down the middle of his scalp and pulled it back with plenty of grease. Very Hollywood, I thought. He was a man with style and money who was 39 or 40 years old. No more than 41. By the ease with which he treated me, as if he owned me, I knew he was from a *kama'aina* family with a prim mainland wife he picked up at Yale, two kids going to Punahou, a summer house at the Pearl City Peninsula, and a residence up on Tantalus. I had these kind of guys all figured out in the first two minutes. He rambled on about macadamia nuts, diversified farming, and the depression which, thank God, hadn't yet hit

13

the islands quite as hard as it could. Roosevelt was sending the country down the drain, he warned me. This was the kind of man who made my future, and I resented him.

I tried to get him to the topic of Sir Duncan, but he didn't know much. He had recently contracted with the British scientist to assist the company with an experimental harvest of macadamia nuts. While Harrison was at the pier, Duncan spent most of his time at the college or in the fields. The most he had heard about Sir Duncan's accident was the scuttlebutt going around town about how the Pali dog had mutilated his body. It takes little time for rumors to spread through this Pacific burg. He seemed to give the ghost story more credence than I thought a man with his background would. Then again, those old families sometimes had been in the islands too long, from my way of thinking.

He started to go on about the legends of ghosts at the Pali, even pulling a copy of Westervelt's folklore books down from the shelf. As he was boring me to tears with his patronizing rendition of the Westervelt tale of Poki, an odd contraption in the corner of his office caught my eye. It looked like an old gramophone but was rigged up with a microphone. I took a closer gander when he cautioned me from touching the device. It was one of those Edison talking machines, the kind that make a record of your voice, and I could damage one of his recordings. I extended my *mea culpa* and asked for a demonstration. He played back for me a record which sounded like fingers scratching a blackboard behind a high, twangy voice that I recognized as Harrison's. It was a speech he recorded the night of Sir Duncan's accident that KGU radio had agreed to broadcast Sunday evening. Since everything was live those days, this was a big event in town—a prerecorded message from the powers that be on the healthy island economy during the world's worst depression. We were used to pie-in-the-sky Republicanism in those days.

As I listened, I heard on the recording in the background the clear sound of a clock which was on the bookshelf chime eight nautical bells. Well, he not only had no motive, I guessed, but if this recording was indeed made on Saturday night, he even had an alibi. Of course, I never even suggested he was implicated in Sir Duncan's supernatural accident. However, just to make sure, I later checked with his secretary. Yes, she confirmed, Mr. Harrison had called her at home Saturday afternoon and asked if she would work with him that evening to polish his radio speech. He had been quite nervous about the recording and had insisted that she help him with rewrites. When he finally went into his private office to record the speech, it was about 7:30 p.m. It was after 8:30 that night when he finished the recording, exited the office and accompanied her home.

The sun had set before I got back to my office to settle into a warm shot of cheap gin made in the back of Manoa Valley by a Japanese fellow named Arakaki. China had been working overtime to get me some names of the women connected with Duncan. I needed to know who the cute Melting Pot doll was in the photograph and the full name of "B." By 7:30 p.m. I had the college yearbook in my hand and the names of officers, trustees and staff of the First United Christian Church. The coed was easy to identify—she was on nearly every other page from Debating Society to sports to racial clubs. I was right about her being Polynesian. What else could she be with a name like Victoria Nalani Nihipali? As for "B," I was less lucky. No ladies connected with the Church staff or board had the initial "B." I figured after a good night's rest, I'd pay a visit to the gorgeous brunette and the minister. Between the two of them, maybe I'd start coming up with some hard facts. I took another hard swallow of the Manoa gin and slipped into a well-deserved world of nightmares. Dog ghosts kept scratching at my face while I spooned down a hot, tasty bowl of mush.

When I woke up at my desk the next morning, my head was still swimming from the cheap booze and my suit smelled of stale cigar smoke. China had already fetched me a cup of hot coffee from the Arcade Cafe next door and was shoving a paper under my nose. It was the list of boys who had gone fishing with Shigetani. She had called them all last night and it seems that they had been fishing at Sans Souci, but one of them remembered that Shigetani, who was always a loner, had gone down to fish under the pilings of Kainalu, the big Castle house. He was gone for over an hour and a half. When he came back, he was empty-handed. He said he got no bites. That was about 9:15 p.m.

I cleaned myself up and drove out to Kalihi Valley, up towards where Kamehameha Schools' new campus was being finished at Kapalama Heights. The Nihipalis lived in a modest house on the heights with a large backyard filled with chickens, dogs, cats and a goat tied to a stake. Victoria wasn't home, her mother assured me, but would be back soon. Would I like a little coffee and donut? Hawaiians were always real generous. I sat down to my hot brew, when an old Ford truck roared up, a door slammed and Mauna Kea itself stormed into a kitchen far too confining for its height and girth. And Mauna Kea didn't look too happy. I was quickly introduced to Mr. Nihipali by his wife and he seemed embarrassed to have been seen so furious. His manner quickly calmed as he asked me what I wanted. When I mentioned the name of Sir Duncan, the volcano didn't erupt, but it was clearly simmering. Here was a man who either hated science or a certain British philanderer who may have gone too far pursuing indigenous beauty.

When she walked in, my eyeballs fell out of their sockets and rolled around on the floor until I could pop them back in. Her photographs didn't do her full justice and, if I hadn't have been twice her age, I'd have worshipped at her altar. Her father spoke a little to her in Hawaiian and she burst into tears and started making dramatic gestures indicating her great grief at her professor's death. Her father seemed less grieved by the accident and indicated to me something about "the *haole* deserved it." Then he started going on and on about how Duncan had come to these islands, taken things that didn't belong to him and desecrated the ancient beliefs. Nihipali gazed over to his daughter, indicating a disapproval at her overemoted demonstrations. I watched her deep brown eyes that were filled with tears and was convinced that she felt absolutely nothing about Duncan's death. Maybe I was fantasizing, but I swear in the midst of her goings-on, I was getting a come-on. I think her father saw it, too. He nudged in between us.

I didn't get much help from her. The last time she had seen him was a week before, when she announced that she was *hapai* and Duncan beat a hasty retreat. Her father had gone over to Duncan's cottage one night to discuss the problem, couldn't find the professor, but admitted to making some threats over the phone. He wanted the *haole* to at least do right by his daughter. He then went on and on again about the legend of the supernatural dog at the Pali that protects the land from vultures like Duncan. I was convinced that the father was not overly found of *haoles*.

I didn't want to press it, but I asked where the both of them had been the night of the accident. Victoria was a few doors down the block at a baby luau with her mother and Mr. Nihipali had had an emergency. He worked for the Territorial Board of Water Supply and had been sent to fix a broken pump at the station near Jackass Ginger. That's only a stone's throw from the Pali, I reminded him. He got very serious, almost frightened, and told me that he had had nothing to do with the accident. The spirits had meted out justice, for when Sir Duncan had died that night, he clearly remembers hearing a banshee-like scream that filled the air of Nuuanu and sent shutters down all the men working on the main. It was a high, shrill pitch of a sound that came from the sea and bounced off the Pali. It was 8 p.m., the time when Duncan was scratched to death and thrown off the cliff.

I thought of explaining to him that the shrill of the dead was probably the siren at Aloha Tower. Since a new warning siren had been installed in the tower last month, it sometimes would short-circuit and let off terrible wails at all hours of the day. The town was getting used to it, even if Mr. Nihipali preferred to see it as the presence of man-killing phantom dogs. However, *haoles* had already said too much in this house, so I held my tongue.

When I left, I was escorted to my car by Victoria. She volunteered to me that she hadn't really been pregnant, but had hoped to force Sir Duncan into some kind of commitment. After all, he was a good catch. She had been going out with Shigetani for about a year when Duncan rolled into town. He turned her head and she dumped the Japanese boy. His death was a terrible, terrible accident, she reiterated with forced emotion. She tightened her grip on my arm but got little sympathy. After all, I was only a middle-aged, overweight private investigator who had about as much fire left as a field of cold *a'a*.

I cruised out of Kalihi to King Street and headed Diamond Head to the public *furo* at River and Beretania. I needed to wash off the filth I was picking up from Duncan's life story. I slipped out of my clothes and joined the men in the public bath, while the sound of girlish laughter on the other side of the partition enticed me to a short nap. I didn't dream of mush.

It was late afternoon when I left the *furo*, determined to make contact with the Iceman. Ask any of the young boys who run errands for the prostitutes and they can tell you exactly where the Iceman is gambling. That afternoon he was making his usual deals in the dark corners of The Blue Note, a racy joint on the corner of Nuuanu and Pauahi, where a local burlesque queen named Orchid did the bumps and grinds. His name was actually "Pinky" Tam, and, although he had been nearly born in Hawai'i, he always insisted on talking the silliest pidgin English like that top chef Me P. Y. Chong, who worked at Lau Yee Chai's in Waikiki. "Me belly sorry, Mac" and all that local Chinaman lingo. I was convinced it was an act that the Iceman cooked up like his stony face expressions and menacing gaze.

Orchid was stripping on a little front stage before the usual front row of baldheaded men to the rhythm of a hot jazz band. One of the first local strippers, Orchid was quite a looker. I slipped into an empty seat at Iceman's table, where he was playing mah-jongg with a few downtown merchant types. Behind us a couple of henchmen looked at me with something less than adoration. Without shifting his gaze or looking up at me, we talked for about 15 minutes about Sir Duncan. Did the Brit frequent the opium dens? Who did he go around with? Seen him with a Hawaiian girl, a knock-out coed?

The Iceman knew Duncan. Seems in addition to being a womanizer, he was fond of gambling, a habit he picked up at casinos around the world. Only his luck ran out in Honolulu's Chinatown. He always gambled alone, paid his debt off regularly, but always came back for more. When he died, he was in for five big ones with the Iceman. I almost think I detected a look of pain on the Chinaman's face when he mentioned the outstanding debt that would now be closed.

What about the opium? I asked. Was Duncan a hophead? Iceman seemed close-lipped on that one. He had never seen Duncan in the opium dens, but who knows? If he had some of the dope in his bathroom, he had to smoke it, right? I knew the Iceman would know where he got the black gold. I wouldn't let up, as Orchid's twirling tassels drew loud cheers.

"Let it go, Mac. Trust me. It's too big, even for you." I knew it! He spoke those words in the finest King's English I had ever heard. I slipped him a fiver for the few rounds I had lost in the last few minutes of mah-jongg, blew Orchid a kiss that went straight to her G-string and faced the glare of the late afternoon sunset. The heat, humidity, cheap whiskey and missing $5 bill didn't sit too well with me. I drove out to the Pali Road again and pulled into the spacious parking lot of the First Union Christian Church. A few minutes later I found Rev. Noah Cunningham, a minister who could have substituted as a Pacific Northwest lumberman. He led me to a small bungalow hidden in a wonderful, verdant grove about 200 yards from the church.

When I entered the parlor, a good whiff of Canadian whiskey gently enveloped my nose, reminding me of earlier glory days when I spent many an evening with my friend to the north. The odor was emanating from Mrs. Cunningham, a pert, full-bosomed young woman in her mid-twenties who was plain in the face, but shapely in the hips. I wasn't surprised when I was introduced to Beatrice Cunningham. My "B" was the perfect candidate for Duncan—lonely, ignored, maybe even unsatisfied. She was a pent-up, nervous lady who chain-smoked half a pack of cigarettes just in the short time I was there. She never looked directly at me, but fidgeted about the bungalow, pretending to straighten up for my account. Rev. Cunningham was as young as his wife, but peculiarly subdued, as if he had just ridden a launch through a hurricane and had finally found safe harbor. Mrs. Cunningham at last excused herself and retreated to a small side room, which presumably was a bedroom.

Rev. Cunningham apologized for his wife. She had been through a trying ordeal, he explained. My mouth dropped open as he then matter-of-factly explained that they had had the pleasure of meeting Sir Duncan, that he was a vile man in league with some devils, and that he had seduced his wife. She, of course, had recognized her sins, fully repented before her husband and God and had resumed her life of wifely devotions and repentance. Funny, I missed some of those qualities in her demeanor, although I didn't tell him so. Of course, he volunteered that on the night of the accident, he had been in his office at the rear of the Church where he worked late preparing his sermon for Sunday. No, no one had seen him since he insists on not being disturbed during his period of study. Mrs. Cunningham, of course, was confined to her bed with a severe attack of guilt.

As I left the Cunninghams to pick over what was no doubt the pieces of their shattered marriage, I thought about how dangerous it was to judge someone based on their cover. Who could have imagined how deceitful the life of an internationally respected man of science could have become? There was no question in my mind whether or not anyone had a motive to kill Sir Duncan. The real question was which of my suspects' grudges, jealousies or greed turned into murder? I decided that it was about time that I took a look at the scene of the fall up at the Pali.

The sun had set on Nuuanu Valley and the road seemed unusually dark, as the moon had not yet risen.

I was remembering Officer Kamaka's story about the legend of Poki, the guardian dog of the valley, and the miraculous ability the creature had to change shape and size. My machine rumbled as I downshifted, starting the long haul past Jackass Ginger and the Morgan estate, passing the halfway house and finally the Cooke place. Why in the hell anyone would want to live in such a remote area was beyond me. Maybe I had heard too much of the squad room gossip about the ghost-gods of the Pali. Over the years, several officers had sworn that they had their car stall on the Pali Road because they had unknowingly had pork in their car. One day, I thought to myself, I would have to ask Kamaka about that pork-in-the-car stuff.

When I arrived at the lookout, the area was deserted. As dark as it was, I enjoyed the grand sweep of the evening windward coast with its few lazy, flickering lights of beach and farmhouses and the electrical glow of little Kailua and Kaneohe towns. The night air felt cool and strong as I walked over to the ledge and leaned into a tunnel of wind swirling up from the cliff below. A crescent moon peaked over the Koolau as I looked over the edge, contemplating the terror Duncan must have felt as he plunged to his death. At that moment a terrible thought slammed into my head like an angry fist. What if the person who killed Duncan hadn't been human? What if I had been too smug? Lonely Hawaiian nights always tended to give me this kind of unsettling thoughts.

The brush about 100 feet to my left suddenly moved as if something was stealthily moving towards me. I turned quickly around, nearly tripping on loose gravel that had been strewn about the outlook. A growl of a dog rose to a snapping bark as a dark shadow lunged for me. I swerved back to avoid the black beast, as I dizzily reached for something to keep me from falling back over the edge of the Pali.

The earth dropped out from under me, as the frothy creature with gaping jaws lunged for my throat. In those split instances you don't think much about anything but clinging to good old terra firma, so I wildly flayed my arms, groping for a vine or exposed root to break my fall as I went over the ledge. A horrible howl of the Pali winds suddenly picked up, blowing insanely around me, as the vicious growling of the monster continued above me. My number had just been called to spit into the eye of death.

Fortunately, a fierce gust of the Pali winds that night saved me from ending up like Sir Duncan. My body was pushed up by the wind against the steep precipice, so I slid down only 10 feet or so when I hit a rock outcrop and caught hold of a strong root twisted around a stone. Upstairs, the beast was leaning over the edge, giving me one of those victorious barks. Then I heard someone shouting, "Oh, my God, what did you do? Down, boy." I called up for help and a human face sheepishly looked down, inquiring whether I was flattened out or still round.

While I was waiting for my savior to drop a rope down to me, I noticed there was plenty of litter strewn about, stuff that tourists must have tossed over which the wind pinned to the lower ledge. A folded envelope with a stationery design I had seen somewhere before caught my eye, so I scooped it up, placed it in my pocket and thought of 15 reasons why and how Beatrice Cunningham might have clawed her British lover up and pushed him to kingdom come.

When I was back up on the Pali Road, I listened to some *haole* bird named Peebles give me lame-brained excuses about his vicious mutt, which was a wire-haired fox terrier the size of my foot. I didn't want him to think a puppy scared me, so I told him it was the howl of the wind that made me lose my balance. "That wasn't no wind howling," he assured me. "It was Aloha Tower. That damn siren has short-circuited three times this week."

He went on to complain about wasted tax dollars while I headed down the Pali Road to the door of a pert, chain-smoking, hooch-guzzling minister's wife. Her husband was in his Church office, divining the ways of God and she was swilling Canada. Sure, she still had a thing for Sir Duncan, she said, she couldn't resist him, even after her pious husband had found the two of them in the hay.

"I needed him, McDougal," she kept repeating.

"Not too much not to kill him," I answered, being a wiseacre.

But Mrs. Cunningham denied killing him. She needed him for her opium. He had turned her into a hophead and, when he spurned her for the younger and better-packed Victoria, she needed her supply. After all, she was a minister's wife. She could hardly be caught frequenting the opium dens on River Street. She met him up at the Pali that night around 7:15 and gave him an envelope with $50 in exchange for a small vial of endless dreams. He took the

Aloha Tower, once the tallest building in the islands. *(Hawaiʻi State Archives)*

money and tossed the envelope away. Then she left him at 7:30 p.m., going back to face her preaching lumberjack and suck on her pipe.

She didn't kill Sir Duncan. I couldn't see her getting her fingernails bloody or shoving her source of opium into oblivion. I asked her who his connection was for the smoke and all she knew was that the Brit made contact with a Chinaman. I had to get hard evidence if the cops were going to nail the Iceman. He had slipped out of every noose they had ever tied for him. As I drove back to my office, I flicked on my Westinghouse to KGU and caught, of all things, that stupid recording Harrison

27

the Third had made the night of the murder. It finally hit me what was missing from this case. I knew my move, if only China would go along with it.

I made her dress like one of Duncan's tarts, with a tight, red dress slit up the side and a sharp pillbox hat with a black net across the face. Then she made a telephone call, promising to exchange certain damaging information for $5,000. The exchange would be made in public at the Blue Note Club. China waited for an hour at a small table in the back of Orchid's place, while I enjoyed watching the bump and grind. When he entered the bar, he crossed right near me, ordered a Jack Daniels and then slid into a chair opposite China. I couldn't hear what they were saying, but when I saw the large black object slide out of his jacket pocket, I didn't wait to find out if it was a wallet or a pistol. I flashed the signal to Chillingworth, who was nearly lost in the twirl of tassels, and we moved quickly into the seats next to him. I placed my .38 into his rib cage, while Sarge quietly removed the big, nasty revolver from Charles Harrison's fist. China fainted.

"What..." he blurted, rising from his chair to make a dash for the front door.

"Relax, Harrison," I said in a soothing voice, my hand pressed hard on his shoulder. "You're not going anywhere for a long, long time."

"What is the meaning of this? This is outrageous! This woman was trying to blackmail me." You could see he was desperate. His whole, neat little *kama'aina* world was going up in opium smoke.

"You and Duncan were in cahoots together for something more than macadamia nuts. Opium is a nice opportunity to diversify the economy, wouldn't you say so, Harrison?"

"I don't know what you are talking about. I..."

"You used the cover of your macadamia company to import the dope into the islands. By my guess, you probably then sold it to the Iceman and other drug lords who put it on the streets for you. Only Duncan found out about the opium racket. He ran up big debts with Iceman and pulled a little extortion job on you, figuring you had a lot to lose with your *kama'aina* reputation. So you agreed to meet him at 7:15 p.m. at the Pali, intending to be late. You knew he'd wait for his dough. By the time you got up there from Pier 7, it was about 8 p.m. You waited until his little tryst with the minister's wife was over and then you jumped him, throwing him to his death. Am I going too fast or is this starting to make sense?"

Charles Harrison was getting nervous. Rich men always get real nervous when they get caught with their hand in the cookie jar.

"I was in my office when Duncan died at 8 p.m. My secretary told you I was there. This is preposterous. I never touched Duncan."

"Your secretary said that you went into your office to make your recording at approximately 7:30 p.m. She heard you giving your speech and then you exited the office at 8:30 p.m. The chiming of the clock at 8 p.m. was recorded by the machine. Am I correct so far?"

"Exactly. So how in the world could I have killed Duncan? I couldn't be in two places at the same time!"

Chillingworth looked over at me like the guy had just slipped out of the noose. "Hell, Mac. You didn't tell me that he had an airtight alibi."

"Not so airtight as it appears, Sarge. You see, what the secretary heard wasn't the recording being made, but the recording being played. When Duncan put the heat on Harrison for money to pay his debt to the Iceman, Harrison figured the only way out of his trouble was to bump off Duncan. So he made a recording of his speech long before the murder and then used his secretary as an alibi. He knew he would have to prove the recording was made that evening, so he set the clock in his office to chime as if it were 8 o'clock. When he entered his office, he stopped the clock, set the recording and used his private back entrance to get to his automobile. He had plenty of time to go up to the Pali, kill Duncan and then reenter his office. When the recording was finished, he reset the clock and stepped out to greet his secretary at about 8:30 p.m."

"How can you prove any of this, McDougal? I made that recording between 7:30 and 8:30 p.m. This is nothing but interesting conjecture."

Normally I would have agreed with Mr. Harrison the Third. However, in this instance there was a fragment of Mr. Nihipali's story that stuck with me. The night Duncan died, he heard the ghost dog of the Pali wail. In actuality, the siren of Aloha Tower had short-circuited, a malfunction that for a few days had been happening repeatedly. Just that night I had mistaken the siren for the howl of the wind. Only, when I was listening to Harrison's speech on KGU driving back to town, there was no such siren wail in the recording. Aloha Tower's loud blast just after 8 would have certainly been heard at Harrison's office at nearby Pier 7. However, if the machine was playing instead of recording, the siren would be missing from the record. When China called, she said she was another one of Duncan's lovers who knew everything about the extortion deal. Although it was a dangerous trump card, it was the only way to get him to play his hand one more time.

During the trial, Harrison confessed that he had hired Sir Duncan to experiment with macadamias, but the overzealous Brit had stuck his nose out too far. Harrison had a side racket smuggling opium into the islands in small containers from Hong Kong, all in the guise of agricultural imports. Sir Duncan found the opium, got greedy and wanted a piece of the action. Evidently the payoff was to be at the Pali, but, instead of cash, Sir Duncan ate several hundred feet of rock. Harrison was found guilty, his wife cried a lot, the kids were moved out of Punahou to public school, and they took him to Oahu Prison, where he was sentenced to life imprisonment at hard labor. They never used to hang *haoles*, certainly never the rich ones.

Shigetani? He went on to win a few medals for the University of Hawai'i swim team and later became a professor at some mainland college. Mrs. Cunningham got a divorce, found redemption and became a famous radio evangelist like Aimee Semple McPherson. By last report she had run off with one of her brawny holy rollers after a tent meeting in Evanston, Illinois. I called Victoria just once, but got Mauna Kea instead. That pipe-dream was quickly buried.

Although the mystery of who had killed Sir Duncan was resolved, there was one last question that never was answered. Harrison admitted to killing Sir Duncan, but he claimed he never scratched up the face. The police publicly stated that the scratches must have been caused by the fall, but they never let the whole truth out. Before his cremation, I saw Duncan's body in the morgue. Those hideous cuts weren't made by rocks. They had been made by claws. One more thing. On his right hip, Sir Duncan had teeth bites. A portion of his flesh was missing with nasty, deep gouges. Some demon had taken a bite out of him. After Harrison pushed him off the Pali, something else got to Duncan. What it was or why it attacked him, I can't say. You'll just have to go ask someone who believes in ghosts.

*[**Editor's Note:** Over the years, many strange, supernatural occurrences have been associated with the Pali*

Road. McDougal's reference, for example, to the stalling of cars that attempt to drive over the Pali with pork in the vehicle has a long tradition in the islands. The so-called "ghost dog" Poki also is a tradition of the valley. His powers to change his shape and size have long been recorded in the oral traditions of both ancient and modern Hawai'i. Although I've never heard or read of any incident where Poki has viciously attacked or killed anyone, his spirit is said to reside in the area near Kapena Falls.

I have found no record of a British botanist dying in a fall from an Hawaiian mountain in 1932. However, Sir David Douglas, the famed Scottish naturalist, did fall into a pit on the Big Island in 1834. Mysterious circumstances surrounded his death, some suggesting that he possibly had been robbed and murdered. McDougal seemed to have no knowledge of the 19th-century case, but was adamant these events took place as described in 1932.]

CHAPTER TWO

The Summer Miss Ash Vanished

It was one of those unforgettable summers when a gentle madness seemed to grip Honolulu. The humidity was soaring so that you couldn't walk a city block without your clothes sticking to you like a death shroud. Everyone was grumbling about the national Prohibition laws going into effect. Our moral guardians had already turned the town dry but, with the Feds coming into the act, where was a man going to be getting his shot of *okolehao*? The "soft drink parlors" like the Miller Street Social Club or the Waikiki Social Club were already going into action in anticipation of the Carrie Nation tomfoolery.

Rumblings on the Big Island had everybody scared that the volcano was going to blow. Even over here on Oahu a few lunatics were preaching the end of the world when the lava started to spew. Some character in Kalihi claiming to be a *kahuna* had a vision that Madam Pele was going to kill everyone in the islands, no doubt in retribution for annexation. The seer announced that only those people within the compound of her yard on School Street would be safe. I drove by out of curiosity, and there must have been a thousand people packed in on her grounds and another thousand lined up waiting their turn for salvation. When Duck Pong and a few of his molls drove up in his sharp Willys-Knight, the

A typical summer day in downtown Honolulu. *(Hawai'i State Archives)*

crowd parted like water to let Chinatown's crime lord join the vigil waiting for Pele's eruption.

If it wasn't the volcanic apocalypse which was going to devour us, then it was certainly going to be the Bolsheviks. The Great War had ended and the Red-White-and-Blue flag-wavers were getting riled up by the French and British kicking Wilson in the seat of his pants over at Versailles. The Hawai'i boys were coming home from the fields of Flanders with stories of how they licked the Kaiser single-handed, so "give 'em a shot at the Reds." Across the ocean, Attorney General Palmer was conducting the Red Raids and the Wooblies were being tried for blowing up the Los Angeles Times building. The Communist sympathizers up at the University of Hawai'i were calling the Bolshevik revolution the greatest social advancement since Carnation milk. A few of the eggheads would have probably liked to have seen Lenin's profile be added with the other four mugs up at Mt. Rushmore.

The Navy was getting ready for a real hullabaloo now that the second naval drydock at Pearl Harbor was *pau*. Six years ago, on February 17, 1913, the first drydock exploded with the force of dynamite when the cofferdam was being pumped and a nine-foot hole appeared in the floor. A *kahuna* had warned them when they began construction in 1909 that the area they had selected for the drydock was the sacred home of Kaahupahua, the shark goddess. Ignoring the warnings, the Navy proceeded with disastrous results. Construction on the second drydock had commenced only after proper Hawaiian blessings had been obtained. When the cofferdam was being pumped on August 21, 1919, workmen found the backbone and ribs of a 14-foot hammerhead shark on the drydock floor. You could hear the "we told you so's" from southpoint on the Big Island to little forbidden Niihau.

Oh, 1919 was also the summer Penelope Ash vanished from the beach at Waikiki.

I hadn't been working at the International Detective Agency more than a couple of months when the rich and beautiful Miss Ash became a missing person statistic. According to the newspaper account, in the late afternoon of Wednesday, July 2, she just stepped right off the planet in front of the Moana Hotel. The last time she had been seen was before sunset, when a beachboy saw her strolling along the shoreline in a red silk evening gown. When her sister hadn't been able to find Penelope about an hour later, she called the cops. She told them that Penelope had been complaining about a terrible headache for over a week, so maybe she had lost her mind and wandered off somewhere. Either that, or she had drowned and her body was swept out beyond the reef. The police commandeered the Waikiki glass-bottom boat to search for the corpse, while Duke Kahanamoku and his brother David paddled back and forth in the waters off the Moana, hoping to find what was left of poor Miss Ash.

When Miss Ash disappeared, I had been working on a "hush-hush" case for one of our local top business executives. He was a dyed-in-the-wool capitalist who thought anyone who advocated anything less than Robber Baronism was a wild-eyed radical in cahoots with Satan. "Our national security is jeopardized by men like this, McDougal," he explained to me as I was hired to shadow a malihini named Paul Dodds, a young, visiting University of California at Berkeley professor who was in the islands to give a series of lectures on the Bolshevik revolution. A storm had already broken out in the press when the proposed lecture series was announced, with freedom of speech advocates squaring off against the redbaiters. For a nice, hefty wad of cash, my client wanted the agency to dig up some dirt on this Dodds while he was in the islands, something to royally embarrass him. The one good thing about being a private gumshoe instead of a cop is that the civil rights of the man you're shadowing doesn't mean twaddle, especially when the price is right.

The evening Miss Ash vanished, I was trying to keep awake during one of Professor Dodds' lectures at the University of Hawai'i. If this fellow was going to start some uprising among the working class, I thought to myself, he would need a better speechwriter. After an equally boring reception held for the Red sympathizer, I followed him back to his rented cottage at Cressaty's Court, a modest Waikiki establishment located on the beach between the Seaside Hotel and Fort DeRussy. About 10:30 p.m. his cottage lights went out and I called it a night, turning the graveyard shift over to Sammy Chun, one of the new young recruits for the agency. On my way home, I stopped in at the social club on Lewers Street, where I indulged in a final, illegal nightcap.

When I got to my office in the morning, China was waiting with my cup of Joe and a Western Union message from San Francisco. It was from Mrs. Harriet Ash, a wealthy widow ensconced in some mountain retreat in Sausalito and the mother of the missing Penelope. She wanted our agency to look into her daughter's disappearance. If Penelope drowned, she wanted some proof of her death. If Penelope lost her mind or was abducted, she wanted her back unharmed. She was willing to pay top dollar for results and I was ready to find them, even if it meant wrestling a shark to extract a bracelet from its belly.

I turned the investigation of the Bolshevik Dodds over to Chun and John Kelly, another gumshoe in the agency, and started digging into Miss Ash's background. The newspapers were playing up this "Socialite Disappears From Waikiki Beach" real big. By the time I got to the Moana Hotel to interrogate her sister, I already had a pretty good picture of Penelope and Jane Ash. They had visited Honolulu in January, intending to stay for only a month. "Falling in love with the islands" (probably read "man"), they decided to extend their stay for a year. They were Northern California women with the edge of sophistication and tinge of arrogance that comes from wealth, status and Frisco "old family" society, which had long ago forgotten how their forebears had made their fortunes from booze and broads. They had been living at the Moana Hotel and working as volunteers at the YMCA downtown. They were with the War Camp Community Service, helping local boys readjust to the farm after they'd seen Paree. It wasn't hard to see from her photograph in the newspaper that plenty of those doughboys must have fallen head over heels for Miss Ash.

I met Jane Ash for lunch under the banyan in the courtyard of the Moana Hotel. Hoping that she would be the same kind of dish as her sister, I learned that good looks don't always run in the family. Jane Ash was 10 years older and 40 pounds heavier, with twice as many chins as Penelope. She knew her mother had lots of money and she used it as an edge over others.

"I suggested that Harriet hire your agency, Mr. McDougal. You were recommended to me by Mr. Clarence Cooke Alberts. Do you know Clarence? He speaks highly of your firm."

"Yeah, I know Mr. Alberts." Clarence Cooke Alberts was Honolulu's walking Christmas tree, doling his fortune out to every pretty flapper in town. He got himself into a scandal a couple of years ago, when his chauffeur sued him for "alienation of affections," after Clarence was caught sending letters and jewelry to the fellow's wife. The whole thing was fairly harmless, but Alberts' family felt the sting.

"Can you tell me something about your sister's behavior before she vanished? You told the police she was suffering from headaches?"

Penelope's headaches had started a week earlier, frequently confining her to her hotel room. The day she disappeared the headaches had increased in intensity. Jane had suggested that her sister see a doctor, but Penelope believed that all she needed was aspirin. She had become a regular customer of Hobron's Drugs downtown, visiting the pharmacy, as well as a Fort Street bookstore.

"My sister was a prolific reader, Mr. McDougal," she whispered, dabbing a tear from the corner of her eye. "I've not been able to sleep since her tragic disappearance. You must find her, you must."

The million-dollar view of Diamond Head from the courtyard of the Moana seemed more beautiful than ever. A few beachboys had taken off on one of those mile-long Waikiki bull waves, then each hoisted up a *wahine* onto his shoulders. Tandem riding was quite a thrill for the visitors and made better entertainment than Jane's sob-sister act. Her tears were about as warm and sincere as the cold, dead shrimp on my plate. With her sister out of the picture, her mother's wealth started to look bigger and bigger. Jane Ash was suffering from a bad case of sibling rivalry and it was all too obvious. She missed her sister about as much as Lorrin Thurston missed the monarchy.

I promised her that I would do my best to find Penelope, finished my lunch and decided to take a stroll down the beach to the Outrigger Club. Manoa Valley had been dry that summer, so the river that cut into the beach was hardly a puddle. I took off my shoes, rolled up my pants and waded through the stream to find a few of the beachboys at the clubhouse, serenading the *haole* honeys while the others were out on the waves. If you needed to know about anything happening on the beach at Waikiki, you had to talk to these guys, who spent their lives surfing and wooing. They proudly called themselves "beachboys," although some of them were hardly youngsters. Everyone got a nickname among them, and it was not uncommon that, if your face was known on the beach, they gave you one, too. For some reason that wholly escaped me, I was known as the "Professor." It could have been that I was always asking them for information.

"Howzit, 'Professor,'" said "Paniolo," one of the landmarks on the beach. "Looking for Miss Ash?"

"How'd you know?"

"I've never seen you down here yet you weren't working, yeah?"

"Did you know her, Paniolo?"

"Sure. She was a good-looking *wahine*. You never miss them, Professor, at Flapper's Acre."

They called this stretch of the beach Flapper's Acre with good reason. Ladies with romance in their eyes and a passion for brown-skinned natives discovered that Iowa just melted away when a husky, strong-voiced Hawaiian sang "Honolulu Maids." To be discreet, they would check into the Moana or Seaside Hotels, pick a man up on the beach, and then get a home in the other hotel for the evening. While the Sunday sermons at the pulpit referred to Waikiki as the "gateway to hell," the hotel owners loved the double-bookings.

In the last few months, the Ash sisters had been doing a lot of double-bookings, especially with a strong, bronzed Kauai fellow named "Turtle Boy" Lum. According to Paniolo, Turtle Boy had set his sights on Penelope, who evidently flirted more than she gave out. A couple of the beachboys who had tried to spark her said Penelope wasn't always what she seemed. Sure she could swill the hooch and walk out to the Queen's pier to mooch, but more often she preferred to be alone.

"Did she often complain about headaches?"

"No," Paniolo told me. "If she had headaches, she never mentioned it to us."

"Did you try to hit on her?"

"No, she wasn't my type. Something was funny about her, like she was hiding something. Some nights she'd get real rowdy, acting real dumb. Then the next morning she'd ask me to go with her downtown to that new bookstore on Fort. If she wasn't flirting, she was reading. I couldn't figure her out."

From Paniolo's description of her behavior, it was almost as if she wanted people to think she was a dumb floozy rather than an egghead.

Jane Ash was just the opposite—an easy mark. According to Paniolo, she had a thing for Turtle Boy, who teased her along, keeping one eye on Penelope and the other on the older sister's fat purse. Turtle Boy was willing to do anything for money.

"He's had plenty of *pilikia*, Professor. I guess he was playing the both of them sisters."

Those type of triangles always lead to either big headaches or gunshot wounds.

I dropped by the office before paying a visit to Turtle Boy Lum, when I saw the late afternoon story in the *Star-Bulletin* that the police had a lead on the Ash disappearance. According to a new eyewitness, a *haole* girl was seen driving away from Waikiki Beach at about sunset in a dark touring car, with a Japanese woman sitting next to her. The girl fit the description of Miss Ash. I made a call to Sgt. Chillingworth, my inside source in the department, to see whether this was a solid lead or a red herring. Chillingworth wasn't certain.

"We've been getting a lot of crazy calls about her disappearance. One lady claims that she saw Ash in a kimono, acting as a servant at one of the Nuuanu mansions."

"There's a reward out for her return, Sarge," I reminded him. Whenever the fish smell cash, they swarm like piranha.

"Do me a favor, Sarge. If you hear anything at all about Ash, call me. Okay? I'm working for her mother. By the way, you know where I can find Turtle Boy?"

"The Waikiki boy?"

"Yeah."

"Sure. He's my cousin's good friend. Last I heard, he was renting a room in Blood Town."

Blood Town was one of the tenements on the *mauka* side of Beretania near Aala Park, which was packed with immigrants, squealing kids, thugs, sleazy brothels and those down on their luck. This section of the town had burned down during the Chinatown fire back in 1900 and, when they built it all back up, they just squeezed everybody into wooden shacks. Turtle Boy was renting a place in a squalid little boarding room watched over by a beady-eyed Chinese landlord, who kept a cig dangling between his lips which dropped its ashes in its own good time. For a crisp, new sawbuck, he let me search through Turtle Boy's tiny room filled with the stink of old cigarette smoke and unwashed dishes. The beachboy hadn't been there for at least a couple of days. I went through his chest of drawers and closet. In the pocket of an old jacket I found a receipt for two steerage tickets purchased for the S.S. *Claudine* leaving for Molokai and Maui on Saturday, July 5, at 6 a.m. I slipped the receipt in my pocket and left everything exactly as I found it—a complete mess.

"You seen Turtle Boy lately?" I asked the landlord.

"No savvy," he answered, the ash on his cigarette approaching a couple of inches. I flashed another sawbuck. Hell, Harriet Ash had deep pockets.

"He no more stay, one...two days."

My next stop was on Fort Street to find the bookstore where Miss Ash spent her free time. The New Thought Bookstore was in the Love Building and was owned by a long-haired gent with a thick Boston accent who peered at me over his thick spectacles like I didn't belong in his highfalutin' joint. The shelves were filled with all those books you hear the moralists rage against but you never read. I sized the place up in two minutes, when I noticed a flyer tacked up on the edge of a bookshelf announcing a speech by my friend, the visiting Bolshevik.

"Looking for something, sir?" he asked, looking at me over his glasses. "A special title?" He posed the question as if he thought I couldn't read.

"Someone, not something. When was the last time you saw Penelope Ash?"

"The police have already been here, mister. I told them everything I know."

"Why don't you try repeating it for me. The name's McDougal. I work for Miss Ash's mother. She asked me to look into her daughter's disappearance."

"She came into the shop twice, maybe three times, a week, usually looking through the oriental philosophy and self-improvement books."

"Did you ever talk with her?"

"Occasionally we had a conversation. She was well-read, but hopelessly bourgeois. The wealth of the leisure class tends to debilitate their intellectual capacities beyond that of self-indulgence, thus the oriental philosophy. But I suppose a man of violence such as yourself wouldn't be interested in such matters."

"Uh-huh. When was the last time you saw her?"

"Two or three days ago. She came in for an hour or so, browsing around. Then she left for the YMCA."

I thanked him for his time, took one more quick look-wise about the joint and started for the door, when the walking Christmas tree came in through the door. Now what would a gent like Clarence Cooke Alberts be doing in a "new thought" bookstore? Maybe the egghead was selling pornography under the counter. Alberts brushed past me and made a beeline for the shelf that read "Theosophy."

"Oh, one more thing, mister…"

"Reed. Robert Reed."

"What's a spiritual fellow like you doing promoting a Bolshevik?"

"Professor Dodds offers an alternative social vision for this country which will not only improve the spiritual quality but also economic condition of the working classes. I would recommend his public lectures to anyone, including you."

"Well, from one working stiff to another," I shot back as I left, "new thought is the opiate of the masses." I slammed the door just enough to rattle the windows, grateful that I had listened to all that garbage Dodds had been throwing around the day I shadowed him.

Fifteen minutes later Alberts walked out of the New Thought Bookstore, headed up Fort and went into the lounge in the Blaisdell Hotel. I sat down next to him at the bar, where he ordered a Coca-cola, which he proceeded to spike with rum from the flask he carried in his inside breast pocket. The lounge was already dry, but no one minded when you poured your own stuff. I ordered the same and nudged my Christmas tree.

"Mind? I forgot my stuff."

"Of course. You were in the bookstore, weren't you?"

He generously poured a double shot into my glass. If he wasn't out of my league, I could have learned to have liked this guy. He was eyeing one of the young dolls sitting alone at a booth in the open garden courtyard. The Blaisdell was a second-rate hotel, with a run-of-the-mill clientele. Just the kind of easy catch for a guy that chases after his chauffeur's wife.

"I was looking into how to get rich quick."

"Oh, the Horatio Alger series?"

"No, the Penelope Ash reward method."

"You're from the detective agency! Of course, I should have known you were a private investigator. It's the hat."

"Never mind my hat," I said, wondering if I should pay my haberdasher a visit. After all, a gumshoe can't walk about looking like a detective. "What can you tell me about Miss Ash's disappearance?"

"Not much. She never paid much attention to me. That is the difficulty when you lure women with money. If they have money, then they are wholly invulnerable to your advances. Jane is a different story."

"Have you been sparking her?"

"She is more accurately sparking me. You see, I met the sisters at a reception my mother held for the women helping with the returning veterans. You know of my mother, of course?"

Who didn't know the name of Grace Alberts? One of the town's do-gooders, she was one of the reasons the Women's Christian Temperance Union was able to turn Honolulu dry.

"Your mother wouldn't approve of the rum."

"My mother doesn't approve of anything I do, least of all the rum. Fortunately she adores my sense of humor, so she has learned to tolerate me."

"And so Jane Ash adored your sense of humor?"

"No. I think she adores the fact that I adore her sister, but she has me."

"Huh?"

"She's so jealous of her sister that if she can seduce any man who has eyes for Penelope, then she believes she has one up on her. Of course, in my case I'm relatively easy."

"Do you think she's jealous enough to harm her?"

"They argued incessantly about everything from men to religion to politics. Penelope appeared demure, but when she got a head of steam, she was impassioned over any subject. During their tirades, Jane would often throw things. It could get quite dangerous to be in the same room with them."

"Had they argued recently?"

"Oh, definitely. How do you think Penelope got that headache? Jane hit her with a perfume bottle."

We had two more rounds and the lights on my Christmas tree were shining real pretty. When I left him, Alberts was falling into a chair next to the lonely miss in the booth, probably already filling her head with diamond dreams.

I stopped by the Union Grill for my usual blue-plate dinner special before dropping by the office. Just as in walked in the door, there was a call from Chillingworth, who had an inside scoop. A woman's half-clad body had just been pulled out of the harbor, right next to Pier 12.

"I'm not certain, but it could be the Ash lady. Someone told me that she was wearing a kimono."

Since Pier 12 was only a hop, skip and a jump from my office, 5 minutes later I edged up to Dr. Faus, the medical examiner, who had the victim on a stretcher in the back of the ambulance.

"Howdy, McDougal. Into chasing ambulances now that you're no longer a cop?"

"I heard they found a body."

About half an hour ago, a drunk sailor reported seeing a lady disrobe and then jump into the harbor from the end of the pier.

"She must not have known how to swim. This isn't much of a jump."

"He said she went in and never came up. The cops dropped some nets and found her right away. Appears like a suicide. We found a kimono, obi and wooden slippers on the dock. I haven't done the autopsy yet, but I imagine we'll find her lungs filled with water."

"Is it Ash?"

"Nope."

"You sure?"

"Take a look for yourself."

I went into the wagon and lifted the sheet concealing her face. For some reason I was praying it wouldn't be Penelope, even though she was worth as much to me dead as she was alive. I took a quick glance and breathed a long sigh of relief.

"Japanese girl, about 16 or 17," added Dr. Faus. "From the bruises on her back, my guess she was hooking for the Hinode gang. Probably couldn't take it anymore."

Every time the cops found some young Japanese woman dead of suicide, they blamed it on the Hinode boys. They were a pretty tough gang that ran the Japanese-style brothels. Most of the women were tricked into the islands as picture brides and then forced into prostitution. For some, the shame was too great and they would commit suicide, usually by hanging. Self-inflicted drowning was rare, but not unheard of.

"What made you think it was the *haole* girl?"

"Just the rumors about her being seen wearing a kimono."

"If you ask me, she took a swim and miscalculated the tides. Either she'll turn up on the rocks or she's in the belly of a shark. What a waste. She was quite the looker, yeah?"

An hour later I was back in my office sorting it all out. The place was bedlam. The rich dame in Sausalito had sent another wire, demanding answers. She said she'd double the fee if we could find her daughter. That put the reward up to $10,000. So far I had a jealous sister with hot pants for beachboys, an overgenerous *kama'aina* with a penchant for scandal, a beachboy with a ticket for two to Molokai and a near-sighted bookstore owner with an egghead attitude. To top it off, China was nagging me for a raise and Chun was shoving a report under my nose, telling me how he got the dirt on the Bolshevik.

"He's a *mahu*, McDougal."

"What do you mean?"

"He's shacked up with some young man at Cressaty's Court. Can you imagine that? A pansy right under nose. Should I call the client?"

"Hell, no," I told him. "When we said we'd get dirt on him, I meant un-American stuff."

"Ain't being a pansy un-American?"

"We'll talk about it later. I didn't get into this line of work to catch people under sheets. That's his own damn business. Now if he was planning to blow up the Bank of Hawaii, that's something different."

I grabbed the Dodds file out of Chun's hand and tossed it to China.

"File it."

"First the raise."

"You're working overtime, aren't you? I'm not giving you a raise, all right? Maybe if we get the Ash reward."

"Can I help?"

"Yeah, tell me what Jan Ash, Turtle Boy, Clarence Alberts and the New Thought Bookstore have in common."

"Maybe nothing."

"Very helpful. *Mahalo.*"

I turned all my scant leads over and over in my head a thousand times, thinking about that shark with the bracelet in its belly. If I was going to get that $10,000 reward, I'd need tangible proof she was dead. Then I jumped up, doffed my dead-giveaway hat, thanked China for the lead and promised her the raise. By 11 p.m. my machine was rolling down Merchant Street, turning up Bishop to Ala Moana Road. If my hunch was right, I was about to become the richest private dick in the business.

The engine died and my coupe coasted silently up to the bungalow at Cressaty's Court at Waikiki which had been rented to the Bolshevik. I switched off my

Paul Dodds' car is parked in front of Cressaty's Court. [This is the Niumalu Hotel. GG] *(Ray Jerome Baker, Bishop Museum)*

headlights and reached under my seat for the Colt revolver I kept there for tight situations. If my hunch was right, I wouldn't need it. If I was wrong, it could come in handy.

I pulled up alongside one of the windows and took a long gander through the blinds that were slightly open. Paul Dodds, professional troublemaker, was in the arms of a slightly effeminate, good-looking young man who looked back adoringly. They exchanged a long, passionate kiss. I came around the front and gave the door a hard rap. Before the lovebirds could break it up, I entered unannounced and closed the door behind me.

They sat on the sofa like Mexican jumping beans, spilling their guts. She was wearing a Panama suit and had her hair cut so short you would have sworn she was a man. She chained-smoked from a pack of Three Kings and mouthed plenty of big dreams about the revolution, her mother's filthy lucre, her sister the playgirl and the disgust she felt for the rich. He egged her on. They knew each other from Berkeley and, in fact, hatched this little plan to sneak off to Russia together last year. They had tickets for the *Korea Maru* leaving tomorrow morning. From Yokohama they would sneak into Japan-occupied Korea and then into Siberia. From there they'd take the trans-Siberian railroad to Moscow to join the Reds in a New World. They clung to each other like magnets and in their eyes you could see they meant every word.

I asked her why she bothered to fake her disappearance. Why not just announce to the world you turned Communist? She looked at me painfully and in a sweet, squeaky voice said, "My mother would rather see me dead than renounce her wealth. I didn't really want to hurt her." She was as beautiful as I had imagined and I thought of the $10,000 reward as I picked up the cottage telephone to call Sergeant Chillingworth at HPD.

"Are you going to turn me in?" She asked. "I never meant to hurt anyone. They'll never really miss me. Mister?" Her voice was soft and plaintive, but I knew my duty.

China had been right. There was no connection between the disappearance of Miss Ash and my suspects. Turtle Boy, I later found out, had a sister with leprosy who was living at Kalaupapa on Molokai. He lived in poverty so that she could have clean clothes and a box of goodies once a month. The tickets were for him and his mother to visit her. Reed was just a bookstore owner with funny titles, and Alberts became my occasional drinking friend.

Last call in a Honolulu saloon before Prohibition. *(On Char, Bishop Museum)*

Mrs. Ash and her daughter seemed satisfied that I had tried my best. As far as I could tell, her daughter had vanished from the face of the earth. Unable to prove whether she had died, I charged the mother $50 for two days' work and $10 expenses for the two sawbucks I gave Turtle Boy's landlord. They both also received my condolences, which were free.

As for Penelope, I guess she's still in Moscow, fighting capitalists and the memory of all that wealth. China got her raise. I don't know where the shark went. Maybe he's prowling around the new drydock at Pearl Harbor.

One night two months later, I slipped into a dark corner of the Beehive Saloon, a dive in the heart of Honolulu, and joined the score of other boozers getting one last "legal" drink before Prohibition and the Feds made us all moral. The air was stale, cheap and lonely, just like my life had become. Funny little memories swirled around in my head as I looked once again into the face of a delicate oriental girl sitting on her mother's front porch telling me it wouldn't work out. "Arthur," she was saying, "my parents would never approve."

A guy can get sentimental now and then, can't he? The bloated face of that frightened picture bride in the back of Faus' ambulance haunted me. Only 15 or 16 years old, she had followed love to the ends of the earth, only to end up beaten, bruised and floating face down in Honolulu Harbor. I thought about that little yard on School Street and wondered if there was space for me if the volcano really did erupt. Maybe it was already erupting.

I poured myself another drink and drowned all that claptrap in my last open shot of rotgut before Honolulu turned totally dry.

[**Editor's Note:** The summer of 1919 was indeed filled with wondrous events as described by McDougal. In Kalihi a seer predicted volcanic eruptions that would destroy all parts of the islands except her yard. The second construction of the Pearl Harbor drydocks had been completed successfully when a shark's skeleton was found on the ocean floor, raising questions about the destruction of the first drydock. And a young woman did indeed mysteriously vanish from the beach in front of the Moana Hotel, never to be found.]

CHAPTER THREE

The Case of the Broken China Doll

The smooth, porcelain skin of the China doll's face was without a single blemish. The cheeks were taut and high and the nose had a slope for which a man in heat would kill. Her eyes were shut tight but still had that perfect almond shape that made me wonder how deeply I could have gotten lost in those hidden celestial pupils. Death had drained her lips of their natural rouge and replaced it with a light blue tint.

The rest of her body looked as if it had been used by the Babe for batting practice. Below her neck, the China doll was broken up into little pieces. A Japanese fish peddler had found her on the train track out at Pearl City Peninsula. She had evidently dragged herself at least 500 yards out of a nearby cane field before dying. I laid the sheet back down over the corpse and grounded down hard on my teeth. My dentist warned me my job was destroying my bite.

"Somebody made sure that her face stayed unbruised, but the rest of her is a mess. Multiple internal injuries, broken ribs, pelvis and two shattered knees, massive internal bleeding." Doc Liu, the assistant medical examiner, wasn't his usual stoic self.

"Either a baseball bat or a crowbar," he added angrily. "At this point I can't determine the exact cause of death, but she wasn't going to live long with all that bleeding. It was a miracle that she was able to crawl as far as she did."

"They wanted to keep her face pretty," I said, imagining what she would have looked like with a smile.

"I knew her, McDougal. Mai Ling Song was a good kid. She had her wild side, but nothing bad. Get the bastards, McDougal. Get 'em."

"I'll do my best, Doc. I promised her parents."

Liu pulled the sheet over the broken doll and we walked out of the basement autopsy room into a balmy Honolulu day. The morgue was located right behind the Territorial Building, where a lone reporter was waiting. Jared Smythe covered the police beat with a nose for scandal. If Mai Ling Song had been a *haole* lady, I thought to myself, the reporters would have been swarming all over the place looking for solid news. If it was an Oriental, only Smythe would be there looking for something sensational.

"What's the scoop on the Chinese girl, Doc?"

"I'm afraid you'll have to talk to the police."

"Was she molested?"

"Smythe," I volunteered, "take a hike. Nothing for your ragsheet here."

"What's a private dick working on a *pake* case for? What's up, McDougal?

I ignored the little weasel, thanked Doc Liu for the information and walked back to my Merchant Street office. A few minutes later I found my secretary, China, trying to comfort Miss Song's parents in the office. They were all jabbering away in their impossible lingo and I was trying to tell them that I would bring in their daughter's killer.

"Kimo Chun killed my daughter," China said, translating for Mrs. Song. "He was her boyfriend, he had a hot temper."

"The boxer?"

"The same, Mac. She broke off with him about six months ago."

I had seen Kimo Chun box several times out at Block Arena up at Schofield Barracks, where Army and amateur boxers used to spar. He was a Chinese-Hawaiian featherweight who had been up and coming in island sporting circles. Only he was a hothead in the ring, throwing wild punches and losing control. The last time I had watched him box a few weeks ago, his timing was all off. He had the anger, but none of the skills. Rumor was he had taken to the bottle and his career at the age of 24 was already washed up.

The Songs were concerned that the police wouldn't do enough to find their daughter's killer.

"The cops don't care about a dead Chinese girl," China translated the parents' words, adding her own slang. "They'd only assume she was some hooker who ended up with a trick in the cane fields and then got herself into trouble."

"Was she hooking?"

"Mac!" China snapped. "You're talking about my cousin. Why do you *haole* men always think oriental girls are cheap?"

"Sorry, China. It's my job to ask, right?"

The Songs apologized about not having much money to pay me, but I told them, "no worry." This was a family affair, since she was related to China. And as I was always reminded by my secretary, I owed her far more than her $10-a-week wage covered.

My first step was to find a wayward boxer named Chun. Since his career took a nose dive, he was drowning his sorrows in the sleazier "soft drink parlors" in Aala Park. One of his hangouts was a downstairs dive under a saimin store called Yamada's. I was on my way down River Street, watching the kids pull "blind mullet" out of the canal, when an overweight flatfoot named John Carney and one of his lapdogs sidled up to me. They had obviously been tailing me since I had left my office.

"What's your pleasure, Carney?" With his pockmarked face redder than normal, the cigar stub in his mouth gave him the appearance of a stuck roasted pig.

"What makes you so interested in a dead Chinese girl?"

"The last time I looked, it was a free country." Everyone seemed to be asking me that question lately, and Carney was the last person in the world to whom I'd have given an answer. When I was on the force back in 1919, Carney was the detective who testified against me during my trial concerning allegations that I had taken a bribe from a Chinese racketeer named Tan. He said I had been chummy with the Iceman and that following his investigation, I was found to have $10,000 in my safety deposit box and a new sailing boat at Honolulu Harbor. The money was from a dead relative and the boat I told them was a gift from a friend—not the Iceman. Nothing was ever proved against me, but I was so disgusted with the force that I quit.

"This town doesn't need dirty private dicks, McDougal. Don't stick your nose into a police department investigation. We heard you were talking to Liu."

Carney was talking tough because the 1928 elections for Sheriff was next month and he had decided to hook up with the Democrats to run for the position. He was trying to get all the publicity he could as a crime-fighter, hauling in bootleggers, busting social clubs and having his photograph taken with babies and babes. Politics and police work, I always said to myself, should never mix.

"All I'm doing is representing the Songs in the death of their daughter. I'm not interfering with the cops. In fact, you'll be the first to know anything I find out, since it seems you're doing nothing yourself to find her murderer."

"She was just some whore who got beat up by her pimp. We're looking into it. You back off."

"Carney, I know kids in elementary school who know more about police work from just reading detective comic books than all you flatfoots put together. So if you don't mind, I've got some work to do." I turned into a little food joint along the canal just to shake him off.

"I'll get your license, McDougal, if you take one step out of line."

"Yeah, yeah," I said, slamming the door behind me. I waited until Carney and his partner turned and walked back towards the Kekaulike fishmarket, and then I quickly walked up to Yamada's stand, where I was waved downstairs to the "parlor." The smoke in the place was stifling, the lighting so poor you could hardly see what you were drinking. The Japanese owner kept his *okolehao* in huge milk cans from which he rationed out the shots with a ladle. I wasn't sure if the poison was sake or gin, but I was glad the place was so dark I couldn't see what I was drinking.

When I asked the poison-dispenser about Chun, he told me I was too late. The cops had already been there looking for the boxer, who had gone on the lam. With his former sweetheart beaten to death, he was lying real low. Everyone in the joint knew the kid, so it was easy to get the story. Chun and Mai Ling Song had been a number for about six months, but she had started to get high-nose by dating some *haole* fellow. When she went for the white meat, Chun had gone for the bootleg.

"Local *wahine* always think that if they can get a white man, they'd be better off," Chun's former sparring partner muttered. "It's not true. They just get haolified and then dumped."

It was nearly sunset when I got back to the International Detective Agency to find a very nervous China pacing in my office.

"Where in the hell have you been?" she snapped at me.

"Wow, lady. Who's the boss here? It just so happens I was working on this little free case you stuck me with so..."

"Shut up, Mac. Come here." She took my hand to pull me into one of the back storage rooms. Sitting on a pile of International Detective Agency stationery was a stewed-to-the-gills Kimo Chun.

"I loved Mai Ling. I would have never killed her. I never touched her, hear me?"

A bell must have rung in his head because he jumped to his feet swinging wildly like I had seen him do to Kid Collins. Collins had laid him flat two rounds later.

"Hold it, slugger. It's intermission, take a seat." We calmed him down so I could get some straight information.

"If you didn't kill her, then who do you think did?"

"The *haole* guy she was dating. He did it to her. He ruined her life. I'll kill 'em if I ever see 'em..." The bell in his head rang again and he started pounding his fist into a box of stationery.

"Stop it!" screamed China, slapping him in the face. "That's expensive stationery." He looked at Mai Ling's cousin and burst out crying like a little kid. The China doll was this kid's Achilles heel.

"Now, tell me what happened between you and Mai Ling. Calmly."

With China scowling over Chun to keep him in control, he finally got out the story without breaking up the office. She had met a *haole* guy who she started to date. Since Mai Ling spoke pidgin, he had encouraged her to speak better English and to dump her has-been boxer. She and Chun finally had a big blowout, and he hadn't seen her for a few days.

"I read that she was murdered. I couldn't believe it, something snapped inside. I swear I went *lolo*, just getting stinking drunk. When the cops came snooping after me, I figured I was in big trouble. That's when I went looking for Yi, hoping to get some help."

"Who?"

"Me, Mac. I'm Yi, remember?"

"Oh, yeah, yeah."

I locked Chun in one of the agency rooms with a bottle of my cheapest whiskey to suck on and told China to make sure he stayed too drunk to leave. As long as the cops were looking for Chun, I figured, I'd have a little leeway to turnover some of my own fresh soil. Chun didn't know the name of the *haole*, but he knew that his girlfriend had been taking an American cooking class at McKinley High School. The *haole* wanted her to improve herself by learning to cook western style so he enrolled her in this class designed to give local women "cultural improvement." Hell, I'd take Chinese food over boiled potatoes and fried shoe-leather meat any day.

At 9 o'clock the next morning I joined 500 ladies in the McKinley High School Auditorium listening to

My machine parked in front of McKinley High School where Miss DuPont's cooking classes took place. *(Hawai'i State Archives)*

a Miss Jesse Marie DuPont wax eloquent over fruit salad. It was trumped up as *The Honolulu Advertiser* Cooking and Homemaking School but it was just a klatch of housewives fussing over recipes and buying fancy appliances like the Kohler Electric Sink that claimed to wash dishes when a penny scrubbing pad did the same job faster. Miss DuPont was on the stage, baking spaghetti rings and making a mint selling every product in town. When she finished her "surprise cake," she asked if anyone wanted to take it home and a hundred screaming voices rang out a chorus of "Yes! Oh, yes! I do." I guess I was the lucky one. She selected me.

After her little performance, I went around the back of the stage to pick up my little surprise and to find out if Miss DuPont knew anything about Mai Ling Song. Up close, her buxom, broad-shouldered body seemed even larger. She was maybe 30 years old, but looked a matronly 40. Her hair was bobbed and she wore no makeup, except a light facial powder to hide a thin mustache on her lip. She peered at me from behind a pair of unattractive spectacles and congratulated me on being chosen for the "surprise cake."

When I asked her if Mai Ling Song had ever won the cake, she beamed.

"Mai Ling is such a dear girl. Are you her gentleman friend? I must tell you, sir, your future wife shows signs of being an excellent wife. After all, as I tell my ladies repeatedly, the way to a man's heart is through his stomach. Now, don't you agree?"

I figured she hadn't read the morning paper yet.

"Mai Ling Song is dead." My bedside manner is pretty *pilau*.

She nearly dropped my surprise cake in the electric sink as she swooned, throwing her hand backwards against her forehead and collapsing into a well-cushioned chair.

"My God, my God," she muttered again and again. "Life is so fragile. She was so healthy, beautiful and young. How did she die?"

"Somebody took a baseball bat to her spleen." I really had to work on this routine. Miss DuPont let out a chilling scream.

"Murder! Murder! My Mai Ling murdered?"

It took two strong custodians to help me carry her to a couch in the principal's office. Arthur McDougal had just received a grade of "F" in tact. Her sobbing continued for nearly half an hour, as the school nurse plied her with cool water, wet compresses and reassuring tones. When I could finally get her to tell me how she knew Mai Ling, I realized she was hardly an acquaintance of the young Chinese girl, who had been taking the home-cooking lessons. Yes, she had taken a special liking to Mai Ling. In fact, the young Chinese girl was so eager to cook *haole*-style dishes to win the heart of an American husband that DuPont agreed to give her some extracurricular lessons. She once had Mai Ling over for dinner at her Nuuanu home, after which they had a long girl-to-girl talk. DuPont gave me the name of a young man, Henry Wadsworth Donaldson, who had been the object of Miss Song's affection. I thought I detected a glint of the green monster in the matron's steel-gray eyes when she mentioned Donaldson's name.

"Please, Mr. McDougal," she implored me, "find the perpetrator of this foul deed. Revenge Mai Ling, sir. Oh, the poor, poor dear." I promised I'd do my best and beat a hasty retreat from the sobbing matron.

As I passed the statue of President McKinley on my way to my machine, I heard a young voice call out to me.

"Mac! Mac! Hold on!" It was Katsumi Odachi, thrusting an excited hand into mine. I hadn't seen the teenager for a while, possibly avoiding the family out of guilt. His father, Naoaki Odachi, had been one of the operatives in the agency. We were partners on plenty of cases, so I had gotten to know his old lady and their son, Katsumi. About two years ago, Naoaki and I were working on an opium racket with tentacles like an octopus, when I received a mysterious message to meet a stoolie at the new Aloha Tower harbor area, where the Boat Day festivities take place. I was supposed to get there after midnight, when the place would be quiet. The booze had been taken a heavy toll on me those days and my head was pretty stretched by the time I got the message. Naoaki volunteered to fill in for me.

The cops found him gunned down along the wharf. The killer had shot him right between the eyes. A single .38 bullet casing was found tossed on his chest. Naoaki's car was parked back along the road, the engine still running like he was waiting for someone. The passenger's door was open and on the sidewalk someone had tossed a deck of cards, a single bullet hole through the ace of spades. The .38 had been meant, no doubt, for me. The case was still unsolved, with no hard clues leading in any direction as to who could have killed my partner.

Kats was an *akamai* kid who supported his mother with a newspaper job while trying to finish high school. Like his father, he had a good nose for snooping around, digging up useful information. I asked him if he had known Miss Song, the Chinese girl who was found dead at Pearl City.

"What a looker, Mac," he answered, smiling. "Everyone noticed her at McKinley." Since McKinley was the only public high school, kids from all over Oahu attended, most of them the children of Japanese immigrants hoping to give their offspring a chance for a better life. "Little Tokyo" High School, as it was called, gave a boy like Katsumi an opportunity to do something other than cut cane. So lots of the students were country boys who ogled every pretty city girl that passed their way. Mai Ling Song must have been the "It Girl" on campus.

"On the afternoon the day before she was found on the train track," Katsumi informed me, "Mai Ling had left McKinley in the back of a taxicab. And, Mac, she wasn't alone. Another woman was sitting next to her."

"Did you see who it was?"

"Nah, I couldn't see her very well. But they were in the back seat sitting *very* close, if you know what I mean."

"Listen, Katsumi, here's a ten spot. Track down the taxicab driver, okay? And get me any dope you can on Miss DuPont."

"The cooking teacher with the mustache?"

"Yeah. And keep this quiet. Let China know what you find out."

I sent Kats on his errand, telling him to give his mom my best while I searched out the *haole* Donaldson.

The city directory gave me an Oahu Avenue address in Manoa Valley for the Donaldson family. As I pulled up to the house, the Manoa trolley car clanged by, came to a stop, emptying its passengers, and then the seats were turned around for the ride back out of the valley. Conductor Hans Ostergaard gave me the nod, as bundles of taro and banana were piled into the cars by farmers taking their produce into Chinatown. Ostergaard was one of those characters everyone who had ever ridden the trolley into Manoa knew and loved. I rang the doorbell to see a tall, medium-built, blond-headed, baby-faced gent answer the door. Now this was the kind of guy I could never like.

"Are you Henry Wadsworth Donaldson?"

"I'm sorry, we really don't need anything," he said with a snotty-air attitude as he began to close the door.

"I'm no salesman. The name's McDougal, International Detective Agency. I'd like a few words with you about Mai Ling Song."

His face fell as he hushed me, stepping out onto the porch.

"My mother's inside. If you don't mind, can we talk in the yard?"

We took a stroll up the valley, which was balmy as usual, with a radiant sky, billowy clouds and those rich, green mountains that almost seemed like giant cardboard background props on a movie set. The taro patches, like checkerboards on the valley floor, glistened in the afternoon sun as the Chinese farmers toiled with their weeding and harvesting. If you had the money, I thought to myself, life could be a bowl of cherries.

Donaldson, a junior account executive with Dillingham Transportation Company, had met Mai Ling when she was taking English lessons from the nice old lady next door. He'd never known an oriental girl before, so he made it a practice to "accidentally" run into her until it became serious. He even promised her that he would polish up this rough little piece of oriental jade to be his bride. Of course, his high-society mother hadn't been told about this quaint meeting of East and West.

"Her old boyfriend Chun must have killed Mai Ling," Donaldson advised me by the time we got back to his place. "He was a violent, terribly violent man." His voice was trembling.

"How do you know that?"

"He threatened me. Actually came to my place of employment and threatened me with bodily harm. He's a boxer, you know."

"So I've heard." Donaldson was gutless all the way around. He wouldn't stand up to his mother and was hiding with his tail between his legs from a washed-up drunk who was standing between him and his China doll. He was crying like a baby at the thought of Chun turning him into mincemeat.

"He told me that if he couldn't have Mai Ling, nobody could. Then he stormed out of the office. It was incredibly embarrassing."

I thought about a pair of permanently closed almond eyes that had once been lured by this weasel's baby looks and social standing. I saw the green flash.

Next door I had a little chat with Mrs. Serrat, a kindly old lady with Victorian manners, who earned a supplemental income tutoring Orientals in English. Twice a week she had been helping Miss Song overcome her pidgin accent. The news of her young student's death had, of course, devastated her but she had known nothing of Miss Song's affectations for "the nice young man next door."

"Did he do it?" she asked with an edge of gossip.

As we were chatting away in her parlor, a stunning brunette came in through the back door with two armfuls of groceries from Central Market. She was grumbling out loud to no one in particular about the red stains her white pumps got in these miserable islands. She cut her tirade short when she saw me sitting in the parlor. I was introduced to a real looker by the name of Edna Serrat, the old lady's daughter. She positioned herself in an armchair directly across from me and crossed her long, well-shaped legs, which were very visible under her summer dress. My temperature soared 50 degrees, as I straightened my tie and plastered down my cowlick.

"We are brand new in the islands and never get out much, Mr. McDougal," she hinted in a sulky voice. "If you have time, perhaps you could give us a little tour?"

"Sure. I know a swell place out on the Windward side. We can go out for a picnic one day." I didn't recognize the voice coming out of my mouth.

"Where is this place?"

"It's called Kaaawa."

"Kaa...what?" She had a wonderful little giggle in her voice.

"Kaaawa. The beach is beautiful." She mispronounced Kaaawa twice before I grabbed my hat, promised to get back to them, and beat a nervous retreat, muttering something about work to do.

Two hours later I had my feet up on the desk, dreaming about skinny dips at Kaaawa, when the ringing of the phone brought me back to Merchant Street. It was Katsumi Odachi, who had tracked down the taxi driver. He took Mai Ling and a *haole* lady to a house in Aiea the night before China doll was found on the train tracks. I jotted down the address, giving Kats a million *mahalo*.

It was nearly midnight before I drove up to a quiet street which wound up Aiea Heights. I switched my headlights off and slowly rolled a few hundred feet away from the address Kats had given me. It was a small cottage with a sweeping view of Pearl Harbor. I went around the back of the house on foot. The lights were blazing inside and there was the sound of jazz from a gramophone. A woman was laughing and a couple of good old fellows let out a belly roar. I reached for the Colt under my jacket and edged up to a back door. Suddenly, a black tunnel straight through the center of the earth to China opened at my feet. As I jumped in, I saw China doll's porcelain face and sealed almond eyes on the other end, her blue lips waiting to kiss me.

A lump the size of a watermelon on the back of my head was throbbing when I came to. The room was pitch black, and my hands and feet were tied to the corners of one of those Murphy disappearing beds that fold up into the wall. In the next room I heard several voices arguing about whether to kill me or not. A woman was making a good case for my demise, but a male seemed convinced that they were in deep enough hot water. He didn't want to go up on a murder charge.

"We've already committed murder once," the woman said. "Another one won't matter now." I wanted to disagree.

There was a shuffle of feet, the slam of a door and a roadster roared away. I thought I had been left alone, when a huge local woman, about twice my size and wielding a baseball bat, entered the room and switched on a light. A sinking feeling in my gut said that the man lost the argument. I lay there helpless, waiting to have my brains bashed in, when I figured I'd try to smooth-talk the Queen of Swat.

"They left you to do the dirty work, yeah? You're going to take the fall for them?"

She lifted the bat above her head, getting ready to use my noggin to hit a homerun. I had to talk real fast, now.

"Killing a *pake* girl's one thing. A *haole* cop's another. They'll hang you for this one. And don't you think they'll find you? Don't you think I gave your address to the police before I drove out here? They know you're the one that rents this joint." I was grabbing at straws.

She lowered the bat as I saw a flicker of fear in her eyes.

"I only do what they tell me, yeah?"

"Sure. The cops will understand. You can cop a plea. I'll vouch for you."

"The Chinese lady had been trying to escape. They told me to teach her a lesson, but to save her face for the customers. Maybe I hit her too hard. I was only doing what they told me."

I assured her that I wanted her boss, not her. If she untied me, I'd let her go. She took off after she cut the ropes. There was no place for her to hide, I figured. The cops could pick her up later.

I was putting on my shoes, trying to decide what my next move was, when I realized that my black leather soles were crusted with red dirt. It was a long shot, but I figured Miss Serrat didn't get her white pumps stained in Manoa soil. That red dirt was from cane fields. I didn't know yet what the connection was, but the female voice in the other room could have been the million-dollar-looking brunette.

Manoa Valley was just waking up, as a dazzling morning sun peaked over the mountains and beat down on the Serrat cottage. They weren't expecting the ghost of McDougal to show up, so I got the drop on Edna Serrat and her Valentino look-alike boyfriend, who were in the act of doing a fast packing job. With my Colt

The corner of Fort and King Streets was the fashionable district where Mai Ling often shopped. *(Hawai'i State Archives)*

pointed at his gut, the L.A. boy did all the talking. They had set up a white slave ring in the islands that recruited unwilling young girls, especially Orientals and Hawaiians, for the brothels throughout the West Coast. Mai Ling Song had caught their eye when she came for English lessons with Edna's mother, who got chummy with the Chinese girl, figuring she'd bring a pretty profit at the high-priced brothels in L.A. Under the ruse that she was going to teach Mai Ling how to dress more high-class for her new boyfriend, Mrs. Serrat picked Mai Ling up after her McKinley High cooking class for a shopping spree at the Fort Street Liberty House.

Instead, they went to the Aiea house, where the slave ring operated. They hadn't meant to kill her. They just meant to give her new occupational opportunities. She tried to escape from one of the rooms and the local woman beat her too hard. In a panic, they dumped her body in a sugar cane field out in Pearl City.

I was backing over to the telephone to call the police, when a bewildered Mrs. Serrat entered from a back bedroom, asking what was going on. I was trying to explain that her daughter was implicated in some dirty business, when that sweet old lady got the drop on me with a gun from her handbag.

"You won't get away with it, lady. This is an island which the cops will sew up as tight as a drum."

Ignoring me, she barked orders to the other two who headed for the door. When they opened it, Donaldson from next door had just stepped up. Fortunately for me, he was on an errand for his dear mother.

"Oh, excuse me. Sorry to bother you but…"

He had just spit out the words, when Mrs. Serrat swung wildly and let off a shot that plugged the young kid in the chest. I snatched a porcelain lamp off a table and flung it to her head. A stream of blood oozed into her white perfumed hair as she crumbled to the floor.

A few days later, I joined China at the Chinese Cemetery in Manoa Valley, where Mai Ling Song was laid to rest. We huddled under large, black umbrellas in a drenching afternoon downpour, as the funeral procession slowly moved into the cemetery. Drums beat and a string of loud firecrackers was lit to chase off evil spirits. A tearful Miss DuPont jumped at the tiny explosions. Kimo Chun had dried out enough to join the other mourners throwing small pieces of white paper punctured with holes to the neighborhood children who had gathered to watch the exotic ceremonies. When a bouquet of anthuriums arrived, sent by a recovering Donaldson from his hospital bed, the boxer got real sore.

With the help of the sensational writing of Jared Smythe, Sheriff Carney turned the white slave ring case into a political football, claiming that he had busted city vice wide open. Mrs. Serrat was really a mainland felon named Mary Ogden out of Chi who had a police record as long as Duke's surfboard. Her "daughter" was a common prostitute out of L.A. who helped with the rackets, controlling the girls and turning tricks. The sheiky boy was some cheap hoodlum who was long on looks but short on brains and guts. The cops later picked up the scared big woman with the baseball bat. I testified at her trial that, although she had beaten Mai Ling, at least she had spared my precious scalp.

What Carney couldn't tell the boys at the *Star-Bulletin* was that I had gone through some of Ogden's private papers before the boys in blue had arrived. As the mourners burned the "hell bank notes" money so that Mai Ling Song would have something to spend in her afterlife, I took a long, hard look at the receipt I had stolen from the white slaver.

"Paid to Sheriff John Carney, $10,000."

A softly sobbing China grasped my hand for comfort as a stinging, bitter rain swirled around us. The dead wouldn't rest easy, I decided, as long as a spoiled cop walked free.

[**Editor's Note:** *Several aspects of this story have a ring of truth to them. In 1928 a "white slave ring" was sensationally exposed for recruiting local women into prostitution. Working from a house in Aiea, the procurers used the women, according to the newspaper, for brothels both in the islands and on the west coast. The story broke during the campaign for the election of Sheriff Pat Gleason, who at that time was also the head of the police department. Another authenticated aspect of McDougal's tale is Miss DuPont's Honolulu Advertiser-sponsored cooking school at McKinley High School, although there is absolutely no proof that the gumshoe was the recipient of the "surprise" cake.]*

CHAPTER FOUR

When Cops Go Sour

For the past few days, Big John Carney was sizzling on a griddle, getting his yolks turned sunny side up by a young, hotshot district attorney named Elias Weaver, who had been earning quite a name for himself by frying dirty cops. In the midst of all Carney's claiming credit for busting up the white slave ring, the news broke that he had been on the payroll of gangster Binky "The Iceman" Tan for a couple of years. Jared Smythe got the inside story from a former Honolulu poi dog who had spilled his guts to the journalist. Right in the middle of the election for Sheriff, Carney was running scared, and I was gloating. There was no need to do anything with the receipt I had found among the papers of Mary Ogden. A bad cop was getting his just due.

Honolulu was having its usual periodic pang of conscience over the Carney case. Old-guard missionaries posing as civic leaders did their expected handwringing about corruption and the moral decay of society. Politicians in glass houses did their typical tap dance, distancing themselves from a fall guy like Carney, who was going to take it on the chin. "Clean Government" committees were set up all over town, attended by the usual flock of "holier-than-thou" do-gooders, who in a few weeks would pat themselves on the back for making this burg clean, not knowing that they only succeeded in driving the dirt deeper and darker.

I was still nursing a lump the size of a mango on the back of my head, received from a brothel baseball bat, sipping a sarsaparilla at Hollister's Drug Store and enjoying Smythe's blow-by-blow account of every alleged corrupt buck Carney ever pocketed. I didn't look up from the gazette when she slipped into the stool next to me. She was the last person on earth I would have expected to ask me a favor, but Kalikolehua Carney was a woman with a lot of surprises. The last surprise she gave me was 11 years before, when she told me she was in love with my best friend on the force, John Carney. I thought we had had a pretty good thing going, but Carney had something better. Losing a gal can be tough, but losing a partner you trusted—that turns you sour. They were still on their honeymoon when he put the screws into me with the graft charges.

I tried not to act too startled to see her. We had avoided each other like the plague and, except for a brief exchange in the aisle of Metropolitan Meat Market, I hadn't seen her in a decade. A quick glance told me that she had added a few inches to her hips, but no more than I had added to my belly. She was still attractive and I felt drab, older and bleached. The smell of a fresh gardenia, which she always wore in her long, silken black hair, brought back memories of gliding across the floor of the Waikiki Park dance pavilion. The sweet scent only made me hate Carney that much more.

"How have you been, Mac?" she whispered, her head bent down as if she couldn't look me in the eye. "You look well."

"Yeah," I lied. "What do you want, Kaliko?"

I spoke sharply to her with a brittle edge to my voice. The small talk was too much.

"Your secretary told me you might be at Hollister's. I have a job for you, Mac."

"I don't need any more work right now," I lied. "The agency has me busy at the moment with an important professional private investigation case." I had been spending my evenings like some damn Peeping Tom, peeking through blinds at a cheating, wayward husband.

"You have to help him, Mac. You're the best in this town and he needs the best."

"Listen, Kaliko, go to the cops if you need help. That's what they are there for."

"He thinks the setup against him is an inside job. He can't trust the cops for help."

"What makes you think that you can trust me?" The words came out choked and my heart was beating faster than normal. Some demon inside me told me to grab her by the shoulders and shake her silly. Who in the hell did she think she was, coming to me like that? I held on to my cold gaze as she went on and on about how they both needed me. I cut her off by pitching a nickel to the counter boy.

"I'm not buying it, sister. See ya."

I stepped outside to the afternoon rush of pedestrians, cars and trolleys on Fort Street. The blast of hot air rising from the city street was stifling as she rushed to my side, pleading for my help.

"He's innocent, Mac! He didn't do the things they say he did. Oh, God, please believe me. He's too proud to ask you for your help. But he needs it."

"If he's really innocent," I said without emotion, "he's got nothing to worry about. If he isn't, he deserves what he'll get."

I took the longest strides I could, but she rushed behind me as we moved up to Merchant Street. As I entered the large glass doors of the Inter-Island Steamship Building, she finally turned back, covering her face with a handkerchief. She had always been quite the weeper, even the day she stuck it to me. I felt a tingle of revenge, but it wasn't sweet.

After chewing China out for telling an absolute stranger where she could find me and being reminded by my hotheaded secretary that it was her job to make sure I got all the business I could to help pay her meager salary, I slammed the door to my office and flung myself into a chair behind my desk. In less than a minute I had ferreted out a half-filled bottle of *okolehao* from the bottom of my desk drawer, poured myself a stiff one and dug out of my pocket a little slip of paper I had found among the belongings of white slaver Maria Ogden. Mrs. Carney could plead her husband's innocence, but the payment of $10,000 to John Carney by a felon suggested to me that hubby was as dirty as hell.

By 7 o'clock I had finished the bottle and convinced myself that Kaliko's *pilikia* was none of my business. By 10 o'clock I was absolutely convinced that I would never talk to her again as long as I lived. By midnight I had dug out some newspaper articles concerning the case of graft against John Carney. By 3 in the morning I guess I knew more about the elections of 1928, Chinatown crime, police corruption and the slime dripping from my former friend than anyone in town. Hell, I had become a real whiz kid.

According to Smythe's exposé, District Attorney Weaver had based his entire case on a stoolie cop by the name of Claus Robertson, a former Honolulu police detective who had been a boot-licker ever since I could remember. Robertson was a bad-breathed, low-down cur who had just been drummed out of the force for protecting crap games, bootlegging and prostitution that went on at the Miller Street Social Club next door to Washington Place, the Governor's home. Evidently, to reduce the charges against him, he had informed the D.A.'s office that he wasn't the only dirty cop on the force. For the last three years, Carney had

A thug is hauled in during the Chinatown crackdown. *(Hawai'i State Archives)*

been receiving $1,000 a month from Chinatown warlord Binky "The Iceman" Tan to turn his back on Chinatown vice operations. Robertson testified that Carney had also been cozy with a *haole* prostitute who had been a little icing on the monetary payoffs. I wasn't surprised when Maria Ogden's "daughter," "Miss Serrat" took the stand, claiming Carney had been her lover.

With the September elections around the corner, this scandal all but killed the political chances of Carney. The Democrats were screaming corruption and their candidate for Sheriff, a good-natured former cop named David De Costa, was a sure winner. Comprised mostly of Hawaiians and old royalists who were still bitter about the overthrow of the monarchy, the Democrats were used to coming in second to the Republican vanguard, which was backed up with *haole* sugar money. For the first time that I could remember, the Democrats now were about to win an election in the islands. As far as I was concerned, the Republican oligarchy could eat their bitter fruit.

The connection between Carney, Maria Ogden, the prostitute and the receipt for the $10,000 dirty money I found among Ogden's papers was now real clear. Ogden had paid Carney off to help protect the kidnapping of young girls to set up her slave trade racket. With the spirit of a broken porcelain doll named Mai Ling Song still restless in a Manoa cemetery, I wanted to be the one to tighten the noose around Carney's neck.

It wouldn't hurt, I convinced myself, to make sure that Carney was guilty. So the next day I sought out

The Iceman for one of our usually cryptic conversations. The Iceman had been nothing but a two-bit henchman for the old-time opium dealers back in the monarchy days. A ruthless bastard, he had earned his name by his murderous trademark—his victim was always found with an ice pick driven into the base of the skull. No murder was ever pinned on him, but in the underworld everyone knew when a Binky Tan victim came floating down the Kapalama Canal.

With all the public heat over the Carney corruption charges, Tan was holed up in the backrooms of his public bathhouse, which also served as one of Honolulu's largest opium dens, at River and Beretania Streets. He was decked out in a white Hong Kong three-piece suit and wore a wide-brimmed, white Panama hat. A compliment on his fashionable attire brought out a wide grin that showed off his gold-capped front tooth. I wasted no time and asked him straight if Robertson and Carney had been on his payroll.

"Prease, Mac, berieve me. Iceman neva giv Calney nothin'." It drove me crazy how he used this phony pidgin and rolling "l" and "r" accent whenever he talked with *haoles*. The more he acted like he couldn't talk English, the less he had to say. Since the *haoles* never thought a Chinese fellow could talk straight English, it was a smoke screen he always got away with. From what I could piece together from his twisted lingo, he had tried but had never been able to tempt Carney. Robertson had been on the take for years. Sometimes he took from The

Iceman, sometimes from other warlords in Hell's Half Acre. But Carney never took a dime from Tan.

He could have been covering something up, but The Iceman had always been fair with me. He let me in on a couple of other interesting underworld developments. Three months ago, the "King of the Underworld," a vicious hood named William Achuck, had organized what he called the "Open Town Hui." Tan had kicked in $5,000 of the $50,000 *hui* collected by Achuck. The money was to be used to get anybody but Carney elected in the campaign for Sheriff. He wouldn't say anything more, but I figured he was letting me in on this dope to protect himself. Weaver had subpoenaed him to testify at the Carney trial, and indictments against The Iceman for offering bribes to a government official were in the works.

"One last question, Iceman. The *haole* white slaver, Ogden. Who set her up and protected her. You?"

"No, Mac. Da haore *wahine*, that's Achuck's business."

I thought I'd pay a call on my three friends from the white slave ring. Only Maria Ogden was locked up in the can tighter than a drum, and the sleazy boyfriend had walked out of the downtown jail when a cop turned his back and now couldn't be found. The "daughter" with the long legs that wouldn't quit had been released on $50,000 bail which was coughed up by a bail bondsman who always took care of Achuck's runners and bootleggers. Her name on the court record was Bridget Halloran, who listed her address as the Elite Hotel, a second-rate joint on Bishop and Hotel Streets.

Tipping the desk clerk a buck, I got Halloran's room number and a few minutes later tapped on the door of Room 210.

"Who is it?" a nervous female voice answered.

"Front desk clerk, ma'am," I lied. I thought I'd be the last man on earth she would have wanted to see.

I was getting ready to jam my foot into the door, when she took her first gander at me. Instead, I was surprised when she greeted me like a long-lost lover, bussing me on the cheek as she pulled me inside the room. Her suitcases were on the bed, carelessly being stuffed with all her personal belongings. She was wearing one of those loose, flowing robes that revealed brief glimpses of her lingerie and long gams. My eyes uncomfortably turned away from her as she continued her packing, all the time in a husky voice begging for my help. She had gotten into something that was over her head and she wanted out of the islands. She was sure they had killed L.A. sheiky boy and they'd kill her next.

"What makes you think your boyfriend is dead?"

"You think he just walked out of prison by accident? It was a setup to get to him. I'm sure he's dead."

She flashed an envelope of ten one-hundred-dollar bills in front of me as her moist lips seemed more sensuous than ever.

"I'll give you the money if you help me get off this rock. From the very first moment we met, despite our falling-out, I've known that you liked me. I can make it worth your while, if you know what I mean."

My notions of honor, love and lust were getting all mixed up. I felt a little dizzy, as I took the envelope and slipped into an armchair to count the dough. She dropped into my lap and put her arms around my neck. I insisted that I needed a lot of information before I took her case—like who did she think had killed her boyfriend and why? Was Carney her lover and why did she have to keep nibbling on my ear?

Bridget Halloran had spent a lifetime lying, so I took most of what she said with a gallon of salt. Achuck, she confessed, had first made arrangements to frame the cop weeks ago by paying her to put a phony receipt into the old lady's papers. The police were going to be tipped off by Achuck about the slave ring. Ogden would take the fall, Carney would be implicated, and Halloran and the boyfriend would be paid handsomely for their help. Only the whole frame-up had been blown apart when Mai Ling Song had been accidentally killed. Halloran and her boyfriend were getting out of the islands when I busted the whole thing up. What made it worse, the planted evidence against Carney had disappeared.

Desperate to nail Carney, Achuck then paid her to claim in court that Carney was her lover. He would fix it that the boyfriend would walk out of jail and they would both be on easy street for the rest of their lives.

That wasn't very long for her boyfriend, who had disappeared right after escaping from jail. She had turned yellow and now wanted out. With a little money she had stashed away, she could get to Frisco on the *Yokohama Maru* sailing that night. She wanted me to give her a little protection. And she would give me $1,000 and a little comfort.

I told her to stay put and bolt herself in the room until I got back. Since the *Yokohama Maru* was going to sail at 9 o'clock, I'd be back around 8 to give her cover to the harbor. She asked me to make it a little earlier so that she could thank me properly and then planted a wet one on my lips. I asked her what such a great-looking dame was doing in this kind of racket.

"I like money," she said coldly.

When the door to 210 closed behind me, I vigorously wiped my lips and spit out a cheap taste of greed.

I wanted to pay Achuck a visit, but that would have been impossible. He had it in for me ever since Odachi, my former partner, and I had busted Achuck's brother during an opium deal a few years back. So, just for the hell of it, I dropped by the Kakaako home of David De Costa to see if the man who had the most to gain by Carney's trial knew anything about the so-called "Open Town Hui."

De Costa and several dozens of his friends and family were busy in the garage painting huge campaign signs like "Democrats for a Clean Police Force." He greeted me with a huge grin and strong handshake. Once upon a time we were rookies together, watching each other's back in Tin Can Alley, where thugs prowled like cats in the shanty-town alleyways. It was good to see him again, and I congratulated him on his impending victory. He made a little remark about Carney and my revenge, then offered me a glass of cold lemonade.

We talked story about the old days for about 10 minutes, when his cousin and campaign manager Billy De Costa stuck his head into the garage and reminded the candidate that he had a political rally at 6 p.m. That's when I brought up The Iceman and Achuck. I had heard about the $50,000 raised by gamblers to unseat Carney by using any means possible. Had the Democrats received any of that cash?

"Hell, no," Billy De Costa shouted. "What kind of *kukae* are you trying to spread, McDougal?"

"Come on, Mac," David added in his usual calm manner. "You know me. If there is any dirt, it's on Carney's hands."

"Yeah, I guess so," I reassured them both.

The smell of people hiding something led me to quietly invite myself to De Costa's Democratic political rally at the Banyan tree near Kaumakapili Church. This was always a popular gathering place for politicos, and the mood was uncommonly festive for the usually losing Democrats. A Hawaiian group was cutting loose with a beautiful falsetto number and the crowd was stuffing itself with stew and poi. Moral outrage rang in the air as speaker after speaker framed in red, white and blue promised no more underworld influence in our island home. Everything seemed on the up and up as I looked over the crowd of hangers-on. I must have received half a dozen name cards of the Democratic candidates printed in English and Hawaiian.

At about a quarter to 7 o'clock I was debating whether to leave, when I saw a familiar pockmarked face at the edge of the crowd, moving in the shadows behind Kaumakapili Church. I hid myself close enough to hear an angry exchange between Claus Robertson and Billy De Costa. De Costa was angry at Robertson for showing up without something he referred to as "the package." De Costa told him to go back and find it "or else." He then rushed back to the rally, as Robertson climbed into a large Willys-Knight and turned out, heading Diamond Head on Beretania.

I couldn't get to my machine fast enough to follow Robertson, so I decided to get back to Bridget Halloran to go along with my little masquerade of being her pal. It was around 7:30 p.m. when I got back to the Elite Hotel with the intention to finagle some info from Bridget on Robertson or De Costa. When the elevator opened on the seventh floor, I noticed that the hallway lights were all burned out. It was pitch dark, except for

the yellow glow from under a few doors. I was moving cautiously along the wall towards Room 210 when a loud shot rang out. A slight, shadowy figure holding a smoking revolver stumbled backwards out of a poorly lit doorway and fled for the staircase. As

Kaumakapili Church. The exchange between De Costa and Robertson took place near the tree on the right. *(Hawai'i State Archives)*

I sprang to action, I ran smack-dab into a cleaning cart left by some lazy custodian and plunged headlong down the hall. By the time I got to the stairwell, I heard the street level door slam. Whoever it was had gotten away.

Bridget Halloran was in bed, propped up on a red satin pillow. A small table lamp illuminated her ashen white face that was darkened at the temple by a large bruise. The slight smell of a perfume reminiscent of gardenia was in the air. Bridget's eyes were open, her lips seductively parted. She didn't make a move or sound. A bullet hole was in the bed's backboard about six inches from her head. As I pressed the pulse in her neck, I realized that the pillow wasn't red satin at all. In the small of the nape of her neck there was a deep hole through which Miss Halloran's blood had poured out onto the goose-down pillow. A bloody ice pick lay nearby on the floor.

"Oh, my God, there's been a murder!" the next-door woman screamed, her head sticking in the door. "Oh, my God! Someone call the police!"

In a few minutes the cops would be swarming around the joint, so I made a quick search of her luggage. There was nothing there but clothes. I grabbed her purse and made a dash past the hysterical nosey-body, ran down the still darkened hallway, leaped over the custodian's cart and scurried down the stairwell, walking briskly into Bishop Street. In the glow of a nearby street lamp I quickly went through the dead girl's purse. I found a storage receipt given by the purser of the *Yokohama Maru*, which I slipped it into my pocket. Since I was guilty of tampering with evidence at the scene of a crime, I quickly tossed the purse into a trash bin and rushed across Bishop to Union Square.

Police cars were speeding up Hotel Street to the Elite Hotel, so I yanked my fedora down over my eyes, pulled up the collar of my coat and slipped around to the Catholic church on Fort Street. By the Blaisdell Hotel, I slipped down Chaplain Lane, half-running to Bethel, where I could scoot down to the harbor without being seen by the cops. As I moved through the shadows of Chaplain Lane, I must have suddenly looked like one of those stupid cats who get frozen in your headlights just before you run them over. A large Willys-Knight with blinding lamps and screeching tires was grinding gears and speeding down the lane, intending to impale me on its hood ornament.

My .45 was blazing as I leaped out of the way of the speeding machine. I must have been doing something right that night, because not only did I manage to avoid being flattened, but one of my slugs ripped into the driver's side of the windshield. The eight-cylinder baby lunged into the side of the Blaisdell, turned over and careened into a street pole on Fort. A slug had entered Claus Robertson's left eye, killing him instantly. Fortunately, the streets were deserted and the cops were busy a block away with an ice pick homicide. I got out of there unnoticed and finished my walk to the *Yokohama Maru*. The ship was getting ready to cast off, when I exchanged the receipt for a little package of greed and death.

I was in my office 10 minutes later, counting out $50,000 and enjoying a few pornographic shots of David De Costa and Bridget Halloran. She had been right when she told me she had gotten in over her head. Blackmailers usually ended up murdered by their desperate clients. As I was twisting one of the photos to get a better view, the door to my office opened and the King of the Underworld and his henchmen paid me a little visit. Evidently Achuck had been having me tailed. He made a motion for me to lift my hands and I was most cooperative, especially with two tommy guns aimed at my gut. One of his lieutenants snatched up the money and photos, and the whole gang left without saying a word. It was all very clean and professional.

When I got back to De Costa's house, an impromptu campaign party was going on in the yard, with bottles of homemade swipe being passed around. De Costa's wife, a rather unadorned Portuguese lady, met me at the door and escorted me to a small back room that De Costa used as an office. He was jittery and he wouldn't look at me. He was guilty as hell, I told him, of corruption, murder, adultery and a few other crimes, including being another lousy friend who turned sour on me.

"Prove it, McDougal."

Billy De Costa entered the room behind me, as cool a customer as you'll ever want to meet. It took only a few minutes to see that the cousin did all the thinking in this family.

"David was being blackmailed by Bridget Halloran. She got greedy and thought she'd make some extra bread before she left the islands. That was a lot of money you turned over to her, David. Where did you get it? From the $50,000 that Achuck paid your cousin to help frame Carney?"

"I couldn't let Maria know, Mac. It would have killed her."

"Shut up, David! He can't prove a thing!" Billy pulled out a small .22 revolver that he aimed at his cousin. "You goddamned weak bastard."

"Billy was behind the whole thing, am I right, David? He had set up the scheme with Achuck to smear Carney and move Tan out of Chinatown in one clean move."

"I'm not a dirty cop, Mac. I never took one bribe, ever, when I was on the force." He was begging me to believe him.

"But you always were a coward, David. You never had a backbone. So what was going to happen, Billy? When your cousin was elected Sheriff, you'd tell him what to do, right?"

"Shut the goddamn up, or I'll plug you. I swear it."

A man cornered either breaks down or bites. I took my chance and kept talking hard.

"So while David plays with his leggy prostitutes, Achuck and his gang have a free run to turn Honolulu into Sodom and Gomorrah. Only Bridget threw a wrench into the plans by being too greedy. She and her boyfriend put the screws to you with the blackmail photographs."

"Yesterday I gave her all the money, to protect Maria," David chimed in. "Only she called me today to say that she hadn't given me all the photographs, that she'd need more money next year after I was Sheriff. So I went to her room tonight to beg her to listen to reason. Those photographs would have killed Maria. She laughed at me, so I lost my head and hit her in the head with a telephone. She fell down and didn't move. I didn't mean to kill her."

"You didn't kill her, David," I explained. He looked at me, surprised.

"What? Billy, you told me ..."

"He sent his dirty pal Robertson back to the hotel to make sure she was dead and to get the 'package' of photographs and money. Only she was very much alive, still waiting for a sappy detective to protect her life. So Robertson murdered her with the ice pick, setting it up to finger The Iceman. Only he couldn't find the money or photographs which Bridget had stashed with the purser on the *Yokohama Maru*.

"When Robertson told Billy at the rally that he couldn't find 'the package,' your cousin sent him back for the second time to look for the loot. They were in a panic by then. The money and photos in the wrong hands could blow the lid on their little political racket. By the time I got to the Elite Hotel, Robertson was watching me. And Achuck was watching Robertson. You're a real friendly bunch of boys."

"You can put the pistol away, Billy," I said, as I reached behind De Costa's desk and poured myself a glass of scotch. "With the girl and Robertson dead and the incriminating evidence recovered by Achuck, I can't touch any of you. It would be my word against yours and I have already been guilty of stealing evidence and fleeing the scene of two murders. As far as I'm concerned, your unholy alliance with the King of the Underworld is untouchable."

Billy kept the pistol aimed at me as I downed the shot of booze, tossed the empty glass to David De Costa and headed for the door.

"We're going to win this election," Billy warned me. "When we do, if I hear one whisper out of you about any of this, I'm going to get your license to practice business. You'll be washed up in this town. You hear me?" His ranting was like an angry little rat, scratching on his cage.

"Mac, I never meant to hurt anybody." David's plaintive voice was begging me for some grace.

"Cut the crap, David," I snapped. "Nothing's worse than when a cop goes sour. It makes all of us stink."

"Achuck's going to be controlling this town, McDougal," said Billy. I passed by Maria De Costa, who had been listening to everything right outside the room. I nodded my condolences like I was at a funeral.

"If I were you," Billy added, "I'd stay on his good side!"

I thanked him for the advice and took a long, lonely drive back to downtown. Just a stupid, lonely gumshoe, I thought to myself, who spent most of his life staying poor by raking through other people's filth.

When I finally got back to the office at about 11 o'clock, I found some cold dim sum on my desk with a note from China that Kalikolehua Carney had called about some urgent matter.

First I rang up The Iceman to let him know that it was a dirty cop called De Costa and his cousin, with their "partner" Achuck, who were setting him up as a fall guy. Tomorrow the papers would report how a young woman was found with an ice pick wound in her brain and he could expect the police to add that murder rap to their charges of police graft. He was very thankful for the information and invited me to his public bath for a free soaking.

Then I called Mrs. Carney. Her voice was desperate, as if she had done something terrible and needed help.

"Kaliko," I said in a voice without any of that old bitterness, "be on Tantalus Road overlooking Manoa in 45 minutes."

She drove up right on time, turned off her headlights and invited me into the front seat of her machine. I could tell that she had been crying for a few hours. The kid was scared silly.

"I've got something to confess, Mac."

"That you tried to kill Bridget Halloran?"

"How did you...?"

"The gardenia scent, Kaliko. The person who pulled that trigger in Bridget's room smelled like a gardenia. But you never killed anyone. You missed."

"What? I..."

"Your aim was lousy, honey. Even if you had hit her, the broad was already dead before you even showed up at the Elite Hotel. Still, it was pretty idiotic, what you did. Did you really think you would help John by committing murder?"

The floodgates opened as I put my arm around her.

"I guess I wasn't thinking straight," she confessed. "Our marriage hasn't been going well for some time, Mac. I've suspected other women. When I read how John was accused of seeing the prostitute, I believed it was true. So I followed her back to her hotel one afternoon and then later returned with John's gun. I fired right at her. I don't know whether I was trying to save John or was just plain crazy with jealousy."

Her head nestled into my shoulder as her body sobbed with relief. I let her know that John was probably going to be cleared. There were no witnesses left to testify against him. It had been a frame-up, just as she had suspected. He had no other woman.

The door of her sedan made a terrible squeak as I got out. Her engine purred on the otherwise quiet Hawaiian night. She rolled down her window and looked deeply at me, as if she owed me a few uncertain words.

"Sometimes, Arthur, I wonder if I made the right choice. Sometimes…"

"Shh," I stopped her. "You made the right choice, Kaliko." A peculiar feeling of peace hit me on the chin, nearly knocking me over. "Trust me," I said, finally with no feeling of remorse or hurt. "You are with the man you need to be with." As she drove off, I was trying to convince myself that I really wasn't a saint.

Two weeks later, I was having several layers of my flesh removed at The Iceman's public *furo* at River and Beretania. I had taken young Katsumi Odachi with me—a little reward for helping me solve the Mai Ling Song murder case. I felt easier now that all the loose ends had been tied up on that poor girl's murder. The hot water opened up all my pores and let out all the slime and grit I had accumulated on the job.

Weaver, by the way, dropped the Carney case after all the carnage inflicted upon his witnesses. Amazingly, my old nemesis went on to win the election by a narrow lead, promising to expose the truth behind the frame-up. A few evenings after the election, David and Billy De Costa were drinking in their garage, when they were trapped in a terrible fire caused by flammable paints used to make campaign posters. Evidently a discarded, lit cigarette had ignited the place like a time bomb. At least that's what the fire department investigators concluded.

The hand of The Iceman also disposed of Achuck, who was found floating in Honolulu Harbor by Pier 22 with the ice pick trademark in his skull. No arrests were made, but the police were still following a few leads that suggested an outbreak of gang warfare. They never found the body of Bridget's boyfriend, though I suspect one day the Moiliili stone quarry will cough up its secrets.

As I drifted into a relaxing slumber, I caught Katsumi holding his breath underwater, peeking beneath the dividing wall that separated men and women in the *furo*. The wall stopped at the surface of the bath, allowing curious youngsters to get an eyeful of the birds and bees. I pulled him up by the scruff of his neck, gave him a good lecture on morals and sent him off to dry in the locker room. After he left, I threw caution to the wind, filled my lungs with air, pinched my nose and cast my own watery gaze on the delights of the Orient.

[*Editor's Note:* In September 1928, Honolulu was rocked by the news that powerful elements in the underworld were trying to control the town. During the trial of a former Honolulu sheriff for graft, it was publicly revealed that an "Open Town Hui" had been established by an unnamed underworld "King" to buy the police force for the protection of gambling, bootlegging, opium and prostitution. This seems to authenticate at least a small portion of McDougal's story.]

The proud boys of the Honolulu Police Department, 1928, with Sheriff Pat Gleason wearing the Stetson in the middle, second row. Hard to believe one of these fine cops could go sour. *(Hawai'i State Archives)*

CHAPTER FIVE

Sharks Always Bite Twice

Agaggle of jazz party revelers packed the passenger car of the Oahu Railway and Land Company train, as tassel-fringed flappers twirled their hips up and down the aisles, bumping into the rest of us who, being either more sober or less agile, cowered in our seats lest the frivolity be contagious. Flasks of *okolehao* were being passed around like a Sunday collection plate, with strawboater-headed young men guzzling down their fiery content while whispering, "Ah, honey, come on," to no one in particular. Never again catch the OR&L train to Haleiwa on a Friday morning, I lectured myself, when summer-vacationing coeds were heading out of town for a three-day weekend. Endless choruses of the "Turkey Trot" and "Bunny Hug" drowned out the little cautioning voice in my head. I never begrudged other folks a wing-ding, unless I was on the job.

The racket finally became intolerable, so I shoved my way through the confusion, stepping out on the back lanai of old Observation Coach 64. There was another gent out there who had also sought refuge from the madness inside.

"Beautiful, ain't it?" he said, without looking at me. "When you remember that 30 years ago this was a hot, barren plain, it makes you proud to be a part of the sugar industry."

Blowing out a long, white stream of cigar smoke that swirled out like a locomotive's stack behind the train, he gazed out on the miles of sugar fields of the Ewa Plantation as if they were his children. We rattled past a string of small plantation camps with out-of-place names like Renton and Verona. In the distance the cloud-shrouded Koolau mountains seemed almost majestic as they tapered towards Waikiki, where they were capped off by the silhouette of Diamond Head.

"Yeah, I suppose the sight of sugar is pretty sweet, unless you have to work in the fields."

"Hell, mister, I grew up working in those fields," he said, exuberantly. Looking down on me for the first time from his lofty six-foot-plus frame, his craggy, white-whiskered face beamed. The Stetson on his head and his flannel shirt gave him the appearance of a well-rode *paniolo*. "Now you ain't afraid of work, are you?"

"I've done my share."

"I bet you have," he said, thrusting his large, callused hands into mine. "McAllister's the name. Lincoln McAllister."

"Of the McAllister brothers fame?"

"The same. And you are…?"

"McDougal. Arthur McDougal."

"Former cop, right? Whatever happened to you? After all that news about the investigation last year, I haven't heard your name lately."

"Being out of the limelight feels good. I'm into the private racket now."

"Oh, a gumshoe. Now there's interesting work."

Lincoln McAllister was one of those men you can take an instant liking to. Gruff, overbearing and demanding, he also had an infectious grin that could melt the Mauna Kea snowcaps. With his brothers, he was a pioneer in these parts, having been one of the family crews who helped tap the first artesian wells in Waianae and Ewa back in the late 1880's. Without the tons of daily water their wells provided, there would have been no sugar which built the profits on Merchant Street, brought immigrants from around the world and stole the lands of the Hawaiians. If sugar was king in Hawai'i, as everyone liked to say, then water was God, which made McAllister the Pope.

From Kahe Point, the train passed into Nanakuli, where the hills took on a bright yellow color. The overwhelming power of the Waianae range always left me a little breathless—the bold, curved peaks standing like armed sentries down the coast. It was as if the land was telling the malihini, "When you come into this district, you better be able to stand on your own two feet."

"Whew, you should bring some of your water out here," I remarked. "It sure is dry as hell."

"Not really. Where do you think we tapped into the first artesian wells? Right here in Nanakuli."

"The place didn't seem to benefit much from all the water."

"Just count the number of streams we pass over, McDougal. This area also gets plenty of water from the moisture on the top of the Waianae range."

"So why's the place so dry?"

"The aquifers carry all the water to Waianae, Makaha and Lualualei Sugar Plantations. Sugar is thirsty. You don't get out this way much, do you?"

"Haven't for a while," I answered. The truth was I rarely came out to the leeward coast unless on business. Going to Waianae always seemed more like sailing to another island than just driving over to the other side.

"The train is the best way to visit," he went on, like a booster of the Hawai'i Promotions Committee. "None of the hassle of broken-down tires like when you take your own machine. And you can't beat the view of Kaena Point."

I enthusiastically agreed that no railroad in the world had a view comparable to the OR&L as it passed around Kaena Point. The conductor would often even stop the train so the passengers could get out to soak in the spectacular view. The train ride from Honolulu to Haleiwa and back again was well worth every penny of the 50 cents.

When the train pulled into the Waianae station, McAllister and I, and a handful of Hawaiians, disembarked. The party revelers were no doubt headed out to the Haleiwa Hotel for a three-day weekend orgy of booze, song and more booze. It was a relief to be able to hear that little voice inside my head again as the train left the station with the noisemakers. Unfortunately, it reminded me, "You're getting too old."

The OR&L station in Waianae. *(Kent Cochrane, Bishop Museum)*

The sun, without mercy, beat down upon us as we stepped off the train platform. Waianae Valley seemed drier, hotter and more barren than I had ever seen it before. As we reached the Old Government Road, a gang of about a dozen young Hawaiian children descended upon McAllister.

"Daddy! Daddy!" they were all saying, jumping up and down and hanging on to his coat sleeves. McAllister began doling out a nickel to each of the kids, patting them on the head.

"Are they all yours?" I asked incredulously.

"Tell you the truth, I'm not sure. Only, if they are, I sure in the hell don't want to disappoint them."

The kids, I thought to myself, had a great racket going. They knew about McAllister's *kolohe* reputation and his generous nature and milked him for everything he was worth anytime he came into Waianae.

"We part company here, McDougal. I'll give you a call if I ever need your services."

From the looks of it, his wife would more likely need my honed skill of snooping. He vigorously shook my hand, stuffed his frame into the passenger seat of a Model A, and drove off with a comely *wahine* with a beaming smile for her weekend man.

"Are you Art McDougal?" a voice behind me called. Turning, I saw a tall, gangling teenager with curly locks and slouched shoulders. "My father told me to pick you up."

"Who are you?" I asked, extending my hand.

"I'm Henry Lauder's son, Chris." His grip was as weak and boneless as Chinese long rice.

Henry Lauder was one of those tight-fisted, hard-driven patriarchs who, like McAllister, had pioneered the sugar industry in Waianae. His Lualualei Sugar Company was smaller than either the Waianae or Makaha plantations, but Lauder had been Johnny-come-lately to the district. Muscling his way in, picking up what government lands he could and grabbing up the older Hawaiian lands, he had started a thriving business.

By the looks of his automobile, he was doing just fine. The large, dark-green Cadillac touring car was gleaming in the Waianae sun, and the distinctive silver radiator cap in the shape of a surfer on his board glistened. The ornament must have cost a pretty little bundle, I thought, as Chris Lauder obediently packed my overnight bag into the rear compartment.

The ride to the Lualualei Sugar Plantation was a long, hot, dusty ride. I tried to kill time by gabbing with the boy, but it was like pulling teeth. With a father like Lauder, I thought, a milquetoast kid like this must have caught a lot of hell. Just by looking at Chris you could see that his old man could break the spirit of a stallion just by grinning it down.

Finally, the teenager got animated when I asked him if the hood ornament meant he surfed.

"No, but my father does. He was quite good when he was younger. He still loves the ocean. Father goes swimming every day."

I could see that for myself 30 minutes later, as I sat in Henry Lauder's private study, filled with stuffed big game fish he had snared, attractive coral pieces he had stolen from the bottom of the ocean, and what must have been the largest Hawaiian shell collection I had ever laid my eyes on.

"Do you surf, McDougal?"

"No," I answered. Hell, I didn't even know how to swim.

"Dive? Fish? You waste your life in these islands if you don't do one or all. I love deep-water diving with a helmet. Ever try it, McDougal?"

He didn't wait for my answer, but went on for 15 more minutes reliving his latest diving exploits, when I finally cut in.

"I'm sure you didn't have me come all the way out here, Mr. Lauder, to regale me with adventures you could have shared over the phone. I don't mean to rush you, but..."

"You're quite right, sir, quite right. Let's get down to business. However, in the future, for the convenience of our working relationship, I prefer to direct the current of the conversation. After all, you will be working on my time."

This six-and-a-half-foot Scotsman, with a passion for saltwater and a shiny gold tooth in the middle of his overconfident grin, was losing a lot of points with me real fast. Then, when he told me what he wanted me to do, he lost the whole ball game.

Lualualei Sugar Plantation, he explained, had always been threatened by a water shortage on the dry leeward side. But this summer they had been really suffering due to an extended drought. Their irrigation system had depended upon some deep artesian wells that were dangerously low. The solution was a good supply of spring water that was available *mauka* in Makaha Valley on property owned by a stubborn old Hawaiian named Keaulumoku. He was leasing the water rights to a Japanese taro farmer named Shigeru Hamano.

"The kanaka won't sell or lease the land to me, McDougal. He says he doesn't want me to divert the water with an extensive ditch system from Makaha to Lualualei."

"I'm not a real estate agent, Mr. Lauder."

"Of course not. Your job is to snoop around until you find some dirt on the old bastard that I can use to extort him into selling. Or maybe you can scare him out. You gumshoes are good at throwing your weight around. And from what I can see of your waistline, you got plenty of stuff to toss."

"I'm sorry, Lauder, you got the wrong guy," I said, instinctively tucking in my stomach. "The International Detective Agency isn't in the business of collecting information to be used as blackmail, making illegal threats or stealing land from Hawaiians. Go find some dirty agency; I'm sure there are plenty. Aloha."

"Who in the hell do you think you are, talking to me like that, you son of a bitch? I'll…"

Before I gave his Scotch blood a chance to boil over, I was out the front door so quick I almost knocked down a couple bounding up the front steps.

"Whoa, mister. Slow down. You must have just met my brother. He has that effect on folks. Are you McDougal?"

Lauder's brother, a far more pleasant gent nick-named "Keone," was on his way in with a shapely *haole* brunette in a swimsuit. Keone was much younger and not as large as his unlikable brother, but was equally tan and athletic. The cute dumpling he had in tow turned out to be Henry Lauder's second wife, Margery. The two of them had just returned from sunbathing at Pokai Bay.

"Don't be put off by my brother's blunt attitude, Mr. McDougal. I'm sorry I wasn't here to present our situation a little more delicately, since we do need your assistance. The plantation depends on it."

"Sorry, I'm sure there are plenty of private dicks who do anything for a fin, but not me. Can I get a lift back to the station?"

"We are not asking you to do anything illegal. We just need to present the old Hawaiian with a good reason to sell his lands to us."

"I'm sorry, it's just not my line of work."

"Now you aren't telling me that you are one of those bleeding hearts that say we stole Hawaiian lands, are you?"

The last thing I wanted was to get into a political discussion about Hawaiians. Ever since Prince Kuhio introduced the Homelands legislation last year, everyone suddenly was an overnight expert on what was best for the kanaka. My gut instinct told me that anything we *haoles* offered to the Hawaiian had some string attached. So anything Lauder or his brother said to me about legal or fair didn't hold any water with me.

"I don't want to get involved, Mr. Lauder. Call me what you want, but I'm not getting my hands dirty."

"Certainly they are a quaint and entertaining race, McDougal. I feel for them as much as any man. But you expect us to hold up the progress of this plantation for one old Hawaiian man? There are hundreds of lives that depend on our sugar crop. We only want what's fair for everyone. Plus we intend to pay the kanaka quite well for the property."

"Could you give me a ride back to the station?" I cut in.

"Chris!" he shot to the youth who was wiping the surfing hood ornament on his father's car. "Take Mr. McDougal back to Waianae town. I'm sorry I can't convince you otherwise."

Chris Lauder apologized profusely for his father's behavior on the ride back to the OR&L Waianae Station. After his mother had died, he explained, his father had become hard-hearted. Margery, his second wife, didn't help matters, he told me. She was much younger than his father and treated him poorly.

"She's a tart," he finally whispered, as if someone was overhearing our conversation. Chris Lauder had no aloha for his stepmother. I just shrugged.

As I waited at the station for the next Honolulu-bound train, I had my eye on two shabby characters who had been watching me since the Lauder boy dropped me off. Finally, the younger of them, bowing apologetically, approached me.

"Excuse me, but did Mr. Lauder hire you?"

"What's it to you?"

"My father and I were bringing our taro to deliver to Honolulu. I saw Lauder's Cadillac. Are you here to kill us?"

"What?" I almost choked. "I'm no hired gun, kid."

There was such a strange, country politeness in Sam Hamano and his father, Shigeru, that you couldn't help but laugh. But I didn't need long to tell that the Hamanos were scared to death.

"My name is Arthur McDougal," I explained, handing them both my business card. "I was asked by Lauder to help him, but I turned him down."

"He wants to kill us. He wants Mr. Keaulumoku's land."

"So he does."

The father and son exchanged some words in Japanese. They studied my business card as if it was a holy sutra.

"How much, sir, do you charge for your services?" the son asked with pained politeness.

"How much are you willing to pay?"

Again speaking in hurried Japanese tones, the father suddenly turned his back, privately examining his wallet. He turned back and spoke in Japanese to his son.

"My father is willing to pay you $10."

"It's a deal," I said, shaking the old man's hand. For a couple of taro farmers, $10 was quite a bit of money. Lauder would have paid me ten times as much a day. But I think I took the better deal.

"*Domo arigato gozaimasu, domo arigato gozaimasu*," the father kept saying, pumping my hand as if I was a water spigot.

"*Do itashimashete*," I answered, throwing around the few Japanese words I had learned from my partner, Naoaki Odachi. It impressed both of the men, as one grabbed my bag and escorted me to their limousine.

The back of their mule-drawn wagon was filled with the *lepo* of taro they had unloaded at the station, plus the few bags of feed they picked up at Waianae town for their chickens. I loaded myself with my bag into the muddy back as the slow mule ride to Makaha Valley began. We passed through the acres of sugar fields, past the swamp at Kamaile, and then turned into Makaha.

The Hamano farm was wetland taro that used the spring water from the Keaulumoko *kuleana* lands. Mr. Hamano and his busy wife, Akemi, spoke no English and only a smattering of Hawaiian pidgin, so their American-born son Sammy did most of the talking for them. They fed me a heaping bowl of rice, fried taro and grilled chicken and plied me with illegal homemade sake, which Mrs. Hamano kept warm and plentiful in our little cups. There was plenty of bowing and smiles and a lot of "I don't understands," but finally it sank in why the Hamanos were so scared of Lauder.

Last week some of the plantation henchmen rode out to the taro farm, set fire to some of the work sheds, destroyed some crops and told the Hamanos to get out of the valley. They even showed me some of the holes in their little house made by shotgun blasts.

Old man Hamano got agitated, sputtering off something in Japanese.

"My father says that his family is from a long line of samurai. He won't run from the *haole*, no matter how much money or guns he has."

"What about Keaulumoku? Have Lauder's men bothered him?"

"The old Hawaiian is very strange, Mr. McDougal. He's very polite to us. He lets my father lease the water rights for our farm. But we don't fool around with him. Some say he has the power of *pule anaana*."

"*Kahuna*," I said, having heard plenty of stories from the men on the force about these people who had the power to pray people to death.

"*Mano*, he *mano*," Mrs. Hamano suddenly added.

"*Mano?*" I asked.

"It's nothing. My mother picks up too much gossip."

"No gossip. He *mano*."

The Japanese woman was trying to tell me in her broken English and Hawaiian that Keaulumoku was a *mano*, or shark. I downed another shot of sake, laughing at the thought that the only human beings whom I had ever met who were "sharks" operated pawn shops along River Street.

I was pretty tipsy by the time I finally nodded off on one of the thin Japanese mattresses that they threw on the matted floor. The wooden walls of the room were old and cracked, but impeccably clean. Everything was as neat and tidy as I always knew the Japanese to be. Though I had never been to Japan, I imagined that I was in some village back in the land of the samurai that I had seen in those silent movies they used to play in Aala Park, where the guy sat in front, narrating all the parts in that singsong Japanese chant. The only thing missing, I thought as I nodded off, was the geisha.

The next morning, the Hamanos took me to the Waianae OR&L station. I promised them that, once back in Honolulu, I'd contact the Sheriff's office about the attacks on their farm, as well as look into the Lualualei Sugar Plantation's financial transactions. If Lauder was doing anything illegal, I promised to nail him.

"My parents are concerned that they'll be back to hurt us. Please, Mr. McDougal, do what you can."

I knew the cops weren't really going to do much about the midnight raid on the Hamano farm. There was no positive identity of any of the masked men. So I had China, my secretary, dig into the Lauders' land dealings at the Bureau of Conveyances, while I pried into Henry Lauder's background. The biography in *Men of Hawai'i*, a self-congratulatory description of prominent island *haole*, with a few Chinese thrown in for good measure, gave me the straight dope. Lauder had immigrated to the islands in 1889 and went to work as a boilerman at the Waianae Plantation. Thanks to the help of his brother, who had brains but no aggressive fire, he was able to parlay some money into nearby sugar lands, which in the boom years of 1911 and 1912 turned big profits for the Lauder boys. Now they were worth a nice bundle, although Henry kept pretty tight reins on the business.

China came up with the angle on how they were able to acquire so much land in such a short period of time. The Lauders made lots of little loans to Hawaiians, who mortgaged the land which their families had held since the middle of the last century when the Mahele first provided them with fee simple rights. When payment on the loans was due, many times the Hawaiians couldn't cough up the dough. So, to get their money back, the Lauders foreclosed on the property and auctioned off the land. In every case, they bought the property themselves. Within a decade they gobbled up hundreds of acres in that fashion, all of it absolutely legal. Now their problem was Keaulumoku, who was too wise for their little land game.

A few days later, as I was taking lunch at very busy Chambers Drugs at Fort and King Streets, who should saunter by arm-in-arm but Keone Lauder, with his very cozy sister-in-law. No harm in shadowing them, I thought, as I kept a good distance between us until she went off shopping at Liberty House. They bussed each other on the cheeks, as he went on towards Merchant Street where, at the corner of Bethel by the old post office, he met a very nervous Chinese man in a nicely tailored suit. Together they walked along until Lauder passed off a small white envelope that I guessed was stuffed with bills.

When they split company, I followed the Chinese man, who led me to Central Honolulu Bank on Bishop Street, where he disappeared through the employee entrance. It came as no surprise when I later checked through a few public records that Lualualei Sugar Plantation Company was one of the major investors in Central Honolulu Bank.

Inside the bank, I couldn't see the Chinese man behind any of the tellers' cages or desks. Maybe he had noticed me and had given me the slip out another door. I was about to leave, when a back office door opened and my Chinese dove stuck his head out, barked some orders to a secretary and then ducked back in. The stenciled name on the door's glass window read, "Robert Lau, Executive Accountant."

Later in the week I decided to drive my own machine out to Makaha Valley to fill the Hamanos in on what little I had found out about Lauder. As I cruised along the old coastal road adjacent to the train tracks in Waianae, I was rattling my car to death, when I noticed a tremendous commotion on the beach before Pokai Bay. I was just in time to see Chris Lauder motoring a small skiff into the bay, screaming for help. His father, who had been using a diving helmet about 300 yards offshore, had suddenly disappeared following a gush of air bubbles. The air line connected to the pump on the skiff had been cut. Chris, who couldn't swim, frantically pulled into shore, calling for help. Except for the airpump, the severed hose, an uneaten picnic lunch, a blood-stained fishbait bucket and a very frightened teenager, the skiff was empty.

Keone Lauder, who had been conveniently bathing in the Bay was right there, taking command. A search party went out looking for the missing Scotchman, hoping that if he had trouble with his air, he had come up on his own somewhere else. In the meantime, the

Hamano men were also returning to shore in their small sampan. They had been much further out than Lauder, doing some offshore fishing. Both of them were soaking wet. They said they had cooled off with a short swim.

In the confusion of the rescue effort, I took a quick look at the hose that had been severed. The jagged, ripping cut told me this hadn't been done with a knife.

The search for Henry Lauder continued throughout the day until sunset, when it was impossible to continue. The old man, everyone agreed, was presumed dead.

Later that night, as I once again ate and slept at the Hamano farm, Keone Lauder paid a very unexpected visit. He knew his brother had been unfair in the water rights issue. Yes, he'd like access to Keaulumoku's water, but he was dropping the whole business. He apologized for any inconvenience his brother's harshness may have caused either them or the Hawaiian.

I couldn't sleep that night, wondering how a powerful man like Lauder, so skilled in the water, could have drowned. Revving up my machine, I decided to take a relaxing drive along the railroad tracks toward Kaena Point. Parked near the entrance to old Makua Cave, I got out to stretch and to soak in the warm evening air. The cave's gaping entrance seemed to penetrate to the bowels of the earth itself. In the old days, I had been told, this cave actually went under the island of Oahu, linking with burial caves on the windward side at Kaaawa. The imagination can be a man's worst enemy, I thought, especially when standing alone at a place Hawaiians deemed sacred.

Uncomfortable, I walked away from Makua Cave, crossing the tracks to the lookout towards Kaena. In town you can rarely see the stars in the Hawaiian skies. But out here on this moonless night, the Milky Way was brilliant with millions of sparkling pins of light that occasionally sparked and fell through the heavens. Some of the yellow stars, I noticed, were shooting up into the heavens from the bright flame of a bonfire burning on the beach. The falling stars and fluttering, upward swirling yellow embers of the fire seemed to blend mysteriously together. Down on the beach someone was feeding the flames, chanting in a monotonous chorus, which I found unintelligible. I followed the haunting chant until I came upon a lone figure silhouetted by the bonfire.

"You are the detective who is helping Hamano. I am Keaulumoku."

He was at least 70 years old, with shocking white, long hair and beard and the look of centuries in his powerful Hawaiian face. He was standing at the edge of the sea, nearly naked, except for a *malo* about his waist and a torn undershirt covering his back. He spoke perfect English, with a vocabulary suggesting that he had been educated well beyond the level of most islanders.

"They say you are a shark," I said, for no particular reason. It was as if my little inner voice was now speaking for me.

"They say many things they do not understand. Do you really believe that a shark and woman can have a child?"

"My knowledge of sex is limited," I confessed, "but I do believe that trick is impossible."

"Is it? There was once a beautiful woman who lived in this area whose name was Kalei. When she bathed in the ocean, it was common that a shark would swim past her, leaving her unharmed, but always watching her. One day, she met a handsome stranger. Kalei and the man fell in love and lived together until she became *hapai*. That was when he told her that his true name was Kamohoalii, the shark god and brother of Pele.

"'I cannot stay with you,' he said, 'but must return to the sea. The child you'll bear is mine. Kalei, you must never feed our child meat.'

"Kalei did as her lover told her after she gave birth to their son, Nanaue. When the baby was born, a small birthmark was seen on his back, a faint mark shaped like the mouth of a shark. Without Kalei's knowledge, as the child grew, his *tutukane* secretly fed him meat. He had not been told by Kalei that Nanaue was forbidden to eat the flesh of animals because his father was a shark.

"One night, as she put her baby to sleep, Kalei noticed that the birthmark was taking on the shape of a mouth. Nanaue was growing a shark's mouth on his back. That is when she discovered that *tutukane* had fed the boy the flesh of pigs, dogs and chickens. Only now, her son had a new appetite for human flesh.

"The mother made a cloak that concealed her son's back. As he grew older, the birthmark became a gaping mouth ringed with the sharp teeth of a shark. He carefully avoided going into the water whenever any other people were around, always working in the taro *loʻi*. Whenever he saw young boys and girls going to the beach to swim, he would greet them.

"'Walina,' he would call. 'Going to the beach? Then be careful, the sharks are hungry today!' And each day, one of the young people would be missing. The villagers suspected that a shark lived among them, disguised as a human being who was feeding on the flesh of their children.

"Finally, one afternoon, Nanaue, working furiously with his *oʻo*, lost the cloak on his back. Everyone saw a gaping mouth of a shark with razor-sharp teeth. Nanaue was grabbed, brought to the beach and was to be thrown into a red-hot *imu*, when his father took pity upon his boy. A wave was sent that engulfed Nanaue, who turned into a shark and escaped his captors.

"Later that night, he returned to his mother, begging to stay with her. His heart was breaking that he could not stay with his beloved mother.

"'No, my son,' she said. 'You must live in the ocean as a shark by day. But at night you must live as a man at Kaneana, the "cave of the man" at Makua.'

"So, Mr. Detective, inside that old cave behind you, the shark-boy resides. If you pass the cave at night, he may attack you, dragging your corpse back into the darkness. There he places your body upon a slimy rock, where he waits several days until the rotted flesh, soft and delicate, tastes very, very *ono*."

The story was told simply, without much emotion or fanfare. He wasn't telling me a legend; he was just talking about someone he knew.

"Good story," I said inanely. I couldn't think of anything else appropriate.

"There were many things which happened in the old days which you could not understand. You *haoles* are in that way blind. But maybe I am wrong about you? Can you see?"

The hairs on the back of my neck rose as if the flag was passing by as he looked up at me from the fire which he was feeding with a large piece of *kiawe*. The sparks shot up like firecrackers as his large, black, cloudless eyes peered at me as if I was a piece of barbecue on the grill. I stumbled back, falling on my *okole* on the sand.

The chanting resumed as he turned back to stare into the flames. A rip in the undershirt on his back blew slightly back, revealing a small portion of a birthmark on his shoulder which, to my mind, resembled a shark's dorsal fin. A thrashing in the sea then caught my attention. In the moonlight, I could see the ocean beyond the surf was churning with the agitated forms of large, deadly sharks.

"The man who always took more than he needed can be found over there." He pointed to a clump of shoreline shrubs, nearly covered in the high tide.

The half-eaten, severed head of Henry Lauder would have been unidentifiable, except for the gold tooth in the skull which slightly reflected in the moonlight. A piece of his torso ripped with jagged teeth marks was rolling in the surf before it finally same to rest on the beach. Everything else of the sugar baron had been devoured by the sharks.

What the sharks didn't eat of Henry Lauder, his family cremated and scattered off the Waianae Coast. The memorial services were poorly attended, and those who did show up could hardly have been described as mourners. Everyone was invited, even yours truly, to a big bash up at the Lauders' plantation home.

"A luau of remembrance was the way Henry would have wanted it," lamented Keone during his heart-rending eulogy.

While the funeral services had been sparsely attended, the party was the social event of the year in Waianae. Just by the jam of spanking new roadsters and classy luxury cars lining the Lauder grounds, you could tell Keone moved in the best of circles. My dirty Willys-Knight felt like a country bumpkin parked near one of those LaSalles. A jazz band was blaring, as ladies and gents kicked out the "black bottom" and servants discreetly passed out the hooch.

"McDougal, my brother would have loved this," Keone said, greeting me at the door.

"If you say so."

"I guess this wraps it up for you. Must have been a hell of an inconvenience."

Yeah, it wrapped it up. The Hamanos were happy and the sharks were happy. The police wrote it up as an accidental death due to shark attack. Everyone was happy but Art McDougal, who cannot stand unraveled threads.

"McDougal! Good to see you again!"

It was Lincoln McAllister, striding through the house like a bull on a rampage.

"What a surprise! Did you know Lauder?"

"In a manner of speaking."

"A real bastard, no?"

I was a little uncomfortable speaking ill of the dead in front of his beloved mourners, most of them now drunk and clinging to each other for comfort at their terrible loss. "Groping each other" may have been a better way to describe it.

McAllister and I did our now-familiar routine of separating ourselves from the noisemakers, taking our drinks and plate of *pipikaula* to the wide outside lanai of the Lauder home. A light rain suddenly fell in the upvalley of Lualualei, cooling off what had been an oppressive air. Now that the old man was dead, it was as if Waianae could breathe again. We chatted on and on, when finally I asked him a question that seemed to come from nowhere.

"You ever heard of people being descendants of sharks?"

"*Aumakua*, Mac. Hawaiians believe they have *aumakua*. Family spirits."

"Sure, I heard of that."

"Some believe that their *aumakua* are animals, insects, or even clouds. In some cases, sharks. Why do you ask?"

"No reason. It's just that I met an old man who gave me the willies. Gossip had it that he was a shark. Old wives' tale, I guess."

"Keaulumoku?"

"You know him, too?"

"Heard of him. One of my *wahine* told me about her grandmother."

"Yeah?"

"Every time her grandmother's husband went into the hills to pick *maile* to make a special lei, her grandmother had a dream that the dark shadow of a man emerged from the sea, entered her bedroom and made love to her. Nine months later, she would give birth to a child from that union. And every child would be stillborn. Taking the dead infant to the ocean, she would feed it to the sharks. Then several nights later, she would return to the place where her babies had been cast into the ocean, submerging herself into the water. A tiny baby shark would then swim to her and suckle upon its mother's naked breasts. My woman told me that she has several aunties and uncles spawned in this fashion who protect her when she swims in the sea."

I'm not sure this was the shark who ate old Lauder or not. *(Frank Davey, Bishop Museum).*

"That's a pretty incredible story, Linc," I said, gulping down a hot shot of *okolehao*. "What do you think?"

"It doesn't matter what I think," he answered. "If anything happens to a man living among Hawaiians, it happens inside. I wouldn't be the first *haole* turned pagan by the mysteries of these people. One thing is for certain—when I go swimming, I stick as close to my *wahine* as I can."

Sharks were on my mind all week as I probed further into the financial dealings of the two-legged breed of shark called the Lauder brothers of Lualualei Sugar Company. At this point, I was working for myself, just trying to convince myself that, although there was no doubt Lauder's death was due to a shark attack, some human hand may have been involved.

The Hamanos and Keaulumoku had an obvious motive to see Henry Lauder dead, but his brother Keone had a more personal goal—money and Margery. Robert Lau wasn't hard to break. I used my most threatening voice on the phone, telling him that embezzlement was punishable by life imprisonment without possibility of parole. Okay, I lied, but an ambitious, greedy gent like Lau takes those get-rich-quick risks thinking he can't ever get caught. We met later at my office, where I explained that if he cooperated, the district attorney would no doubt go light on him. When reality sank in concerning the shame he was about to bring to the Lau family, I got him whimpering like a baby.

Keone Lauder had paid Lau handsomely to set up a separate account at Central Honolulu Bank under a phony name. Every month, a portion of the Lualualei Sugar Company funds would be siphoned off into the fake account. They were slowly bleeding the plantation dry, providing Keone with a substantial monthly revenue, while Lau kept the whole operation looking on the up-and-up. As far as Henry would be concerned, the business was sluggish due to the drought.

After asking Sergeant Henry Chillingworth to keep Lau on ice until I had a chance to talk to Keone Lauder, I took my third drive to Waianae in a week. I must have lost an inch on my silvertones, maneuvering the district's rough roads. But if my hunch was right, this last drive would wrap up all the loose ends.

Lau had not been able to talk with Keone, so the news that their little gig was up should come as a shock. I found him sitting in his brother's office, which had been stripped bare of the stuffed fish. After getting rid of his brother, Keone was in the driver's seat at Lualualei.

"Tell me, Lauder, do you know a fellow by the name of Robert Lau?" I asked the question straight off.

He didn't flinch, but looked me in the eye and smiled.

"I don't believe I do."

"Lau says you do. He's saying a lot more right now to the district attorney."

He let out a long sigh and slumped in his chair, as if he had been deflated.

133

"I deserved everything I took from my brother. I worked as hard as he did to make this plantation successful. The tight-fisted bastard gave me an allowance like I was a kid. An allowance! Sure I skimmed the business, but it was nothing compared to what he owed me."

"With him out of the way, you could have it all. Including his wife."

"What are you getting at?"

"That day you were sunbathing at Pokai, you decided to erase Henry from the picture. The 300 yards to where your brother was diving would have meant nothing to you. The way I see it, you swam out, cut the line and probably stabbed your brother underwater, leaving the corpse to the sharks."

"I see you're no watersportman, McDougal. A neat theory that falls apart. I couldn't have dived without equipment to the depths my brother was at, certainly not without getting the bends. And wouldn't Chris have seen me surfacing?"

Not all my theories are fully worked out before I present them. He kept putting holes in my logic.

"As for my motives, why would I need to kill Henry when I was getting everything I needed? As for Margery, he didn't care any more about her than he did for me or Chris. My brother tossed her to me like a used bone. She used to sleep in my room right under his nose and he never said a word."

Swiss cheese suddenly came to mind as my forehead burrowed. "Is that checkmate, gumshoe?"

"Maybe on the murder charges, but there's still the embezzlement racket you cooked up with Lau. Why don't you pack your things? You'll be going away for a while."

I left him frantically calling his lawyer while I drove down to the Waianae station, where I sent a telegram to Sarge.

Sgt. H. Chillingworth, Honolulu Sheriff's Office. Stop. Keone Lauder has been told of Lau's confession. Stop. Proceed as you think best. Stop. A. McDougal.

While it may have sounded superstitious, I had one last suspect to interrogate. A sharkman named Keaulumoku.

I found the old man in front of his grass-thatched house, shaping small fishhooks from bones. He was even more dark in the daylight than he had appeared that night on the beach near Makua Cave. I checked for the strange birthmark. It was still there.

He looked up at me with those cloudless black eyes and noted in recognition. If I hadn't known it was 1921, I'd have thought I had stepped back 300 years in time. There was really nothing for me to say. If he could turn into a shark, and I'm not saying I believe he could, then how would I be able to prove that in a *haole* court of law? And if as a shark he killed Lauder, who's to say he didn't have his reasons? For the first time in my life, this wiseguy's tongue had nothing to say. I was there because I wanted to listen.

"The sharks did not murder the *haole* man," he suddenly volunteered with his uncanny wisdom. "They only feed upon other life, just as we feed upon pork or beef. But sharks never feed off other sharks. The *haole* man, he had a taste for human flesh that could never be satisfied. He, too, was a shark.

"Did I kill him, you're thinking? I know he killed many people when he took the land that gives us life. Now they give back a few acres of the land that they have dried out and tell my people they may live as homesteaders on this barren rock. The lands they have given to us are lands they no longer want for their sugar.

"That is why I hold on to this *kuleana*. One day our *akua* will prevail once again in Hawai'i, and they will need this land. However, it is for the *akua* to deal with men like Lauder. Not me."

He offered me some poi and dried fish, with a gourd of fresh water from his spring. We didn't talk much for the rest of the afternoon. I got lost listening to the scraping sound of his tool against the little bones being given a fine, dangerous point. I thought about all the human sharks I had seen turn on their own species and I felt just a little dirty.

When I returned to the Lauder place that evening, the Honolulu detectives were just showing up. John Carney spit a few words in my direction, which I ignored. My former partner had already put the knife so far into my back that my silence had become my only alternative to murder.

"Before you haul him off to town, I think you had better also take in the murderer of Henry Lauder," I said.

"You can't pin my brother's death on me, McDougal!" Keone was being handcuffed as the sorrowful widow, Margery, looked on in anguish at her lover who was being sent up the river.

"I know that. It's your nephew who's going to have to face the music over Henry Lauder's death."

Lauder and Margery's mouths must have hit the floor when I made my little announcement.

"Chris? Why, he's only a boy. He couldn't hurt a fly." Keone had sincerely liked his nephew and was aghast at my accusation.

"You see, sharks never attack other sharks," I tried to explain without sounding too strange. "An old man explained that to me this afternoon. If they attacked, it was because they were feeding on other prey. They smelled blood. There was an empty bloody bucket on the skiff that day which, if my hunch is correct, was used by Chris as bait to call in the sharks. The airhose was cut as they came in to feed.

"But why would Chris kill his father?" Margery asked.

"His father ignored him, you saw to that. The kid was humiliated by all of you. Maybe by killing his father he was proving he was as good, if not better, than the old man."

While baiting sharks with bloody fish and guts was a pretty chancy way to kill someone, Chris could have always tried again another day. It was only a matter of time and he would have committed a perfect murder.

We found Chris Lauder in his room, surrounded by stacks of dime novels and magazines. He knew what we were there for and he began to shrivel up on his bed, whimpering. The cops tried to pry him out of his fetal position.

"Come on, boy," I said gently, stopping them. "We know you hurt your father. We'll get you some help." He unfurled himself and left quietly with the officers, as Carney fidgeted. He never said thank you.

An alienist at the University of Hawai'i later testified that Chris Lauder had suffered deeply following his mother's death. His father's second marriage to a woman that he regarded as immoral only intensified his hatred for his old man. The continual rejection of his father, who saw his son as a pansy, built up an emotional storm that was unleashed that afternoon at Pokai Bay.

Chris Lauder was committed to the Territorial Insane Asylum and his uncle spent a couple of years in Oahu Prison, thanks to Lau, who turned witness for the prosecution. Lualualei Plantation went bankrupt and the Hamano taro farm did so well that, when Sammy got married a few years later, his folks could afford a luau for the whole Makaha Valley. Oh, they paid me $10, plus a $5 bonus, in crisp bills.

As for Keaulumoku, I saw him only once after that on the corner of Hotel and Bishop. Totally out of place in *haole* clothes, he cut a fine figure with his long white hair and flowing beard under a fine new straw hat. He had come into town, he said, to help some of his neighbors sign up for the Hawaiian homelands which had recently been made available in Nanakuli and Waianae. We shook hands and were ready to part, when he looked at me intensely with those round, black eyes.

"You don't still think I'm a shark, do you?"

I didn't answer as I watched him glide effortlessly through the human rush of downtown Honolulu, submerging finally beneath the mass of fat crabs which sharks find so tasty.

*[**Editor's Note:** The descriptions given by McDougal of the water situation in Waianae were fairly accurate during the early part of the century, when the sugar plantations dried out the lands. Water rights is still an important issue to taro farmers and others in the district who seek access to the rich resources of water. The rendition of the Nanaue shark story given to McDougal by "Keaulumoku" is very similar to one recorded 10 years later by Norah Stearns.]*

CHAPTER SIX

The Case of the Fallen Missionary

Two things I quickly learned after moving to this Pacific burg. First, don't take raw pork over the Pali Road if you expect to get to the other side. And, second, don't talk stink about missionaries to a *kama'aina haole* if you expect to keep your job. Either way, you may be bucking some real old chain-rattlers that have a funny habit of creeping along lonely highways or into family trees.

Ruth Eleanor Keegan may have cooked her pork, but she sure didn't learn to keep her mouth shut. Next to Babe Ruth hitting a home run out at Moiliili Stadium last October, Keegan's nasty little novel about missionaries had become the talk of town. *Blest by the Lord* was selling hotter than *manapua*, and gossip was a few of the missionary clan had gathered in white robes up in Manoa one night and, with a burning cross, put the torch to a pile of the potboilers.

Keegan had moved to the islands a few years back and had been working as a librarian in the Archives building. She had spent her lunch hours across the street at the old mission library, raking through the old documents and letters. I guess no one suspected she was looking for skeletons in the closet until one of the big New York firms published *Blest by the Lord*. The way Keegan spilled the beans, seems some of the first band of

Calvinists that came to these islands were more anxious for terra firma than heavenly mansions. From the hullabaloo that followed, I guess some descendants couldn't sleep at night thinking the old saints had clay feet.

Course, I had been far more interested in Babe Ruth, Jimmy Fox and Lou Gehrig's Honolulu All-Star Team visit than I was in the silly book. My literary interests suddenly changed early one morning, when I was greeted in my office by a nervous little petunia named Eddy Carlson, who offered me a handsome bundle to do a little snooping. If you can say one thing about Art McDougal, it's that his feet are pure clay. Carlson was Keegan's literary agent and, from the looks of it, his client had gotten herself into an unsavory scandal. He threw across my desk a copy of the morning edition of the *Star-Bulletin*, which I hadn't yet seen. Splashed across the front page was a gruesome photograph of a Chrysler "75" sport coupe with two legs sticking out of the roof. One of Honolulu's most respected businessmen, Samuel Grimes Hollinshead, had taken the big leap from the roof of the Alexander Young Hotel at about 11:20 last night. The Chrysler was a mess, not to mention poor old Hollinshead.

"So what does this have to do with you, Carlson?" I had seen this type of slick bloodsucker lots of times in my line of work. They pretty themselves up in Panama suits and spats and then leech off some dumb, talented jerk dreaming of stardom. He fumbled putting his cig in an effeminately long holder. With a gold-enameled lighter, he lit up and took a short draw and quickly blew out a gush of white smoke.

"About one hour ago, Mrs. Keegan's husband was arrested by the police for the murder of Hollinshead," he explained, quite matter-of-factly. "Last night, there was a big argument at the Roof Garden Cafe between Hollinshead and Keegan. Hollinshead is one of those missionary descendants who want to ban *Blest by the Lord*, and my client's husband is a consummate alcoholic who likes to pick fights with everyone. If it's true what the police are saying, there'll be a dirty scandal that Mrs. Keegan just could not live through."

He stopped me short when I suggested that such a sordid scandal might help to sell books.

"Books, Mr. McDougal, but not a movie. We have a very good chance to sell the rights to *Blest by the Lord* to a major Hollywood studio. However, with all the moralists watching the movies these days, a murder scandal would destroy our chances of making a profitable deal."

"Mr. Keegan might also have an interest in his innocence," I suggested. He didn't seem impressed.

"Mrs. Keegan is estranged from her husband, Mr. McDougal. They haven't spoken to each other in over six months. In fact, he is shacked up with a little oriental hussy somewhere in the Waikiki jungle."

Images of Mrs. Keegan as a little, old, white-haired librarian saying "Hush" with her finger to her lip flooded my mind. How could a librarian hook up with someone capable of murder and adultery?

"What kind of case do the cops have on Keegan?"

"That's what I'm paying you to find out. You'll get a $5,000 bonus if you get that drunk cleared of the charges."

As he was about to leave, he took a final, long drag on his cigarette, blew a last smoke storm into my office and, with a raised eyebrow, threw me one last blessing.

"Whatever you do, sir, keep Mrs. Keegan out of this." After the door shut, I offered Mr. Carlson a gesture that I learned as a kid from a foul-mouthed Greek.

I gave China two assignments before I sped out to Oahu Prison to interrogate my new client. First, call Sergeant Chillingworth at headquarters and see if he could get me the scoop on the case against Keegan. Secondly, do a file check on Samuel Grimes Hollinshead.

About 45 minutes later I was sitting in a small interrogation room at Oahu Prison, listening to Steve Keegan plead his innocence. He was a real big, affable fellow—the kind of guy you could spend an evening with chewing the fat at Two Jacks Saloon until they shut the place down around you. He had been a doughboy, seeing action in the trenches of France before a Kaiser bullet sent him home with a crippled right leg. Like a lot of the boys coming out of the Great War, he had had pretty bum luck. He had tried to make a career for himself as a journalist. But the Crash hit him pretty bad. He had been out of work for nearly six months, when his wife got a job offer in the Hawaiian islands. It wasn't easy, he said, for a New York boy to make the change, but he tried it. A year later, he was hitting the bottle awful hard. When his wife made it big with her novel, he moved out of their house.

"I still love her, McDougal. But that pansy Carlson soured her on me. He said I wasn't good enough for her; that I'd ruin her career. I guess he was right, considering I'm not worth much now. I met Fumiko during one of my binges. She hung me up and helped me dry out for awhile. I got a real hankering for Fumiko, but I still love Ruth."

Fumiko was the Japanese barber girl who cut hair in a Pauahi Street shop. Keegan stumbled into her place one night after getting drunk. I guess a woman couldn't resist his good looks, even if he did have a lame leg and a bad drinking problem. They were living in a little cottage in Waikiki.

"If you're so innocent," I asked him bluntly, after listening to most of his life story, "what in the hell are you doing here?"

Last night, he explained, he had followed his wife to the Roof Garden Cafe at the Alexander Young Building. She was up there with Carlson and some of her literary-type friends, having dinner and taking in Bina Mossman's Hawaiian show. He approached their table, causing a little commotion by telling her he wanted to come home. Only, Carlson stuck his nose in and they all started to argue. He had been drinking a little too much gin and he made a fool out of himself.

On Keegan's way out, he saw Hollinshead on the other side of the rooftop cafe, seated with his wife and

Hollinshead took the plunge from the rooftop of the Alexander Young Hotel. *(Hawai'i State Archives)*

companions under one of the large, colorful tent awnings. He had been reading Hollinshead's nasty letters to the *Star-Bulletin* about his wife's book, so he made some pointed remarks. They exchanged a few hot words and then he left. Next thing he knew, the cops arrested him because, they said, he had threatened Hollinshead's life.

"Did you threaten him, Steve?" I was watching Keegan. You could see that too much boozing had begun to wipe out some of his brain cells.

"Maybe I did, McDougal. The guy had been writing some pretty terrible things about Ruth in the papers. I guess I wanted to show her how much I loved her by defending her. But I didn't kill him. I swear it. It was about 10 p.m. when I left the hotel. I was too drunk to

One of the open-aired trolleys on King Street at Nuuanu Avenue. *(Hawai'i State Archives)*

drive, so I left my car at the Bishop Park Auto Stand and took the trolley to Fumiko's."

"Which trolley, Steve? Try to remember. If you want me to get you out of this mess, I need every bit of information I can get."

"Hell, McDougal, I was drunk."

"Did you catch it on Alakea?"

"I guess so. Yeah. It was one of the barrel cars. The number 28. Ask Fumiko. She'll tell you. When Hollinshead took his dive, she and I were just hitting the sack."

I wanted to believe Steve Keegan. I always felt for a guy who went through life carrying around a big ball of pain in his gut. By noon I was parking my machine under the world's largest banyan garage next to the Archives building and catching my first sight of Mrs. Keegan, who was on her way to lunch. She didn't look anything like what I expected of a dowdy, white-haired librarian. She had a young and full, but firm, body and a pretty face that was younger than her 33 years. I thought about all the fun I had missed by not reading, introduced myself, and asked if I could treat her to lunch.

We sat in the Chick Inn, picking at their 75-cent fried chicken plate, as I listened to her sob story about Steven and his bad luck, drinking and womanizing. It seems Fumiko hadn't been the first local flower he had plucked. There was still a warm spot in her heart for him, she explained, but she could no longer tolerate his immature antics.

"He needs help, Mr. McDougal. I'm grateful that you've taken the case. If you get him cleared of these charges, I'll see to it that he gets medical treatment."

I gnawed away on a thigh and then I asked her point-blank if she thought her husband could kill a man.

"No, Mr. McDougal," she answered, with the sincerity you expect of a librarian. "He's an alcoholic, but not a murderer. You didn't know him before the war. He was popular, good-natured and considerate. He's been through hell. But he's not capable of killing anyone."

She had a sadness in her eyes, remembering a younger Steve Keegan. A little sinister voice wanted to say that she probably never used to think him capable of adultery.

Fifteen minutes after I returned Mrs. Keegan to the Archives, I was at the Pauahi barbershop where Fumiko

Yamashita plied her trade. She was working on the scalp of some bolohead, trimming the few hairs he had left, when she noticed me plop into an empty chair. A slip of the scissors nipped the top of her client's ear and he let out a yelp. As Fumiko frantically put a steamy hot towel on the tiny wound, he let out a louder scream from the blistering heat and uttered a few oaths as he dashed for the door. I don't think I have ever had such an exciting effect on a woman.

"I'm not a cop, lady. I only look like one. I was hired to help your boyfriend."

"He's innocent. I tell you, he's innocent." Small-bodied and demure, Fumiko was fumbling about with her scissors and combs when an older Japanese man came out from a back room. Looking at me with a scowl, he started to scold her in a tirade of thick pidgin and Japanese lingo. I couldn't totally understand what he was saying, but I knew it had to do with white men and it wasn't too complimentary. When he went back into the room, I sat down in her barber's chair.

"I tell you what, since your *luna* isn't too happy with you talking to a private dick, why don't you give me a trim and a shave. Then I'll be your customer."

"He's not my boss," she explained as she draped a sheet about me. "Take is my brother."

"He doesn't seem to like *haoles* much."

"He nevah like me stay with *haole* man. After our parents died, he wen watch me real close kine. I told him what I do is my own business."

She was one of those plantation kids that came to the big city and was taking the hard knocks. To be honest, I didn't see what Keegan saw in her. She had what some of the boys in the agency called "*daikon* legs," crooked teeth and an ironing-board shape. But she was sweet and I figured, "any port in a storm."

"Doesn't approve of you and Steve, uh?"

"He says that I should marry one good Japanese man. I told him, bullshit, I over 21. I marry who I like."

"So what did you tell the police, Fumiko? I need to know what you said so that I can help Steve."

"I told them the truth," she insisted, nearly snipping my ear.

She was one nervous butterfly. Evidently the cops had interrogated her earlier that morning regarding the whereabouts of her *haole* boyfriend last night and they hadn't totally bought her line. She told them he had gotten home from town on the trolley at about 10:45 p.m. He was crazy with drink and passed out once he hit the bed. She told me there was nothing else to add.

"You telling me the truth? You and Keegan went to bed at 10:45 p.m.? How can you be so exact?" She had a straightedge razor in her hand to trim my sideburns, when her hands started to tremble. I grabbed the knife.

"Forget the trim, okay? Now, how do you know what time you went to bed?"

"I looked, okay? You really trying to help Steve? Then you believe me, yeah?"

When I finally got back to my office, I found a soaking-wet China behind her desk, muttering something about being caught in a downpour while fetching a report from Chillingworth. "Damn streetcar had no damn window, Mac." I was still laughing as I looked through a somewhat drenched police report and some autopsy photos. The police had nothing more on Keegan than I already knew, except for one supposed eyewitness. One of Bina Mossman's dancers, a young girl with a great comic hula routine by the name of Iolani Luahine, had been at the lady's *lua* just before 11 p.m. She claimed that she saw Hollinshead and another man go towards the staircase leading to the *makai* six-floor tower roof. The man had a limp.

I then read the file on Hollinshead. Fifty-two-year-old president of the Central Honolulu Bank. Good missionary stock going back to 1823 with the arrival of his great-grandfather, Dr. Thomas Grimes Hollinshead. Graduate of Yale, an avid hiker, student of Hawaiian language, and philanthropist. Married for the last 25 years to Harriet Sullivan Reynolds, a Vassar graduate and heiress to a Brahmin Boston family. They had three homes. One on Ferdinand Street in the shadow of the Manoa Castle. The second at Haleiwa, and the third at Waimea on the island of Hawai'i. He was another well-heeled oligarch cut from a common stock of cloth.

It took me three phone calls to finally get through to Mrs. Hollinshead's secretary, who informed me that her highness was too much in a state of shock to see me.

After a little snooping, I figured the widow was holed up in Manoa Valley, so I paid a little unexpected visit. Flashing an old police badge I kept just for such occasions at the oriental doorman, I brushed past an astonished secretary and into a large, well-furnished library, where Mrs. Hollinshead was holding court. Several well-tailored, double-breasted suits stuffed with flesh stood about looking officious. Mrs. Hollinshead was of course dutifully draped in black, while a handsome younger man who I quickly identified as Phillip Jeffreys leaned over her shoulder, directing her where to sign some lawyer-drafted papers. Jeffreys was one of the better-paid lawyers in town, with a Stangenwald Building address.

Their mouths dropped open as I burst into their little party. There was a lot of outrage and inquiry into my background and not a few attempts by the stuffed suits to lay their hands upon me. Funny thing about the double-breasted-suit boys, though. They back off real quick when a working stiff gives them a nod that he means business. The only one who didn't react was a quiet little Japanese man who sat stoically on an oversized sofa. Behind his wire spectacles, he kept his eyes on me without ever parting his lips.

After a brief introduction I plunked down into a chair straight across from Mrs. Hollinshead. Jeffreys positioned himself as if to protect his former client's wife. I told them I had only a few questions about what happened last night at the Roof Garden Cafe.

Mrs. Hollinshead was very cool. She did Vassar proud. This drunken Mr. Keegan, she said, accosted her husband just before the Hawaiian show at 10 o'clock. He said he was defending his wife's honor or some such nonsense. When Keegan took a swing at Hollinshead, her husband floored him with a punch to the jaw.

"Was your husband an athletic man?" I asked.

"We played polo together every Sunday," volunteered Jeffreys.

"My husband was a pugilist at Yale, sir, and he has kept in shape all these years."

"That's a boxer, McDougal," Jeffreys said, with a patronizing air.

She then explained that just as the dancing began at 11 p.m., her husband excused himself to go to the restroom. In the excitement of the dancing, they didn't notice that he hadn't returned until 20 minutes later, when the cafe was thrown into turmoil by screams below. Mrs. Hollinshead passed out when she learned that her husband had fallen from the tower roof.

"What did your husband have against Mrs. Keegan's book?" I finally asked. "It's just a harmless novel."

"Harmless? Obviously you haven't read the scandalous tripe. Samuel was quite proud of his lineage. Mrs. Keegan's sensational attacks on his ancestors as mercenaries and land thieves are without any truth. He viewed her work as libel not just against his great-grandfather, but the entire missionary cause. So he boldly voiced his opinion and, for doing so, he is now dead."

I suggested nothing was so bad about saying missionaries made a few bucks. We're all human, ain't we? Every comic in town knows they "came to do good and did very well."

"To suggest that Dr. Hollinshead was a greedy man who used his religious influence to steal land is an affront to the memories of those early pioneers who made many sacrifices to bring Christianity to the islands, Mr. McDougal. But, really, I haven't the time or emotional energy to give you what is obviously a much needed history lesson."

"Maybe you could give me a crash course when you're feeling better," I said, apologizing to them for taking their precious time. Since it was late, instead of going back to the office I just went home to my ugly, empty bungalow in Moiliili, thanking goodness that my ancestors hadn't done any more good for anybody than stealing a few Scottish horses. Plantation Music Hour was on KGU radio when I drifted off to sleep, only to be interrupted by the ringing of the telephone. It was a frightened, thin and foreign voice inviting me to his home on 10th Avenue in Kaimuki. He needed my help. He hung up before I could ask him if it had to do with Keegan.

It was raining by the time I pulled into the driveway of a simple, but well-kept, Kaimuki house. As I dashed for the front porch in the heavy storm, I was reminded of poor China's drenching that afternoon. The lights in the parlor were blazing, but no one answered my knocking or ringing. Finally, I sloshed in the mud around to the back, found an open bathroom window and crawled in over the sink.

He was slumped over his desk in a back room used as a private office. In his hand was a .44 revolver, the barrel of which was stuck in his mouth. The back of his head was splattered across the venetian blinds. On the desk, written in broken English, was a simple confession. "Last evening, I kill Mr. Hollinshead because he find out that I steal from the bank. I am sorry." It was unsigned.

The dead man was the stoic little Japanese gentleman who had been sitting so placidly in Mrs. Hollinshead's library. I looked around for something to identify who he was, but everything was in Japanese. Finally, I called homicide and spoke with Chillingworth. I told him to get the wagon out to the 10th Avenue address. I could almost taste my $5,000 bonus, as I made myself cozy in one of the victim's stuffed chairs, downing a tumbler of his sake. Thunder and rain pelted Kaimuki as I waited in that lonely death chamber, realizing how stupid I had been. I guess greed had made me blind.

By the time the homicide boys showed up, I had finished two more tumblers of sake and was feeling pretty sorry for myself. Not only had I lost my bonus, but I had lost a drinking friend even before we had gone drinking. Sergeant Chillingworth was the first of the cops to examine the unfortunate bloodied corpse.

"Hell, Mac, I never get used to this. I can't see how you can sit there and drink that crap with this guy's brains all over the room."

Picking up the confession note, he let out a long "Ah soo! No wonder you're so cool. So I guess this sets Keegan free."

"Maybe. What's it look like to you, Henry. Suicide?"

"What else?"

In all my years as a cop and a detective in Honolulu, I had seen quite a few Japanese suicides. Some were by jumping off cliffs or bridges, some by self-inflicted knife wounds or poisoning. But most were by hanging, not with a pistol. And the position of the body also seemed odd. If he had put his mouth over the barrel of a .44 and pulled the trigger, his head and body would have been thrown back, not forward. The little tabletop scene was too neat. A round stain of blood on the carpet behind the corpse proved that the body must have fallen backwards to the floor after the shot.

The confession note was also suspicious. First, the guy calls me up and tells me to get over here, he has something to tell me. Then he writes a murder confession note and kills himself? Plus the scrawl is in English when every written book or letter in the room is in Japanese. Why would a desperate man about to kill himself use a foreign language to make his confession? Unless, of course, someone made him write the note, then put the gun into his mouth, pulled the trigger and then set up the scene to look like suicide.

The victim's name was Seiji Shintani, chief bookkeeper for the Central Honolulu Bank. Evidently he was a topnotch number man even though he spoke little

English. Judging by the fixings in his house and a stash of cold cash we found in one of the cubbyholes of his desk, he was doing real well by Central Honolulu Bank. A little too well for a 100-dollar-a-week man. I asked Chillingworth to do me one last little favor, then I went home to romp through lullabyland before my big day.

The missionary graveyard where I nabbed Jeffreys is directly behind Kawaiahao Church. *(Hawai'i State Archives)*

I found the clan of stuffed double-breasted suits, Phillip Jeffreys and Mrs. Hollinshead attending her husband's funeral in the little plot of earth reserved for missionary descendants behind Kawaiahao Church. Hundreds of the mourning relatives, friends and associates were in attendance. It was a Who's Who of Power in Hawai'i. Following a simple graveside ceremony, Mrs. Hollinshead was whisked into a waiting sleek, black Oldsmobile by Jeffreys, who was most solicitous of the grieving widow. As the sedan sped away, I caught him by the arm and asked if I could have a few moments.

As we walked back through the graveyard, I asked him if he had heard about Seiji Shintani's death. He had been Hollinshead's bookkeeper, wasn't that true?

Jeffreys was very sober as he said how shocked he had been when the police called earlier that morning to inform him of the bookkeeper's suicide.

I asked him if he had any theories on the suicide.

"Well, I suppose the note says it all, doesn't it, Mr. McDougal? You really must excuse me. One of my best friends has just been laid to rest and this is no time for business."

"What note, Jeffreys? Sergeant Chillingworth never told you they found a note. I asked him to leave that little detail out when he called you."

His foot was so deep into his mouth, he had to gasp for air.

"Well, everyone leaves suicide notes, don't they?"

"Maybe yes, maybe no. Only you know he left one, because you wrote it."

He bolted like a frightened rabbit who, having nowhere left to hide, just runs in terror. I was in no shape to chase him through the graveyard, but fortunately he tripped on a little footstone that marked the graves of old Hiram Bingham's infant sons. When he started to get up, I was right behind him.

"Hold it, Jeffreys."

He swung widely at me as I packed my fist into his nose like it was a punching bag. Blood spurted forth as he fell back, knocking himself out on the tombstone of someone named Levi Chamberlain.

"Gee," I said, to no one in particular. "Am I a pugilist?"

A few boys in blue helped me haul Jeffreys through the Kawaiahao churchyard to Chillingworth's patrol car which was waiting on Punchbowl Street. Not all missionaries were bad, I thought to myself, as I thanked Mr. Chamberlain for performing the *coup de grace* on Jeffreys.

By nightfall his fancy lawyer had admitted to the murder of his fellow embezzler, Shintani. For a year the bookkeeper, Hollinshead and Jeffreys had been quietly siphoning off bank funds. It was a perfect conspiracy where the top executive, the bank's bookkeeper, and lawyer arrange to make themselves filthy rich. Only Hollinshead had been having some pangs of guilt. He told Jeffreys and Shintani that he wanted to terminate the embezzlement scheme. They had already made enough and what if they got caught?

So when Hollinshead fell off the Alexander Young building, the Japanese bookkeeper got scared. He figured that Jeffreys had killed their partner and it was only a matter of time before Jeffreys would get rid of him. Jeffreys saw the bookkeeper was acting strange and tailed him. When he overheard Shintani calling me for protection, he murdered Shintani and set up the whole suicide scam. When you get dirty, I guess you can't trust anyone.

"So Jeffreys killed Hollinshead?" Sarge asked.

"No, it wasn't Jeffreys. He had an airtight alibi."

"Who did it?"

"You already got the man who killed Hollinshead."

"You mean Keegan."

"The same. He lied to me when he said he caught the No. 28 barrel trolley to Waikiki that night. It was China getting drenched on the streetcar that reminded me that the barrel cars had all been pulled out of service at the beginning of the year. The barrel trolleys had those fancy glass windows you could pull down to protect yourself against the rain. Lots of folks missed those cars on rainy days. Course, since he didn't use trolleys very much, Keegan evidently didn't know about the pulling of No. 28."

The way the prosecuting attorney argued it, Keegan was drunk and hotheaded. He wanted his wife back and thought he'd show his love by protecting her honor. He never left the hotel, but waited for Hollinshead to go to the men's room. There he challenged him to fisticuffs. Iolani Luahine must have seen them going out to the tower roof. I guess the Yale pugilist was no match for the younger and stronger ex-doughboy, who finally admitted he accidentally knocked him off the roof during the fight. In a panic and too drunk to drive, he called Fumiko, who used her brother's car to pick him up and then give him an alibi. When you think of it, it's pretty stupid what some people will do for love.

As for Mrs. Keegan's book, the studios never picked up the options. She got a divorce and moved to San Francisco, where I last heard she's working on the sequel. It's about the sons and daughters of missionaries. Keegan was found guilty of manslaughter and was sentenced to Oahu Prison for 10 years at hard labor.

A few months after the trial, I drove out one afternoon to the old mission house on King Street and ate a ham sandwich while parked under one of the big kukui trees. They had fixed the old place up real nice, turning it into a museum. I couldn't help wondering what other skeletons would one day fall out of its closets. I gulped down my last bite of sandwich, told myself it was none of my business, and rolled my big machine toward Waikiki, where there was more than enough greed to keep me busy for another few years.

[*Editor's Note:* There is absolutely no resemblance in the character or biography of the Ruth Keegan described here and Ruth E. McKee the authoress of The Lord's Anointed, a novel which caused a small stir in the 1930's when it was first published. As James Michener learned when he wrote Hawai'i, "talking stink" about missionaries used to make you persona non grata among Hawai'i's old social set. Glimpses of factual data, however, are contained in McDougal's story. Iolani Luahine, the famed hula dancer, as a young woman did do a comic hula routine with the Bina Mossman show at the Roof Garden Cafe at the Alexander Young Hotel. The barrel cars which provided shelter from the rain did go out of service in 1934 and, on October 22, 1933, Babe Ruth hit a home run out of Honolulu Stadium in Moiliili. So did Lou Gehrig.]

CHAPTER SEVEN

Banyans Bleed in Saipan

I was four days out of Honolulu, leaning over the railing of the *Empress of Tokyo*, upchucking chipped beef and cursing the name of Katsumi Odachi. It was Katsumi, the son of my former, murdered partner Naoaki Odachi, who had hornswoggled me into this little Pacific adventure. A few months ago he had gone gaga over a cute number named Elizabeth Yamaguchi, a svelte, cat-eyed beauty who worked at the counter at the Japanese Bazaar, an import business at Pauahi and Fort Streets. Last week her parents received a telegram from Tokyo that her brother, Ichiro, had disappeared in the backwoods of Saipan while on a Bishop Museum archaeological expedition. He was a research assistant for one of the big name anthropologists that the museum had sponsored to go to the Marianas to find out if there was any solid evidence that Hawaiians had migrated from Saipan. The wire said Yamaguchi had been missing in the islands' most rugged terrain for several days and was presumed dead.

Elizabeth Yamaguchi was, naturally, beside herself. She couldn't believe her brother could get lost like that—he was a mountain goat when it came to hiking. The official report by the Japanese authorities in Saipan suggested that he had gone off into the wild, northern regions of the island and may have fallen off a gorge or been attacked by a feral pig. They couldn't find his body. Since Elizabeth didn't have much dough, Katsumi figured he'd impress her by getting his gumshoe pal to take on the case for next to nothing. I told them they should get a Boy Scout troop to go tromping off into some godforsaken island backwoods. Art McDougal is definitely a city boy. Anyway, what could I do that the Japanese authorities hadn't already done?

When they look at you with those begging eyes, I turn into Honolulu's biggest sucker. She agreed to pay my passage and living expenses, and I promised her I'd turn over whatever rocks I could to find her brother, dead or alive. Katsumi sat there beaming like he had just scored a touchdown against Punahou.

Before I left town, I went out to the museum to get the scoop on this Saipan expedition. I was ushered into the office of the director, a big, gangling gent named Dr. Paul Gregory, whose nose had a striking resemblance to W.C. Fields'. He wasn't the warmest or friendliest fellow I'd ever met. In fact, he was downright evasive. Seems a Dr. Herman Goodmeyer, a bigtime Pacific anthropologist with a list of publications as long as Binky "The Iceman" Tan's rap sheet, had been in charge of the archaeological expedition. Yamaguchi was his assistant. The museum team had been given permission by the Japanese government that controlled Saipan to locate ancient sites of the Chamorro race that had once inhabited Saipan before the Spanish either wiped them out or married them. From the way Gregory talked, I figured some big bucks and reputations were to be made

One of the earlier Bishop Museum expeditions in Agingan, Saipan, at the Latte ruins. *(Hans George Hornbostle, Bishop Museum)*

if they could prove that Hawaiians and Chamorros had a common ancestry. My cynical little voice told me that everybody's got some kind of racket.

"Mr. McDougal, you understand that you do not, and should not, represent the museum in this personal venture. I'm completely satisfied that Yamaguchi had a most unfortunate accident. We want no trouble with the Japanese authorities caused by a private detective who earns his money by digging up trouble."

I told him I didn't like his tone. A man who worked for the museum was missing and his sister was hurting pretty bad. I would have expected more enthusiasm, I told him, even if it was a wild-goose chase. In addition (now I was really building up steam), I told him, I didn't like his nose and if he wanted to keep its shape, it should stay out of my business.

By the time the *Empress of Tokyo* arrived in Yokohama, I had lost 10 pounds, turned permanently green at the gills, and read Goodmeyer's *Peoples of the Pacific* twice. As a self-professed semiliterate, I have to admit I don't know much about writing, but that guy could turn a phrase. I was actually anxious to meet a man who could be so clever with words.

I checked in with the operative who represented the International Detective Agency in Japan—a thin, toothy fellow named Adams, who stared at me through thick spectacles that tripled the size of his eyeballs. I wondered how the chief had ever assigned such a sap to our Yokohama post. He helped me make arrangements to take a Japanese sugar transport to Saipan and transferred my greenbacks to yen.

On the night of my departure, I met Adams for a few beers at a Japanese saloon along the wharf. It was a humid summer night as I downed my Kirin and listened to my fellow gumshoe rattle off some information he had gotten from the U.S. Embassy boys. Seems they didn't like my going to Saipan, either. Adams leaned forward with those oversized eyes bulging and whispered in hush tones like we were in some Cagney movie. "Watch yourself, McDougal. The pin-striped diplomats have never called me in two years. You show up and they get excited."

"How do you figure it?"

"Goodmeyer and Yamaguchi may be doing something other than digging up old rocks."

It was July 17, 1937, when I got my first sight of Garapan, the main city of Japanese-controlled Saipan. I had no idea of what to expect on this little island, which the League of Nations had mandated to Japan after the Great War and which Tokyo entrepreneurs had transformed into a major sugar plantation. Garapan was a little honky-tonk town, with colorful Japanese banners flying from wooden buildings that looked like they had been lifted out of the ghost towns of Nevada. Once in a while you'd see dark-skinned Saipanese in Spanish-looking costumes or Carolinian natives leading their oxen-pulled carts down a dusty lane. But more dominant were the hundreds of Japanese merchants, blacksmiths, swordmakers, umbrella-makers and tradesmen invariably followed by their kimono-clad wives. They had a hotel, a few geisha houses, a movie house, a cane-hauling railroad and a hospital. The smell of burning sugar from the harvest of the great cane fields permeated your hair, skin and clothes. Hell, it reminded me of Waipahu.

After I got settled in at the hotel, I paid a call at the government building known as Nanyo Cho. It looked somewhat like the Mormon Temple at Laie, with that white marble gleam that you imagine resembling the halls of heaven itself. Since I didn't speak their lingo and they didn't know English, it took me nearly half an hour of gobbledegook with the guards to make them understand that I wanted to speak to the police authorities. I was taken to a small anteroom for

The village in Saipan where Miguel lived. Those folks are members of Miguel's family. *(Yoshio Kondo, Bishop Museum)*

another very uncomfortable hour where I watched white-linen-suited bureaucrats come and go, obsequiously bowing to me with bright smiles as they passed my lonely bench.

Finally, I was escorted into the office of some high-ranking military officer who I soon learned was an Oxford-educated young man by the name of Captain Takeo Hiraguchi. He offered me a cig and a smooth shot of Glenlivet Scotch whiskey, inspected my passport and asked me point-blank what I hoped to find by coming all the way to Saipan.

"A young woman is crying her heart out in Honolulu. She wants a little proof that her brother is either dead or alive."

"As I informed your government, Mr. McDougal, the young man has vanished quite without a trace. We did a thorough search of the rugged Kagman Point district, the area where he was doing archaeological surveys. If he fell from any of those steep cliffs, I'm afraid his body was long ago washed out to sea in the rugged currents."

I suggested that he wouldn't mind, then, if I did a little snooping of my own. He made some remark about my poor physical condition. Compared to the captain, I admit that I felt like an out-of-shape sumo wrestler.

"There is one more thing I believe you should know, Mr. McDougal. The young Yamaguchi lad had earned in a very short time a disreputable reputation for himself in the geisha houses. It seems as if he was quite the playboy. He was acting very irresponsibly, if you know what I mean."

I congratulated Captain Hiraguchi on his impeccable English, told him I expected his support, and left the efficient military climate of Nanyo Cho to take in the sights of Saipan and find Dr. Goodmeyer. I'll admit I was a bit disappointed in the scenery. The flat land of Saipan was covered with sugar cane production, but the mountains were smoother and more whitish than the Koolau, almost what Oahu would look like with a million more years of erosion. The north and east ends of the island were rugged and precipitous like the Pali. Kagman Point is on the eastside and was accessible only by mule train.

Two hours after leaving military headquarters, I was sitting in a field tent enjoying my second glass of expensive Scotch and noting the clumsy but laughable manners of Dr. Goodmeyer. I had expected a brilliant, aloof genius, but found a friendly, almost absent-minded, old-world gentleman who puffed away on Lucky Strikes and spewed out Pacific words like he was a native himself. He was dressed in a khaki uniform with a campaign hat that reminded me of Teddy himself storming San Juan hill. For 20 years Goodmeyer had roamed the Pacific Islands, gathering up bits and pieces of culture here and there, tossing them into a huge, good-smelling stew. I took an instant liking to him when he unthinkingly lit up a second Lucky Strike, not realizing that his first cig was only half-smoked in the ashtray.

"Terrible, terrible what happened to Ike. Warned him not to explore that territory alone. But he insisted. Of course, I've sent a full report to Dr. Gregory. This has put a real damper on the expedition. Can't do much work without Ike."

"I heard he was slacking off. A playboy?"

"Oh, I guess on his own time he found Garapan's pleasure dens enticing. Can't say I haven't found a few smiles there. But no, McDougal, the boy was a good archaeologist. Trained at Stanford, you know. He thought for sure that Kagman Point would be a good place to do a dig. Lattes stones, you know."

"Excuse me, professor?"

"Lattes stones. Huge, carved stones that the ancient Chamorro used to build their houses on. Protected them from the wild pigs. I'm quite convinced, sir, that the origins of the Hawaiian people can be traced right here to Saipan. At least that's what we are here to find out."

A cloud of Lucky Strike smoke filled the air around his head as he took a drag on this cig, then the other.

"I'd like to take a trip out to this Kagman Point, professor. Would you accompany me, perhaps tomorrow?"

"No, no, son. Bad legs. However I'll ask Miguel Guerrero if he'll take you out there. He's an excellent guide. A native of Saipan who is also quite fluent in English and Japanese."

He extended a very warm and firm hand and I returned to the hotel with young Guerrero in tow. He was a good-natured kid, maybe 18 years old. I had wanted to get this over with as soon as possible, but he convinced me to delay my trip to Kagman Point. We made an appointment to leave on the morning of July 20, three days away.

Since I was on the International Detective Agency's payroll, I didn't waste those three days in idle leisure. If Ichiro Yamaguchi had been spending most of his free time in the geisha houses of Garapan, then I felt obligated to investigate, against my will, the pleasure dens. After all, there were possibly some clues to his disappearance in these dens of iniquity if foul play was involved. Anyway, I had always heard about geisha girls and this was my opportunity to do a little of my own anthropological research.

I dragged my translator, Miguel, along with me as I made the rounds. I gotta confess, the sake flowed real steady for the next two nights. You could tell the women were mostly Okinawans, Miguel pointed out, because they had tattoos on the backs of their fingers. Despite the thick, white paste-like make-up they all used, they weren't bad-looking at all. As we downed our sake, the girls would sing out-of-tune folksongs to us, while playing their banjos, and laugh at anything we said. Hell, I was convinced I was as funny as Bob Hope and made plans for my first film, *The Road to Saipan*.

It was in one of the dingiest houses that Miguel introduced me to a hefty geisha by the name of Miwa who, I was told, had been an intimate friend of Ike Yamaguchi. Rotund with a flat, oval face, Miwa's breasts were larger than papaya, her thighs under her thin robe thicker than melons.

"She's pillow geisha," Miguel explained to me.

"What do you mean, pillow geisha?"

"Some of the high-class girls that sing or play the *jamisen* aren't for screwing. The pillow geisha you can sleep with."

Miguel was giving me a real education in the nuances of Japanese sex life. He also found out that Ike had been sparking this Miwa almost every night. She spoke little English, but was taken with the American boy with the Japanese face. Yamaguchi must have been hornier than hell.

I was recovering from my usual bout with too much sake from the night before when I decided to pay an off-hour visit to Miwa, hangover and all. I must have looked terrible when I tracked her down to a little bungalow near the main street of Garapan, because she took my shoes and hat, offered me a hot cup of tea, and whipped up a bowl of saimin. I didn't know what I expected to learn from her since she hardly spoke English, having acquired "*sukoshi* American." But using hand gestures and pidgin I had learned to use with the old-timers in Hawai'i, we spent the day bridging East and West.

Ike wasn't her boyfriend, she admitted, but just a good friend. He felt sorry for her because she was "good girl" who had to sleep with so many men, every night. Although I had thought she was at least 25 years old, I was shocked to learn that Miwa was only 16 and had been a "pillow geisha" for two years.

Being a good kid from Hawai'i, Ike had probably been just as shocked. He was trying to figure out a way to smuggle her back to Hawai'i, to help her to become a good girl. That's why he spent so much time in the geisha house.

"Neva touch me," she pleaded. "He respect me." The kid started crying, but quickly held it back, trying to smile. She didn't want to burden me with her sorrows. I could see with Ike's death, Miwa had resigned herself to the life that fate had dealt her.

I asked her if Ike seemed upset or worried when she last saw him. No, she assured me, he promised to be back in three or four days.

"He go Lagua Katan. Come home, take me Hawai'i. Three or four day," she said, holding up her fingers. "Three, four day he make me good girl."

173

I left her putting the white gooey make-up on her face, a cigarette dangling from between her lips that made her look more like a dried-out whore than a teenager. Since Miguel and I were to leave Garapan right after dawn the next morning, I first paid a short visit to Dr. Goodmeyer to confirm that Ike had gone off to explore a Lagua Katan site, not Kagman Point. He kindly corrected me that the area Ike was surveying was indeed Kagman Point.

"Lagua Katan," he instructed me like a good professor, "is quite on the opposite side of the island."

When I told him that the girl had said Yamaguchi had gone to Lagua Katan, he laughed that most of the Japanese who had moved into Saipan didn't know which end was up.

"That site is absolutely devoid of archaeological sites," the doctor explained. "The museum surveyed Lagua Katan in 1930 with no success. The girl must have been mistaken."

"Well, after we search Kagman Point," I informed him, "to be on the safe side, Miguel and I will check out Lagua Katan."

"You really are wasting your time, Mr. McDougal. I understand his sister's concern, but everyone has really done their best to find poor Ike."

The next day I was huffing and puffing on the bluff overlooking Kagman Point, finding just the right words for Katsumi Odachi and this damn escapade. I didn't know what I was trying to prove, except that a middle-aged blimp could still keep up with 18-year-old Saipanese mountain goats. We turned up no clues—not a trace. Captain Hiraguchi was turning out to be a very rational fellow. I told Miguel that we might as well check out the Lagua Katan area. Maybe the kid had gone there, not Kagman.

Miguel's face dropped about five feet, hit the ground and bounced back with a slam. "No, Senor McDougal. We should not go there. Chamorro spirits will kill us."

I'd lived in Hawai'i long enough to know that when the subject of ghosts comes up, everyone shuts up. I wasn't about to let any superstitious nonsense sour my desire for exercise, so I didn't want to hear any more about bogeymen murdering us. Only, Miguel volunteered the information.

"We call them Taotaomona. They are evil spirits of ancient Chamorro that live in banyan trees and haunt the lattes sites. They dwell at Lagua Katan. I'm a Catholic, senor, but even Jesus himself can't protect you from Taotaomona."

I didn't want to argue. I asked him to take me as close as he could go and then point me in the direction to Lagua Katan. It was sunset the following day that Miguel planted himself in the middle of a narrow footpath, pointed his finger to a short, but very steep, plateau and said he'd wait for me. I trudged off with a small pack, consumed by a skipping tribe of mosquitoes and hating every second of my island adventure.

The moon was full and exceedingly bright by the time I came to an open clearing with two magnificent lattes stones sitting as pretty as a picture in the shadow of a large banyan. If Goodmeyer had been in this territory before, I couldn't imagine how he had missed this Chamorro site. Not far from the lattes stones was another small rise that opened up to a beautiful vista of the north end of Saipan. I edged to the precipice, which must have been at least half a mile high. I had heard that this end of the island was relatively deserted, but not so on the flat plains far below. There were small structures, some of which looked like airplane hangars, bordering what was a long runway. There was a mile-long line of heavy armored vehicles parked just adjacent to the airfield. The island was a source of sugar for Japan. What in the world was all that military hardware for?

I retraced my steps to the lattes site, retrieved my pack and decided to rejoin Miguel rather than spend the night at Lagua Katan. I don't know why I felt someone was watching me or why they should be in the banyan. I won't admit that Taotaomona crossed my mind. Or that I felt a desperate spasm of fear when my flashlight reflected dried, red blood splashed on the trunk of the banyan. I swung the light upward and caught the gaze of what I imagined might have once been Ichiro Yamaguchi. He had a hideous grin in death. I don't know where his body was, but his head was like a gross jack-o'-lantern propped up in the branches of the tree.

I rolled back at least 15 feet, emitting a scream that must have been heard in Garapan, 40 miles away. As my feet scrambled to position themselves flat on the earth, the butt of some heavy object smashed into my back and I fell forward.

"Well, Mr. McDougal, I warned you that you were out of shape. We've been waiting a long time for you. Like Sergeant Preston, 'You caught your man.' And we've caught you."

Captain Hiraguchi was with a dozen other armed members of the Imperial Army who took a delight in escorting me down the plateau of Lagua Katan to a few waiting jeeps that drove us to a small prison along

Amelia Earhart at Wheeler Field. I swear this is the woman I saw in a Japanese prison in Saipan. *(Bishop Museum)*

the beach south of Garapan. I was thrown into a cell with a couple of rodents and the large iron doors slammed be-hind me. I struggled to peer through the high, barred windows to the right, where I saw Miwa, beaten and manacled. On the left side of the cell, I heard a man and woman talking in English. I lifted myself up to a high window to see who my neighbors were, when I recognized the rather boyish-looking Caucasian woman.

She looked up at me, shocked to see another *haole*. Her male friend started towards me, when another crashing blow from a blunt object sent me headlong into my cell. I remember one last, silly thought before I drifted off to lullabyland—"What in the hell was Amelia Earhart doing in Saipan?"

A Saipanese crow was wailing its head off as a warm Pacific sun rose over my barren beachside prison. A knot the size of a pigskin twisted up in my belly. My tongue was so dry and brittle I couldn't even spit.

My friend Captain Hiraguchi came into my cell about high noon and started drilling me. He wanted to know my true connection with Yamaguchi. Was the International Detective Agency some cover for U.S. intelligence? Why had the U.S. Embassy in Tokyo shown such an interest in me? Did I know Yamaguchi was a spy? Who was the Saipan contact? The Okinawan girl? It went on like this for at least an hour. When the captain wasn't prying me with questions I couldn't answer, one of the guards was practicing his soccer game with my solar plexus.

The way I figured it, Yamaguchi had stepped over the line. He was fraternizing with Miwa and maybe acting a little sneaky about getting her into Hawai'i. Then he heads out to Lagua Katan and, like me, stumbles onto what is obviously a Japanese military build-up in violation of the League of Nations' mandate. Only, instead of arresting Yamaguchi, they execute him on the spot and put his head in a banyan to frighten ghost-fearing Saipanese out of the area. Then yours truly shows up on his errand of mercy.

"I don't know nothing. I'm here because of Yamaguchi's sister. Let me go or it may be worse for you. After all, you've killed one American. And you don't really expect to hide a fighter airplane base, do you? Be realistic. The Navy boys don't need to send a private investigator in here acting like a bull in a china shop to know that you're fortifying Saipan."

I was talking fast, slick and nonstop. It didn't make any sense to me, but I was hoping to keep my head attached to my neck.

A look on his face told me that my act was sinking in. He probably beheaded Yamaguchi without authority from the brass in Tokyo.

"You could cover up Yamaguchi, but who's going to believe that two of us mysteriously dropped into the Marianas trench? I'm sure you don't want this international incident to get any worse than it already is."

Bingo. He jabbered something to one of the guards and started to make an exit, when my smart-aleck mouth just had to step in with the last word.

"And it'll be even worse if you hurt that white woman and her friend."

"I'm sorry, Mr. McDougal," he uttered as his composure suddenly returned, "that your curiosity has now caused your death." When the cell door shut behind them and I was left alone, I expected my whole life to rush in front of me. Instead, the rats came out to feed.

I spent several hours rationalizing why I should be back at the Inter-Island Steamship Building handing in my resignation, when a noose slipped around the bars of my prison window and the tug of a Carolinian water buffalo tore open my adobe confinement. Miguel Guerrero at that moment was Fourth of July, Christmas and Chinese New Year all rolled into one. My deliverer tossed me an old shotgun and I followed him along the shore, expecting the entire Imperial Army to be blazing around us. Instead, I heard distant shots like a firing squad.

"They kill the *haole* man and woman. I knocked out one guard they left with you. Hurry, my uncle and me take you in his fishing boat to Tinian."

"Wait. We got to get Dr. Goodmeyer. They'll kill him for sure."

"No time. They'll find you."

"Miguel, I'll wait with your uncle. Just tell Dr. Goodmeyer that I must see him. Bring him to me. Don't tell him that I've been in prison or escaped, it'll frighten him. Then, when he shows up, we'll take him with us, even if he doesn't want to go."

I waited on a deserted beach, watching Miguel's uncle rig the sails in his little fishing skiff. It seemed an eternity before Miguel returned with the professor. The moon came up full, but dark thunderclouds passed before the orb, casting strange shadows on our anxious faces. I tossed Goodmeyer the shotgun and told him he may need it. The Japanese had executed Yamaguchi, they were going to kill me and they may very well have just shot Amelia Earhart.

"No, no, no, my boy. You must have Saipan fever. Amelia Earhart, my word."

"Let's go, Doc. You're not safe here now. To hell with your museum project."

He raised the shotgun level with my chest and let out a long, toneless whistle.

"You should have stayed in Honolulu, McDougal. First Yamaguchi acts like a Boy Scout and now you take on the Japanese Imperial Army."

I told him I didn't get it.

"I'm here not only to dig up history, but to spy for U.S. Intelligence. Only, the Japanese pay me just a bit more. They move a few guns into Saipan, the U.S. Navy is satisfied the island is nothing but a huge sugar plantation, and I earn 50,000 in good American dollars."

"Only, when a Japanese flag is over Iolani Palace, you ain't going to be spending it."

"Don't be juvenile. The Japanese are only interested in Asia, not Hawai'i. Let them have it, Mr. McDougal. They can't do any worse than the British, French, Germans or Americans. Now, I really must get you back to Captain Hiraguchi."

"Miguel, point your hunting rifle at the professor's head. You can give me the gun, Doc. It isn't loaded."

He seemed a little surprised, but I assured him it didn't take a doctorate to know that he was the weak link in this soiled business. No one knew I was going to

liss Earhart, Her Plane And Navigator Noonan

Honolulu Star-Bulletin

LAST EDITION

70 PAGES—HONOLULU, TERRITORY OF HAWAII, U. S. A., FRIDAY, JULY 2, 1937—20 PAGES ★★★★ PRICE FIVE CENTS

MELIA LOST! HUNT ON

TITUTE IS POSED FOR ON COURT | BASEBALL | BAN URGED ON HUSBAND-WIFE TAX RETURNS | Boy Dies; Given Christmas Visit Before Passing | AGREEMENT IN SOVIET, JAPAN ROW REACHED | **Cutter Prepares For Search; Flier's Fuel**

I should've gone to the newspaper with my story, but I knew no one would believe me. *(Hawai'i State Archives)*

Lagua Katan except Goodmeyer. Even Miguel didn't know. Yet the captain was waiting for me.

"Somebody had to tell him, Goodmeyer, and so you were elected."

I never thought he brought his own gun. He had it out in a flash, but the blast of Miguel's hunting rifle was faster. The traitor hit the beach with a gaping hole in his head.

I never looked back so I didn't turn into salt. From Tinian I was smuggled into Guam by Miguel's second uncle, twice removed. I offered Miguel protection in Hawai'i, but the kid insisted that he wanted to stay in the Marianas.

"First the Spanish, then the Germans, now the Japanese. One day, senor, the Saipan people rule themselves. I like to raise the flag."

I told the U.S. Navy at Guam everything that had happened on Saipan. Some second lieutenant wrote out the report and had me sign it. I watched as he put it on a stack of other worthless documents. They must know everything, I figured, or else they would have acted more interested. The authorities then told me how Earhart and her companion Fred Noonan had gone down July 2 in the Marshall Islands. When I told them I saw the two on Saipan, they laughed and took my temperature. No one ever believed me except Miguel and the world's most famous woman aviator. She had won the heart of America as "Lady Lindbergh" and was executed in some lonely Saipan jungle.

I never learned what happened to the Okinawan geisha girl. But the Doctor's reputation remained intact. The Navy didn't want the truth out, so the Bishop Museum was informed that Goodmeyer died of cholera and was buried in Garapan. No questions asked. Elizabeth Yamaguchi received a simple-worded telegram from Guam informing her of her brother's death.

Aloha Tower never looked so sweet when I arrived by ship on the first day of August. China and Katsumi greeted me at the pier. Kats was shaking my hand, thanking God I was alive and saying how sorry he was to have gotten me nearly killed. I told him it was nothing. China thrust a newspaper in my face and started running off the handle in Chinese. You could tell she was furious. The headlines said that the Japanese Imperial Army had invaded Peking. The war in Asia was escalating and in Honolulu's movie houses fistfights between Chinese and Japanese were breaking out during the newsreels. The world was going to hell.

That evening I went to the Smile Cafe, paid off my long-due chit of $5 and, while enjoying pork chops, tried to decide between seeing Otto Kruger in *Living Dangerously* or cheering for Sailor Arnold to pin Biggie Joy to the mat at the Civic. Then I thought about a blood-stained banyan in Saipan and a good-hearted American kid who was dead because governments play fast and furious with our lives in their pursuit of power. I had had enough violence to last me through the week, so I took in the Honolulu Serenaders at the Royal Hawaiian. I felt safe and comfortable being home, even though the rest of the world was in the hands of fanatics.

"I thought we made the world safe for democracy back in '19," I said, to no one in particular.

"Come on, Mac," my waitress said. "We lucky we live Hawai'i."

"Yeah," I sighed. In the summer of '37, we were still America's impregnable fortress.

*[**Editor's Note:** There is absolutely no historical proof that American aviator Amelia Earhart and her companion Fred Noonan were kept prisoners on Saipan by the Japanese military. This long-circulated speculation, kept alive on Saipan, should not be accepted merely through the testimony of McDougal. The first woman to make a solo flight over the Atlantic Ocean in 1932, Miss Earhart*

was the first woman to pilot an airplane from North America to Hawai'i, landing in the islands on March 18, 1937. A monument to Amelia Earhart overlooks Black Point Beach on the slopes of Diamond Head. During the first "Round-the-Equator" attempt with her navigator Fred Noonan, Amelia Earhart left New Guinea on July 1, 1937, heading for Howland Island. From Howland, she intended to fly the 1,900 miles to Honolulu and then back to the U.S. continent to complete the 29,000-mile journey. A massive search for Earhart and Noonan failed, although one theory suggested that they were taken captive by the Japanese. The prison where McDougal had been confined to this day is shown to visitors to Saipan as the place where "Lady Lindbergh" had been kept before her execution. The Japanese build-up on their League of Nations' mandated islands did occur during the 1930's in their preparation for the Greater East Asian Co-Prosperity Sphere.]

CHAPTER EIGHT

Death Visits the Volcano

I ain't got no green thumb, preferring hot lead, spiked juice and a broad with legs that don't quit to plants, ferns, flowers, birds or orchids. If it's green and growing, I'm not interested, unless it's my bank account. I wouldn't give a plug nickel to know anything about tides, tsunamis or volcanoes. But I'll never forget May of 1924, when Halemaumau blew its brains out—it was the same month I fell in love. When you think about it, there's not much difference between being in a volcanic explosion and falling hard for a stunning lady.

I met her in the last week of April, down at Flapper's Acre in front of the Moana Hotel. I was treating myself to a steak dinner at the Banyan Court, when she caught my eye. A sultry, dark-eyed beauty with high cheek bones, she wore a superficial smile that couldn't hide a secret melancholy. It didn't take an alienist's degree to know with one look that this soiled dove had a broken wing. I'm a sucker for lame birds.

Another, older woman with a fat bun of red hair and a pinched face was hovering all over her as if she was her nurse. I finished up my steak and potatoes and carried my cup of kona over to their table.

"Visiting the islands?" I asked politely. Sure it was a hackneyed line, but it had always worked before.

"We have no need for a tour guide, thank you," the pinched-face lady answered. "You'll excuse us?"

I sat down at the table, looking directly at the brunette.

"Well, I'm not a tour guide, ma'am, but I'd love to show your friend here the beauty of our island."

"We've seen everything, mister...?"

"McDougal. Arthur McDougal. No malihini can see the real Hawai'i without the assistance of a *kama'aina*. Would you like a little?" I showed the brunette a small flask in my inner breast pocket.

"Heavens, no! We don't drink. Perhaps you would benefit from obeying the laws of the nation." An odd odor of sweet perfume swept around this annoying creature.

"Yes, I'll have a small shot," the brunette suddenly spoke up, showing her first real vital signs. I poured a small amount of the *okolehao* from the flask into her tea.

"Just a little more, Arthur." No one had called me Arthur in years. I complied willingly, filling her teacup to the brim with the Manoa bootleg.

"My sister shouldn't be drinking at this time of day."

"Catherine! Please. Sit down and take just a little."

"I'll sit down, but don't expect me to partake in illegal liquor. Not in the wide-open. The redhead acted like I was committing a mortal sin. She had enough tinge of a prude to make the staunchest missionary proud. Shrugging, I fixed my eyes on her better-looking sister.

"I'm Jay Ann Farrell, Arthur. Are you a native of the islands?"

"No, but I've been here about 20 years."

"What kind of work are you in?"

I was about to answer when Paniolo, a beachboy with the Nui Halu o Honolulu, called over to me from the beach.

"Hey, Professor! What are you doing in Waikiki? Somebody wen *make?*"

"Naw, just getting some lunch. How's the surf?"

"So-so. Anytime you and the ladies like to try surfing, ask for me, okay?"

"Sure."

"Very quaint," said the redhead. "A friend of yours?"

"I like to think so."

"Are you a professor, Arthur?" Jay Ann looked at me with a bit more respect, I imagined. I thought about leading her on, but decided to come clean.

"No. Everyone on the beach gets a nickname. Paniolo gave me mine. Actually, I'm a private investigator."

Catherine was in the midst of sipping her unspiked tea, when she sprayed forth a good dose of it all over my new tie.

"A detective? My word, what a horrid profession."

"Not at all, Catherine," added Jay Ann. "It takes a remarkably strong man to work in that profession. Now tell me, Arthur, is your friend Paniolo's invitation sincere? Will he take both of us surfing?"

I didn't want to let on that I couldn't swim, so I went on about my bum leg which I had gotten in a gunfight in a downtown saloon with a cheap hood out of

Seattle. She didn't need to know the bruise came from a cupboard in my kitchen. I set up her first surfing lesson and watched later that afternoon when Paniolo guided her through some of Waikiki's gentler waves.

In the evening I escorted Jay Ann over to the newly renovated Waikiki Park by Ena Road, where we rode the carousels, the death-trap loop and Noah's Ark. Unfortunately, Jay Ann insisted that we bring along her sister who was making a career of being a thorn in my side. The only way to duck her was by dancing, so Jay Ann and I clung to the pavilion dance floor like two collegiates. By the time I got them back to the Moana Hotel, my feet were sore, my head was spinning from bootleg, and my heart had fallen hard.

The next few days I decided was my long overdue vacation leave, as I showed the Farrell sisters the islands. Jay Ann and Catherine were out of Santa Clara, California, where their father, Lucius Farrell, had plenty of dough from lettuce farms, so neither one of the sisters had ever needed to work. I spent a wad escorting the *wahine* tourists to dancing parks, the Kaimuki Playhouse and the rooftop Garden Cafe at the Alexander Young Hotel. We did all the tourist activities, including riding the train to Haleiwa, swimming by Chinaman's Hat, eating poi and *kalua* pig at Manuel Richards' luau, and being blown off the road at the Pali Lookout.

The instant dislike Catherine and I had for one another never went away. Maybe I was reading into things, but I could tell Jay Ann was falling for me, too.

The Volcano House where Jay Ann and I stayed during our Big Island visit.
(Bishop Museum)

Yet, despite all our good times and laughs, underneath I could still sense her ocean of pain. Sometimes when she didn't know she was being watched, you could see her eyes turn watery, her brow furrowed.

The first week of May, the sisters took off on the steamer *Haleakala* to the island of Hawai'i. The manager of the Volcano House, an old friend of their father's named C.J. Lovejoy, had offered them free lodging as long as they liked. So I closed up shop, gave China an unexpected two-week vacation, paid my $50 for fare and joined the Farrell sisters on the *Haleakala*. Two days later we had landed at Hilo Bay, took a motorcar to Kilauea, and settled into the Volcano House.

The first one to greet us was Uncle George Lycurgus himself—the living legend of the Volcano House. The Greek was in his late fifties then, a dignified white-mustached gentleman who loved to sit in his koa rocker, smoke cigars and gaze out from the back lanai of his old hotel overlooking the fiery domain of Tutu Pele. He told us that he was expecting a big eruption—at least 100 earth tremors had been reported at Ka'u during the last few days. Down in Pahala village two *paniolo* also claimed to have seen a Hawaiian woman dressed in white, talking gibberish, walking along a country road. As they rode towards her, she mysteriously disappeared. Jay Ann was acting giddy over the excitement of folks actually claiming to see Pele.

I was less excited over the way Lovejoy bent over backwards to make sure the Farrell sisters were comfortable. I don't know how they knew each other, but I didn't like the way he looked longingly at Jay Ann. The little green monster was taking hold somewhere down in my gut, as it always did when I liked a woman too much.

There were about 20 other guests who joined us at one of the big spreads put on by Uncle George. Festoons of *maile* laced the tables and high-beam ceilings of the dining room, as we consumed ducks, chickens and taro, all of them steamed in Pele's vents. It was a feast fit for royalty, and I wouldn't have been surprised if Lili'uokalani herself hadn't once sat here with Lycurgus, being regaled in this fashion. After all, in the days of the monarchy they had been friends. The Greek had even spent some time in jail when he helped in an attempt to restore the Queen back in '95. An evening didn't go by that Uncle George didn't mention those "good old days."

Some of the other guests at the table were as distinguished in the annals of Hawaiian history as Uncle George. Governor Wallace Rider Farrington and Lorrin Thurston, accompanied by their wives, were there, along with Rev. William D. Westervelt, the distinguished collector of Hawaiian tales. The fact that Thurston and Lycurgus had been on opposite sides of the fence during the overthrow of the monarchy did not escape the discussion at the table. If I were Thurston, I would have thought twice about eating the duck on his plate.

The other hotel guests were less interesting. There was Miss Worthington and Miss Hampshire, two middle-aged secretaries who took the vacation of their lives to get a repast from Washington, D.C. A burly *haole* by the name of Bennett was making plenty of noise with his hunter friends, boasting about the number of crows he had bagged that morning. If he and his buddies kept it up, I figured the Hawaiian crow was soon going to be as extinct as the dodo bird.

Then there were the honeymooners—the Thompsons out of Seattle, a handsome couple who fondled each other throughout the serving of the *haupia* dessert. A couple of military men and their wives, a Colonel Speer from the Presidio and Major Tyler from Schofield Barracks, pretty much kept to themselves. Captain Speer's wife, I noted, consumed a great quantity of fluid from a very hidden flask.

After dinner we all posed for the photographer Tai Sing Loo, who was up at the Volcano House to document the anticipated eruption of Kilauea. I was hugging Jay Ann close, with an evil eye cast by big sister, when Loo's flash pan blew. As my eyes were clearing up from the glare, I could see him make his grand entrance. His tweed, double-breasted jacket was a cool, tailor-made cut worth at least $100. It was worth almost as much as his patent leather thigh boots. The rest of him was equally well-manicured. His thin eyebrows and mustache looked as if they had been painted on his face with a fine brown ink pen to offset a handsomely sculptured Anglo face. A pipe jutted out from his jaw, sending smoke signals to some imaginary tribe on the other side of Kilauea Crater.

Jay Ann suddenly slipped off my arm and was rushing back to her suite. Big sister took a long, sweet gander at Mr. Hollywood, who was also known as Clifford Updike, and then rushed off to join her sister. The well-chiseled face made his bold entrance, secured a room and, with a valet in tow, climbed the stairs to his second-floor suite.

An hour later I had cajoled Jay Ann into taking a short walk on the crater rim. The glow from the lake of fire in the crater far below cast a soft, beautiful red shadow across our faces. I told her straight that I knew something was wrong and offered my help.

"You can't help me, Arthur," she quietly answered, giving me a simple kiss on the cheek. If anyone else in the world had ever called me Arthur, I would have broken his nose. When spoken from her lips, "Arthur" made me sound special.

"You seem to know the slick-looking gent. Friend of yours from California?"

She held the tips of her fingers together, separating the thumbs.

"Arthur, you've opened up one layer of my life. But there are many more that I can't reveal to you just now. Maybe when the time is right."

I spread apart her index fingers and assured her that she could trust me. After all, my business was trouble.

She took me in her arms and kissed me hard. I wasn't sure whether the rumblings I felt beneath my feet were caused by Pele or Jay Ann.

At around 6 o'clock in the morning I fell out of bed when an earthquake shook the Volcano House like a $5 martini. All the guests were in a pandemonium, half-dressed and disheveled, rushing to the lanai lookout. The Governor and Thurston were absolutely ebullient.

"Never seen anything like it in my life," Thurston was muttering.

"Glad you asked me up here with you, Lorrin," replied Governor Farrington.

Below us a column of fire, ash, smoke and rocks blasted out of Halemaumau crater. The hotel swayed under the impact of the repeated blasts.

"Not in a hundred and thirty years has there been anything like it," pronounced Thurston.

Miss Worthington let out her own blast of hot air at that moment, nearly causing me to fall off the lanai.

"My God, there are people down there!"

Sure enough, the hunters had gone down near the crater early that morning hunting crows and could be seen like little ants running for their lives, being pelted by flying stones. No one had expected such a tremendous eruption. When they got back to the hotel—bruised, frightened and exhausted—they told us that some Army privates from Kilauea military camp were near the crater when it blew. They must have been consumed in flowing lava. Another man named Taylor, a plantation book-keeper from Pahala, had been killed in the barrage of stony missiles.

"I swear, it was just like France," said Bennett, who evidently had been a doughboy during the Great War.

By noon, Superintendent Boles and Observatory Director Finch had informed the guests and manage-ment of the Volcano House that we were in no immi-nent danger, but that they had marked off a forbidden zone with painted white stones, over which we were restricted from venturing further. Loo was going crazy taking photos and the rest of the guests were transfixed as they watched the gorgeous display of fireworks. To be honest, I wanted to get back to Hilo, but Jay Ann, who seemed exhilarated by the excitement, refused to leave while her frightened sister Catherine confined herself to her room.

It was approaching 11 o'clock that night, when most of the hotel guests had finally pulled themselves away from Pele's extravaganza. Bennett had gotten drunk, boasting more than ever about walking through the mouth of hell. He and his gang had mostly passed out from their carousing and then dragged themselves to bed. Lovejoy, Lycurgus, the military couples and middle-aged secretaries had all gone off to their rooms, as had Updike. I had kept my eye on him most of the day, feeling maybe a little jealous by the way Jay Ann had run off when he showed up. He kept to himself, but was acting increasingly nervous with each eruption.

By midnight, only a handful of us were left on the lanai. The Governor, Thurston and Rev. Westervelt had sent their wives off and formed a private little group, smoking cigars, sipping brandy and trying to impress each other with their wealth of knowledge about volcanoes. I was getting bored with all the *kama'aina* pomposity, but Jay Ann was transfixed by the fires. I had just gone off to fetch a fresh glass of water to mix with a little bootleg whiskey, when I heard a sharp crack and the splintering of wood in one of the porch beams. Jay Ann let out a scream, and I saw Thurston wrestle the Governor to the floor.

Someone had taken a shot at the group on the lanai. I pulled an hysterical Jay Ann off the porch, as two more bullets ripped into the hotel, shattering glass and wood over everyone. We were all hugging the rug, when the firing finally stopped. Dashing to my room, I grabbed my revolver, checking that it had six slugs. The only place where anyone could have gotten off any shots was along the crater rim, towards Waldron's Ledge. The fire glow from Kilauea was bright enough for me to move fast through the *ohia* woods, but not fast enough. Fifteen minutes later I found a little nest where the sniper had perched. With a scope he would have a clear, but difficult, target on the lanai, 300 yards away.

When I got back to the hotel, most of the guests had been awakened by the commotion and were buzzing about. First Pele was erupting, and now an attempted murder. Jay Ann was nearly in a stupor.

"It was God's punishment, Arthur," she murmured. "It was God's punishment."

"What are you talking about, honey?" She was trembling in my arms.

Catherine came bolting into the room, her eyes wild, as if she had seen a phantom. I smelled whiskey on her breath.

"My God, Jay Ann, are you all right? Are you hurt?"

"She's all right," I assured her.

"It is God's punishment, Catherine," Jay Ann repeated.

"No!" her sister screamed. "No!" She then ran off to her room, as if the bullet had been meant for her.

Governor Farrington and Thurston no doubt harbored the same suspicions. As prominent targets on the lanai, the bullets could have been meant for one, or both, of them. When that high in the oligarchy, I reasoned, there is always someone who has a bullet with your name on it.

Captain Speer helped me dig the bullets out of the beams. They were .30-.30's, a caliber used by the hunters.

When I finally got around to counting heads, they were all there. Lycurgus and Lovejoy were apologizing profusely to the guests, trying to usher everyone back to their rooms. It was curious that only Updike hadn't been aroused from his sleep. I had had to knock on his door to make sure he was there. He smelled like whiskey mixed with an expensive perfume I had learned to tolerate. He was dripping with the scent of Catherine Farrell.

I drowned Jay Ann in a quart of hooch to help put her to sleep. I didn't tell her that the bullet holes were grouped in an area near where she sat, but I was determined to get her out of the Volcano House in the morning. Whatever hidden layers she possessed, I suspected something very rotten was at the core.

She was calmer but tight-lipped when she woke up late the next morning. When I told her we were going back to Hilo, all she could say was that it was no use. God was going to punish her. At lunch, a few of the guests were discussing the shooting, some of them making arrangements to leave. Superintendent Boles, acting like he had more than enough problems with the volcano, called the sheriff in Hilo, who agreed to come out as soon as he could. From his voice you could tell he wasn't going to go near Kilauea just now.

In the midst of the discussion, a couple of Hawaiian cowboys burst into the dining room, announcing they had just seen Pele. Rev. Westervelt seemed real interested, taking notes on their story about riding up here and seeing a woman down on the crater floor about an hour ago. She had long, red hair and was wearing a thin gown, walking in the danger zone towards the erupting Halemaumau. I wasn't paying too much attention till they said Pele took the form this time of a pale *haole* woman. I dashed to Catherine Farrell's room. She wasn't there, but a note was on the bed.

Some soldiers from the Kilauea military camp and I, braving showering rocks, fumes and smoke, found her body about 300 yards from the thundering pit. At first I thought she had been struck by a deadly rock as she approached Pele's fiery home. Only after we got the corpse back to Volcano House did I see the bullet hole in the nape of her neck. Someone had robbed Catherine of her last willful act of self-destruction. There was no use alarming Jay Ann or the others, I thought, so I kept the murder to myself, letting everyone else think it was a case of suicide.

I found Jay Ann lying face down on her bed, heavily sobbing into a pillow. I quietly took her sister's note out of her hand and reread it slowly, trying to unravel its meaning.

You didn't kill them, Jay Ann. I drove the car that night. I let you think you were driving because I wanted to destroy you, the way you and father have destroyed me.

He is here to kill us. Only I won't let him kill me. God forgive me. Kate.

I turned Jay Ann over and shook her hard.

"I'm not letting you go until you tell me what this is about," I said in a firm tone.

Pele was groaning and coughing, as a frightened Jay Ann Farrell peeled off several layers of the onion. My job is discovering the truth but, when it's from a woman you love, you feel like the earth just fell away, leaving you with nothing to hold on to but air and lies.

Eleven months ago, the woman I loved, spoiled and beautiful, had been one of those rich floozies who took her men like she took her booze—cheap and easy. Hearing about the one-night stands and doped-up lost weekends put a hard, jealous knot in the pit of my stomach. She had even gone so far as to steal Clifford Updike away from her poor, drab sister. Updike was just another conquest for Jay Ann, but it made her sister wild with grief. She had tried unsuccessfully to take an overdose of pills.

Then at one of the fabulous Farrell parties where the hooch, opium, and Charleston were wide-open, Jay Ann overindulged. She didn't recall much after that, except that he and Catherine had gone out for a joy ride. The next thing she remembered was waking up with a lump on her head behind the wheel of her Hupmobile roadster in the early morning darkness on a lonely highway outside Santa Clara. Catherine was in the backseat, her head bloodied. Across the road, scattered like heaps of old clothing, were two small, dead children. A fire was burning under the hood of a car smashed into a highway sign. Someone was trying to get out of the wrecked vehicle when the engine exploded, consuming the survivor in a terrible white flame and agonizing scream.

The roadster was hardly damaged, so Catherine took over the wheel and sped on to their father's large estate. It wasn't hard for Lucius Farrell to protect his most beloved daughter from the police. As far as the newspapers were concerned, a family of six traveling overnight from San Francisco to Santa Clara were the victims of a horrible hit-and-run accident. No suspects were ever found.

After the accident, Jay Ann sank into an uncontrollable depression, wracked with guilt over the six deaths. She wanted to turn herself in, but her father wouldn't hear of it. Suddenly Catherine became the strong one, dominating her sister. To bring Jay Ann out of her grief, the doctors ordered an extended Hawaiian vacation.

Judging from Catherine's note, she was driving the car that night, not Jay Ann. After the accident, Catherine put her sister behind the wheel, letting her take the blame. Great sisterly love. But for someone who never had her father's affection or sister's respect, it was Catherine's way to get all the attention. Jay Ann had turned into an emotional cripple and the older sister was her nurse. No wonder Catherine resented me for putting a smile back on her tormented sister's face.

"She says here something about 'He is here to kill us.' Who do you think she meant?"

Jay Ann had no idea. The family had perished in the flames. Their father had hired a private detective to make sure the cover-up was perfect. No one else knew who had driven the car that night.

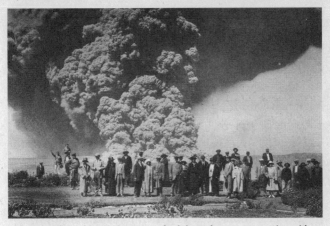

This is the photo that Tai Sing Loo took of the Halemaumau eruption with the guests of the Volcano House. I was driving back to Hilo with Jay Ann when this was taken. *(Tai Sing Loo, Bishop Museum)*

I asked about Updike. She said that she dumped him after the accident. When I told her that he had been with Catherine in her room the night someone had taken a shot at her, Jay Ann didn't act surprised.

"Clifford is a dear man with a deep streak of vanity and an empty pocketbook. He followed us to Hawai'i, either to get me back for his pride or Catherine for her money. I don't think he would have taken a shot at either one of us, Arthur."

That evening, as Jay Ann slept as sound as a baby and Kilauea became ominously quiet, I made arrangements for a coffin to be brought up the next day so as to get Catharine Farrell's body to the coroner in Hilo. In the meantime, I kept an eye on the Volcano House guests who, with the explosions, attempted murder and apparent suicide, seemed appropriately subdued. I played a few rounds of checkers with Uncle George, who said he was considering closing the hotel up for a few days until all the *pilikia* in the air blew away.

The volcano was still quiet the next day when, during lunch with the other guests, Jay Ann and I got into a terrible argument.

"I want to leave this afternoon, Jay Ann. I want to get you back to Hilo."

"I'm sick and tired of you watching over me like a hawk. Who do you think you are?" she snapped back.

My face turned red as I tried to calm her down.

"Don't touch me. I'm going crazy inside here. I've got to get out."

When I tried to hold her back, she slapped me in the face and raced out to one of the parked cars. She drove off in the direction of the crater road.

I excused myself to the guests, said I didn't give a damn what she did, and announced that I was packing my bags. I slipped out a window in my hotel room and onto the back of Uncle George's favorite steed. I figured that by horseback, cutting through the *ohia* forest, I could get to the ancient lava tube at least 20 minutes before Jay Ann, who was taking a longer, circuitous auto route. It was a risk and a very long shot but, if someone wanted her dead, this could very well be their best and last chance.

I entered the Thurston Lava Tube from the backside, where tourists usually exited. In the damp wall I found a small recess where I could hide. The cavernous tube was pitch-black, except for the glow at the entrance. A loaded Colt revolver held tightly in my hand helped me feel very comfortable.

A few minutes later, a lantern glowed at the entrance as Jay Ann walked carefully into the tube. I pulled her into the recess beside me and told her to blow out her lantern. She whispered that she had been followed by a large touring car a few minutes after she left the hotel. It was only a few minutes later that we heard the crunch of bootsteps on the chinky lava floor. The shadow of a figure in a yellow light moving towards us loomed larger and larger. Goblets of water dripped incessantly from the thin strands of lava that hung like skeletal fingers from the ceiling of that underground tomb. The shadow was nearly upon us, when I sprang forward with my Colt aimed at the intruder's heart.

"That's far enough, Captain. Put down your rifle, please."

"Step aside, McDougal. I'm not a killer; I'm an executioner." I could tell it was going to be a Mexican standoff. His manner was so calculating and cold, it turned my blood to ice.

"What's this all about, Captain? She never hurt you."

"She and her sister killed my little Julia. She was in the car that morning, going to spend the weekend in Santa Clara with her girlfriend's family. Her father's money could cover her identity up to the police, but I found out the truth. The detectives I hired found in the bushes near where my daughter died a small receipt for caviar that must have fallen out of the car during the accident and then blew into the bushes. It didn't take long to find out who had bought the caviar. Everyone knew the Farrell sisters."

He held the little piece of paper up that had been his ticket for revenge.

"First her sister paid, now her. Step aside, Mr. McDougal."

"You've gone too far, Captain. Don't make it worse."

"It can't get worse, McDougal. My life is ruined with my daughter gone. You saw what my wife has become. I've got nothing to lose."

Jay Ann didn't move a muscle. She was like a sheep going to the altar. Captain Speer raised his rifle at a level right between her eyes. I knew I couldn't kill him, but was ready to catch the bullet myself, when suddenly all hell broke loose.

The earth heaved, twisted and then settled as a blast of dynamite the size of a city block ripped through the air. We were all thrown to the ground, as it seemed the lava tube was cracking around us. I dragged Jay Ann to her feet as we scrambled for the entrance, the Captain struggling behind us. The earth was still heaving as we got into the open air.

In the direction of Halemaumau Crater, an unbelievable white-ash cloud of steam, rock and soot consumed the sky and sun. It seemed as if night had fallen, although it couldn't have been later than 3 o'clock in the afternoon. The air was filled with a powdery ash that covered the cars and road. Pulling a terrified Jay Ann into the backseat of the auto, we took off for the Volcano House, half-expecting to see the hotel falling into the crater. The explosion was sending rocks so furiously into the sky that the friction caused large bolts of lightning to dance above the bellowing eruptive clouds. The car swerved all over the road.

In the distance, Halemaumau was a raging avalanche of rock. Boulders that must have weighed a ton were being hurled miles through the air. The pit had nearly doubled its size, and my guess was that before she was done, Pele would consume us all. In my rearview mirror I saw Speer also navigating the cracked and vibrating road. The captain's car suddenly veered into a gaping crater opening alongside the road, turning over and over until it came to a crashing stop on the caldera's bottom. My guess has always been that he would have rather died right then and there by his own hand than face a court-martial for avenging his poor daughter's death.

At the Volcano House, the first panic had already subsided to reverent awe as we drove up to the entrance. The floor of Halemaumau caldera must have suddenly collapsed, Thurston explained, causing the lake of fire to pour into the earth. As the hot lava came into contact with an underground stream, the crater erupted, sending steam, gas and rocks into the sky. The resulting explosion had widened the pit and saved my life.

Tai Sing Loo set up his tripod and camera and photographed the eruption with all the hotel guests standing in the foreground, looking nonchalant. I refused to step into that sweet little scene, preferring instead to take the body of Catherine Farrell and a very subdued Jay Ann back to Hilo, where all sane human beings belonged at that moment. Captain Speer's wife was under the care of military authorities who escorted her back to San Francisco, where her relatives could care for her. It was hard not to feel a lot of aloha for the grieving mother and widow.

Jay Ann talked about maybe setting up house in Honolulu with a well-known detective. But I encouraged her to go home to Santa Clara first and settle things with the authorities. She wasn't guilty of killing those people, but she needed to set the record straight.

I received letters from her once or twice a week for about six months. She talked about what it would be like when we were together. Suddenly, however, the letters tapered off, until I got nothing but Christmas cards for a couple of years. She just signed them, "Your friend, Jay Ann."

The wiz kids have a saying these days that "a woman is like a streetcar; there's another one coming in ten minutes." I stood at Hotel and Bishop one lonely day for about 20 minutes, and no streetcar or woman came by. So, I walked back to the Inter-Island Steamship Office and purchased a roundtrip ticket to Hawai'i. A few days later I hurled a full bottle of Duck

Pong's very best bootleg gin into Halemaumau and gave a very special woman thanks for my being alive.

[**Editor's Note:** *The account of the cataclysmic eruption of Halemaumau Crater, the legendary home of Pele, in May 1924 has an extraordinary ring of truth, both to the natural events, as well as the social events at the Volcano House preceding the blast. However, after exhaustive research, I can find no proof that an attempt was made on a guest's life which imperiled either Governor Farrington or Lorrin Thurston.]*

CHAPTER NINE

Pilikia at the Haunted Mill

BACHI. That's what the Japanese call divine punishment—the retribution that hangs over your head because you've said or done something to anger the gods. Point your finger at a grave, speak ill of the dead or mock fate and you'll hear a local Japanese warn you, "*Bachi!*" For the next few days you'll walk around town looking out for a Thayer piano to come crashing down on your head.

The old sugar mill ruins at Kualoa had *bachi*. Back in the 1860's two *kama'aina* families named Judd and Wilder nearly went broke trying to make a go of the plantation. This was long before the days of the reciprocity treaty which brought profit to sugar. Dr. Gerrit P. Judd, a former missionary physician, had acquired the lands of Kualoa, including the island of Mokolii, or Chinaman's Hat, from Kamehameha III. Before the sugar plantation went belly-up, one of Dr. Judd's young grandsons, Willie Wilder, was killed on August 20, 1868, when he fell into a clarifier of boiling cane juice. With the financial ruin of the plantation and the death of the boy, the mill was abandoned. Some folks referred to the ruins as the "Obake" or "haunted mill," since the spirit of the dead child was said to haunt the premises. Other old-timers simply called it "The Mill of Tragedy." Jade Kealoha Ah Lum found out too late how deadly it was.

The Ah Lums ran a noodle factory out of a joint like this. [This is the Sumida Building at Pauahi & Smith Streets. GG] *(Ray Jerome Baker, Bishop Museum)*

It was 3 p.m. on July 5, 1929. I was in my office playing poker with Sgt. Henry Chillingworth of the Honolulu Poi Dogs. I was taking Sarge to the cleaners when my secretary, China, burst in, announcing that one of the bigtime Chinese merchants, Daniel Ah Lum, the eldest son of Chung Ah Lum, Honolulu's last Chinese emperor from the old days, was on the phone. Ah Lum said he wanted to see me pronto at his social hall. Ever since I had brought in the murderers of the Lims—a Chinese man and his wife brutally slaughtered in their store at Moiliili—I had become something of a celebrity in Chinatown. If a detective was ever needed by a Chinese, I was the first one they called.

China walked with me over to the Four Colors Club, at the corner of Maunakea and Pauahi, a Chinese clan meeting hall, market, noodle factory and import business that Chung Ah Lum founded 40 years ago. Ah Lum's dynasty was an expansive family affair run by the Ah Lum brothers—Daniel, Mark, Luke, John, and the youngest, Matthew. Their Hawaiian mother had been a devout Christian who had named each of her *pake* sons after one of the twelve disciples, but quit producing after number five. The oldest son clearly was in charge of things at Ah Lum Enterprises—the other brothers seemingly hard-working, sober and dutiful assistants, who managed various aspects of the business. Matthew struck me, however, as a bit more Americanized. He had dropped the sober colors of his brothers for a slick new outfit right off the racks at Liberty House.

"So, how can I help you boys?" I asked in my most business-like tone.

"It is about our niece, Jade Kealoha Ah Lum."

"You need her shadowed or something?"

"Mr. McDougal," Daniel said in the King's English, "we are concerned that our niece, Jade, is getting married to a man whom we hardly know. He is a *haole* from California whom she met a few months ago."

"Maybe a marriage counselor is what you need," I quipped.

"This man is very smooth-tongued and has turned my niece's head. We are very concerned that she may be making a very tragic mistake."

When I pushed for more information, Daniel Ah Lum informed me that Jade's father and mother had been killed in a car accident when she was an infant. Consequently, the patriarch of the dynasty, Chung Ah Lum, took her in and raised her as his own daughter.

"My father's health is very poor," Daniel explained. "As his sons, we want to make certain that the young *haole* is a good man. Since you have a very trusting reputation among the Chinese, we'd like to hire you to look into the man's background."

"For the right price," I told the eldest son, "I'll take the young fiancé to the laundry and bring him home bleached, starched and clean-as-a-whistle. Now, what's the fellow's name?"

Mark Ah Lum was starting to give me the handle, when Matthew burst forth in staccato fashion to Daniel, throwing Chinese syllables out like a machine gun. During his tirade, Matthew kept poking his finger in my direction, giving me snarling looks. I got the name I needed and China and I excused ourselves.

Since we were in Chinatown, we decided to stop by Wo Fat's Restaurant at the corner of Maunakea and Hotel Streets. Although China always insisted that the cooking was more *haole* than Chinese, I told her that's exactly why I liked the joint. Over my usual plate of *chow fun* and sweet-sour pork, China translated Matthew's little speech.

"He didn't like you, Mac," she said tactfully. "He said that this was a family matter and they tainted the family by bringing in a detective to investigate this man. Matthew claimed he could do the same thing for free."

Through several telegrams back and forth between our offices in Honolulu and L.A., it took only about a week to get the full dope on Jade's good-looking fiancé. I met the Ah Lum brothers one more time at the Four Colors Club to share what I had uncovered concerning Stewart Evans, a 30-year-old womanizer from Santa Monica, Calif. He had been entangled in a nasty scandal with a rich, buxom matron, who took a near-fatal dose of arsenic rather than fess up to her husband that she was fooling around with a man young enough to be her grandson.

Without his sugar mama, Evans turned up two weeks later in Honolulu, where he met Jade at some Waikiki night spot for the collegiate crowd. I turned over to Daniel a file of photos, witnesses' statements and other incriminating evidence that the gumshoes in L.A. turned up for us.

What I hadn't told Daniel Ah Lum was what I had found out about his niece. A student at the University of Hawai'i, Jade Kealoha Ah Lum had been setting up her own personal League of Nations on the Manoa campus. I had spent a few hours one day at the "Chicken Coop," a coed hangout behind Farrington Hall. All I did was mention the name Jade Ah Lum and every student had something to say about her, most of it laced with a heavy dose of envy.

"That *wahine* takes pleasure in collecting men, like conch shells."

"She one real choo-choo."

"Choo-choo?"

"Yeah, you know, butterfly flitting from one man to another."

According to the gossip mill, there were two *haoles* on her dance card—a husky fullback on Otto Klum's Roaring Rainbow team named Jackson and a well-heeled gent from Nuuanu named Charlie McCreely. Jade had also taken a fancy to Matsuda, a Valentino driving a snappy coupe; a muscular surfer named "Spider" Aiona; and a high school dropout named Tom "Cracker" Rapoza. Rapoza was a mechanic at Schuman Carriage, across the street from Washington Place.

"So she sees all of them?" I asked.

"No," said one anxious informant, "she dumped them all a few weeks ago."

"Why?"

"The choo-choo met an older man who she said treated her like a woman. He drives a Hupmobile and wears Beverly Hills double-breasted suits."

"Who could have resisted?" I sarcastically added. The comment set off a brief debate about Prince Charming.

"So, how did the other boys take it?"

"Oh, they begged for Jade to take them back. All of them, only, she said 'no.'"

The bleeding hearts could tolerate sharing her with each other, but not losing her forever to some mainland slick.

The "Mill of Tragedy" at Kualoa. The rear of Big Ben Naauao's touring car is to the left. *(Hawai'i State Archives)*

There was no point telling the Ah Lum brothers any of the dirt on their niece, so I sealed up the old pucker, sent my invoice for services, telegrams and help from the L.A. bureau, and waited for the check. I was surprised three weeks later when the *Star-Bulletin* reported that Jade Kealoha Ah Lum had been found dead behind the Kualoa Mill of Tragedy. Police announced that she had been sexually assaulted and then strangled. Their prime suspect was a missing Stewart Evans. Her half-clad body was found on the mountain side of the mill, lying on a wool blanket in a field of tall weeds.

The connection to Evans was thin, but logical. The police had been told that the couple had once been engaged. Jade, however, had broken off the engagement when she learned from her uncles that he was a two-timing gigolo out of L.A. who was more interested in her family fortune. In a fit of passion and rage, he took

Jade to Kualoa Mill, a popular place for young folks to spark, at about 10 o'clock. There he must have begged her to change her mind. When she refused, he raped and then strangled her. His Hupmobile was later discovered parked at Pier 21 near Honolulu Harbor, where foreign freighters frequently moor. After murdering her, the police believed that he must have left the islands as a stowaway on one of the freighters.

I suppose the whole matter would have disappeared from the public eye except for a heavy storm that dumped 15 inches of rain on Oahu in a couple of hours during the month of October. Massive flooding led to the evacuation of Windward valleys, as residents sought shelter from the torrential downpour that caused extensive damage to homes and businesses.

The next day, a Board of Water Supply mechanic on the leeward side of the Waiahole Tunnel got the surprise of his life. Gushing through the ditch under the Koolau mountains was a bloated human corpse. Stewart Evans no longer appeared human, the features of his face swollen beyond recognition. As Dr. Liu told me after he identified the remains, "Thank goodness for dental records."

The Jade Kealoha Ah Lum murder case was reopened with plenty of fanfare in the press. Soon after Evans' body was discovered, Chung Ah Lum, the emperor himself, summoned me to his mansion along the Waikahalulu pond near Nuuanu Avenue. Since my machine had been in the shop with a broken axle, I took the trolley up Nuuanu Avenue to the fashionable homes above School Street. The Ah Lum mansion was an old Victorian home with gingerbread trim. I was greeted at the front porch by Daniel, who defiantly told me that my services were not required.

"I'm here to see your father, Mr. Lum," I said with an air of authority, pushing past the eldest son to greet the youngest son inside. Matthew and one of his thuggish-looking friends were blocking the entrance down the hall.

"Excuse me," I said politely, as I shouldered them aside to find the royally appareled emperor in a private sitting room, propped up in a fancy sandalwood chair with a carved dragon back. He had come to the islands over 60 years ago as a very young immigrant laborer. He

Fashionable Nuuanu Avenue above School Street where the Ah Lum clan lived. *(Hawai'i State Archives)*

skipped out of his contract and escaped into Chinatown, where he went to work at one of the merchant stores. Pulling himself up by the bootstraps, he had married a Hawaiian woman with whom he had five sons. That introduced him to the whirlwind life of Hawaiian royalty, which he enjoyed until the overthrow of the Kingdom. His life story had been written up and published locally as a "Horatio Alger" success story. Chung Ah Lum spoke deliberately, with a heavy Cantonese accent.

"You will help me find my granddaughter's murderer? She was my only happiness in my old age."

"Your sons seem reluctant to hire me," I said.

"They are afraid I'll spend their money. I am going home to China, Mr. McDougal, to die there in peace. I leave everything now to these sons to fight over among themselves. They want as much as possible to grab."

Although I told him I didn't want to get into the middle of a sibling rivalry, I felt sorry for the old guy. He just wanted some peace of mind before he returned to the homeland. As beneficial as the islands had been to the old guy, Hawai'i in some ways must have always remained an alien land. I agreed to take the case for my usual fee plus expenses.

About an hour later I was sweating bullets, hoofing it over to the morgue at Punchbowl and Queen, cursing the pothole that broke my axle. According to Dr. Liu, although the body had been greatly decomposed and bloated, there was evidence that the cause of death had been strangulation. Bruises indicated that Evans had been badly beaten. It sounded like Jade and he had suffered the same fate.

Although the cops had pretty much sifted through everything at the murder scene, I thought that a visit to Kualoa beach wouldn't hurt. I hired a taxi driven by old Big Ben Naauao to drive me to the Windward side. Big Ben was one of the best tour taxi drivers in town and on the way out to Kualoa he regaled me with legends of Kamehameha, Maui the Demigod, the gods Kane and Kanaloa, and other ancient deities associated with sites along the Kamehameha Highway.

"You know, Ben, you can save that tourist stuff."

"Hey, Mac, I love talking story about the old things. You don't enjoy them?"

"No, I do. Go ahead." I figured some guys do these things only for a living. Big Ben did it as a way of life.

We were winding our way past Waiahole when I told him that we'd need to stop by the old sugar mill near Chinaman's Hat.

"Mac, please. Don't call 'em 'Chinaman's Hat.' The *haole* wen give Mokolii that name, but it's no good."

"What's in a name?"

"Everything. Our ancestors give everything a name for a meaning. Mokolii was a *moo* that had a great battle with Pele's sister, Hiiaka."

"*Moo.* Like a gecko?"

"No, a supernatural lizard. With a body 20 feet long, black-skinned and round, the *moo* had a head like

221

a dragon. Mokolii lived at Kualoa. When Hiiaka was passing by, he attacked her and they had a great battle. Hiiaka finally broke the back of Mokolii, killing him."

"Tough luck for the lizard," I said sarcastically.

"Look, you can see his body," Big Ben said, enthusiastically pointing to the Koolau mountain range as it bent towards Kualoa. "Mokolii's great tail fell into the ocean, the tip rising from the sea."

We were now sailing straight towards Kualoa, past the ancient fishpond. The tail of the *moo* rose up beautiful from a blue-green sea, placid in the afternoon sun. Billowy clouds passed overhead in an azure sky—a scene that always left you a little breathless in awe of the beauty of God's handiwork. Too bad human beings had to mess it up.

"Now that you mention it, the island does look more like a tail than a hat," I said.

"Old Hawaiians knew best, Mac. So do me a favor, yeah? No more Chinaman's Hat, okay?"

We pulled off the side of the road by the old ruins of the mill. The heavy rains in the past month had pretty much obliterated the crime scene. Walking through the creepers and *kiawe* produced nothing but sticky thorns attached to my pant legs and socks. The sun was setting when Big Ben insisted on showing me the profile of Kanehoalani, the great mountain peak right around the bend in the road.

"Really, Ben, I gotta get back to town."

"Mac, you gotta see this."

Since I had come this far empty-handed, I figured there was no harm in picking up some Hawaiian lore before returning to town.

We drove to Kaaawa valley so that Big Ben could point out the profile of the face of an ancient chief wearing a Hawaiian helmet, looking up to the skies. A thin sliver of a moon had just started to rise, as I twisted my head this way and that to see the profile.

"See it, Mac?"

It took a minute, but I finally saw the image of the ancient chief.

"The point is called Lae o Ka Oio," Big Ben explained, "and just back from the road is a cave entrance. Come, I'll show you."

We took a short hike into the valley to see a small cave entrance leading straight into Kanehoalani.

"This is Pohukaina Cave. My *kupuna* say that this cave leads underneath the island. Somewhere deep in the cave, Mac, are ancient bones. This place is very sacred."

I lit a match and started to peek in. Big Ben grabbed me, pulling me away.

"No one goes into that cave, Mac. I show it to you, but nobody ever goes into it."

I had never seen Big Ben more adamant. The usually congenial and cooperative tour guide who would bend over backwards to make his client happy was now sullen, determined and in retreat.

By the time we got back to the car, it was already 8 p.m. It would take us a while to get back to town, so I urged my tour guide to give me a raincheck on the rest of his storytelling. We were cruising back towards Kualoa, with the thin crescent moon rising above Mokolii, as we passed the Mill of Tragedy. Looking in the sideview mirror, I suddenly saw a large, flickering flame burning in the road behind. I turned to see it floating about 200 feet above the road at the point Big Ben had called Lae o Ka Oio.

"What do you think that light is, Ben?"

He looked in his rearview mirror and hit the brakes so hard that it nearly threw me into the dashboard. He started talking to himself in Hawaiian as we came to a stop alongside the desolate mill, now made even more so by the darkness of the night.

"Get out of the car, Mac. Get in the bushes, *wikiwiki*."

Dragging me out of the machine, he was running like a frightened rabbit into a thicket of creepers. I looked back and the huge, yellow flickering light had been joined by another one.

"What are they, Ben? Look, there's another one."

At the moment I spoke those words, six more torchlights, each hundreds of feet high, ignited, floating high in the darkened sky.

"Wow!" I said, like a kid looking at fireworks for the first time. They clustered in the sky like candlelights on top of a birthday cake.

"Don't look!" screamed Ben, pulling me violently to the earth. His big hand took hold of the back of my head, thrusting my face into the earth.

"What in the hell?" As the words came out of my mouth, a few creepers suddenly went in as my face was held tight by Big Ben.

I cannot swear that I heard them as drums, but a thumping sound began to reverberate off the Koolau mountains, as if a giant baseball bat was striking against the cliffs, emitting a dull, rhythmic beat. Big Ben's hand was trembling. I tried to move, but his grip was almost superhuman. The beating slowly faded away, as my protector's hold upon me relaxed. Bewildered, I was starting to ask him what in the hell was going on when he suddenly cut me short.

"Shhhh," he said, with a long whistle of air. "Listen."

A sobbing sound rose from the ruins of the old mill, a sobbing—pathetic and lonely. Was it a child, a poor child who was burned alive in boiling sugar? Or were they the sobs of a lovely young woman, her life terminated on this holy ground?

"Do you hear it?"

"Yes."

The sobbing continued for a few minutes and then vanished, just as the drumming and lights had vanished into the night illuminated only by a thin crescent moon.

As I was pulling myself up, ready to have Big Ben tell me what the hell was happening, I saw something gleaming among the creepers—a silver chain entangled in the vines. I picked it up, then drilled Big Ben.

"What was…?"

"Nightmarchers, Mac. You had a great privilege tonight to sense the nightmarchers. The lights and drums. Look at the moon. I would bet anything tonight is Pokane."

"Pokane?"

"The twenty-seventh phase of the moon when the ancient spirits walk. They walk on paths they walked in life. Lae o Ka Oio means the 'point of the nightmarchers.' This was their path."

"Incredible," I muttered. I had seen those huge lights floating in the sky. The drumming? Something was pounding against the mountains.

"I'm sorry for being rough with you. But my aunties always said, never, never look at the nightmarchers. Throw yourself to the ground and bury your face in the earth. It was for your protection."

Both of us were pretty excited on the ride back to town, telling each other over and over what we had heard and seen. The sobbing from the mill could have been the wind blowing through the place, I said to myself again and again. There had to be a rational explanation for all of it. As we were chatting away, I fingered the silver chain in my hand, looking at it hard. It wasn't supernatural, but it was the key we had come to find. And spirits had helped us find it. The Schuman Carriage chain could have come from anywhere, but I had a date with a young, hot-headed mechanic named "Cracker" Rapoza, who had grease under his fingers and blood on his mind.

There were probably 10,001 explanations as to why a Schuman Carriage key chain was lying in the dirt at Kualoa Mill. Only, I wanted to hear how "Cracker" Rapoza explained it and find out where he was the night the young lovers kissed death.

The next morning I was still thinking about last night's nightmarchers as I strolled over to Schuman Carriage, at the corner of Richards and Beretania, right across from the Governor's home at Washington Place. I went in through the back entrance to the garage where Rapoza was busy working on an engine. A radio was blaring "Barney Google with the goo goo googley eyes," as I stalked my pigeon. Rapoza was leaning under the hood of the car, tightening up a spark plug.

"Rapoza? I'd like a few words with you."

Maybe I was too dramatic, dangling the key chain in my hand, or maybe I smelled like a gumshoe. At any rate, I wasn't prepared for the plug wrench that went sailing past my head or for "Cracker's" athletic shove as he dashed towards Beretania Street.

The last time I was in a foot race I had dark brown hair and a lean frame. I was no match for Rapoza, who darted across the street in front of the trolley, raced past Washington Place and then ducked into Miller Street by Queen's Hospital.

Luckily, a motorist on Punchbowl clipped my fleeing pigeon. When I showed up huffing and puffing, Rapoza was bleeding from a gash on what could have been a broken leg.

"The way I figure it, 'Cracker,' you killed your old girlfriend and her lover."

"I don't know what you're talking about," he pleaded. "I need a doctor."

I placed my foot on the place where his leg was broken and applied just enough pressure to help Rapoza belt out a beautiful aria. The folks milling around saw the bulge under my coat and instinctively backed away.

I could have lost my license for what I did, but I held back the medics with threats and put my boy through an ancient medieval torture. He buckled like cheap tin.

"I never touched one hair on their heads, I swear."

"But you were there at the mill that night, weren't you?"

"They'll kill me if I talk."

"You won't be much better off with me if you don't," I assured him. "Talk, Rapoza, and talk fast."

A little more pressure on the leg and he told me what I needed to know. He admitted he had followed the victims out to Kualoa Mill and that the green monster had taken hold of him. He'd parked his car up the road, then hid by the mill and watched them start to woo. It started to hurt so bad watching his lady screwing another man, he sobbed like a baby.

When he couldn't take it anymore, he started digging in his pants pocket for his keys and slowly walked back to his car. It was then that he must have dropped the key chain to one of the sedans that he had been working on. Before he could get to his car hidden by the mill, a black touring car suddenly drove up and two men got out. Rapoza went back to his hiding spot. The men descended on Jade and Evans, "Cracker" said. It was over in minutes.

The two men carried Evans' body back to the automobile. One drove off in the touring car and the other in the Hupmobile. They must have dumped Evans' body into the Waiahole ditch and abandoned his car at the pier to make it look like he had killed the girl and then skipped town.

Scared at what they'd do to him if he talked, Rapoza kept quiet.

"Who was it, Rapoza?"

"I don't know, but it was a car I had seen before. Up at the Ah Lum estate in Nuuanu."

I turned "Cracker" Rapoza over to the medics just before he passed out. Half an hour later I hopped off the trolley at the Nuuanu mansion looking unsuccessfully for the black touring car. Nobody was home.

Cursing that pothole and broken axle again and again, I boarded the trolley for the short ride to the Four Colors Club on Maunakea Street. The Ah Lum boys weren't to be found in the social club area, but I finally located Daniel inspecting the ground floor noodle factory.

"I want to talk to you, Ah Lum," I said.

"I don't think so, Mr. McDougal. At least I don't want to talk to you."

"It's about one of your family cars and a filthy deed at Kualoa Mill. Putting a hit on a stranger is one thing. Knocking your own kin off is another."

He barked some orders in Chinese. The place emptied so fast you'd have thought it was *pau hana* time.

"What are you threatening me with? I warn you that I won't let you extort me."

He seemed more afraid than bold.

"What kind of man would kill his own niece just to protect his money?"

"I don't know what you're talking about. We hired you to make sure that my father wouldn't give Jade half of his wealth, as he intended to do, so it would go into the hands of some stinking *haole*. He wouldn't have dared put that kind of money into her hands after she announced she was going to marry *haole* trash. But the old man got weak and sentimental. He didn't care who she married, as long as she was happy."

"So, then, you killed her?"

"Don't be preposterous. I am a rich man with or without my father's inheritance. I despised my brother's daughter, but I would have never killed her."

A brash Chinese voice burst out a string of angry sounds from over my shoulder. It was Matthew and his buddy, both packing mean-looking revolvers. Whatever they were saying was directed at me. I didn't wait for a translation, but hit the floor, rolled through noodle droppings and pulled my Colt. The barrel flamed and smoked.

One bullet hit Matthew's friend in the gut, his gun blasting away as he flew back dead, right through the store front window onto Maunakea Street. I saw Matthew from the corner of my eye, lowering his sights on me while I lay helpless on the floor. I was bracing, getting ready for the hit and swinging my Colt around. Before Matthew could fire the shell that had my name on it, the young Chinese boy went flying forward into a huge table stacked with raw, white powdered noodles. The back of his head had been split open and blood oozed from the wound, flowing into and staining the white noodles a rich, deep red.

"Thanks," I said to John Ah Lum, as he stepped forward with one of those Chinese noodle rolling pins that looked like a baseball bat. He said nothing, just pulled Matthew out of the dough.

Daniel Ah Lum was furious. He spewed more orders in Chinese, and John forced a barely conscious Matthew to the floor, on his knees. I still couldn't figure out what they were saying, but I knew an execution when I saw one.

"Hold it, Ah Lum. I don't know what's going on here, but I know that if you didn't hurt your niece, doing this is just going to make matters worse."

Matthew started babbling. He and his buddy had killed Jade and Evans. She had shamed the family by fraternizing with a cheap *haole*, and she didn't deserve the money. His brothers were too weak to set things straight, so he and his friend took it into their hands.

The sibling rivalry between Daniel and Matthew was thick in the air.

Daniel took Matthew's gun and put it right between his younger brother's eyes. The cop sirens were finally getting close.

Matthew was taunting his brother to kill him. Just then, a wry smile came over Daniel's face. He uncocked the pistol and handed it over to me. Turning his back on Matthew, he walked out without another word.

The family disowned Matthew Ah Lum. When he went to the gallows at Oahu Prison nine months later, none of the family watched the show. Only the boys in the press showed up.

The Ah Lum business is still going strong. Rapoza settled down with a sweet Portuguese girl in Punchbowl. Chung Ah Lum finally left for China, to die in peace after turning everything over to Daniel.

As for me, I spent the $3,000 I had earned as a bonus from Chung Ah Lum on speakeasy hooch and playing poker. For months I told anyone who would listen about the nightmarchers I had seen that night at Kualoa. *Haole* friends laughed at me, saying I was getting weak-minded. The Hawaiian guys on the force seemed to understand. They'd smile at me, nodding in agreement. Then in a few months, the miracles of that Kualoa night seemed so mundane, so normal that I asked myself if it had ever really happened. So many wondrous things happen in this world, I knew, but most of my life was sunk into seeing the uglier, dirtier face of life. In time I became thankful for the blessings those torches had brought my jaded soul, but still wondered why everybody's *bachi* always seemed to mosey home to me.

*[**Editor's Note:** The nightmarcher encounter described by McDougal has an uncanny resemblance to my own sighting of torchlights above the Waianae mountains in August 1994, while walking in the parking lot of Hickam Air Force Base Officer's Club. The huge torchlights appeared floating above the mountains for about two or three minutes, and then vanished. This sighting can be verified by one other witness. It took place on the night of Poakua, the night of the gods when there is no moon in the Hawaiian skies. The legend of the Mill of Tragedy and the background of Mokolii as told by Big Ben Naauao also seem fairly accurate renditions of history and lore. The admonition of Big Ben to use the proper name of Mokolii and to slowly dispense with erroneous nicknames that reveal nothing of the islands' past is a sound recommendation.]*

CHAPTER TEN

A Simple Case of Suicide at Schofield

I was killing time at Duke's Waikiki Shell station that Monday morning, July 23, 1934, pumping premium into my thirsty Willys-Knight and listening to the boys in the station boast that their boss, famed surfer Duke Kahanamoku, was going to take the Roosevelt boys surfing when they got to town.

"You better not let Duke hear you talk like that," I reminded them. "He doesn't take to bragging."

For all of his fame and achievements as a U.S. Olympic Gold Medalist, movie star and world's most famous surfer, Duke Kahanamoku was extremely shy and self-effacing. I didn't know him real well, but I never heard him once say anything boastful about himself. Indeed, he really hardly ever spoke much at all, preferring to listen. The fact that the President of the United States was going to meet the most famous citizen of Hawai'i who would take his boys, Franklin, Jr. and John, surfing excited the boys at the station, but never phased Duke. It was all in a day's work for the islands' beloved official greeter.

From the look of the fancy red carpet that Honolulu was getting ready to roll out for FDR and his sons, you would have thought that the islands were a Democratic stronghold. Actually, there wasn't one sugar boss in town who didn't mutter a hateful epithet whenever he heard the band strike up "Happy Days Are Here Again." Republicans held sway in the islands, although I was certain a lot of the men and women eligible to vote would have cast their ballots in the last election for FDR. However, when a fellow went into the voting booth in a lot of rural districts where his job depended on his Republican boss, he voted to please his employer. In some places, they hung the pencil used to mark the ballot from the ceiling above the curtained balloting booth. If the string swung to the left, then they knew which party's candidate you had voted for. So much for the secret ballot. Although Roosevelt was for the little guy, most of the little guys in Hawai'i went along with the wishes of the fat cats.

When I finally got into the office, it was already 9 o'clock and China was all excited about the presidential cavalcade that was planned to pass down Fort Street right below our office window. She was so busy calling around town for bunting and little American flags to wave that she nearly forgot to give me a wire that had arrived that morning from Lawrence, Kansas. A Dr. Samuel Wright, who taught at the University of Kansas, was requesting the services of the International Detective Agency in the matter of his son's suicide. When the Honolulu operator finally patched me through on a long-distance hookup with Kansas, Dr. Wright talked on for nearly an hour. I let him go on and on. After all, he was paying for the call.

His son, William, he explained, had always been a roustabout, never settling down. It got worse when his mother died a few years back. The boy dropped out of college when the Crash came, took to the rails and was living out of Hoovervilles. The father was able to finally track him down and forced his son to enlist in the Army. Although he was hoping military service would make a man out of his son, I could have told him that putting khaki on a boy doesn't put hair on his chest. Last week, Pvt. William Wright hanged himself in the stockade at Schofield Barracks.

I told Dr. Wright as nicely as I could that I thought he was wasting his money by bringing a detective on this case. The military was pretty thorough in such matters. I knew, being a former Spanish-American War veteran who served his country in that "splendid little war" in the Philippines.

"The Army," he retorted angrily, "be hanged. They have decided that it was a simple case of suicide. My son would never have taken his own life, I told them. But they won't dig any deeper."

"When boys get stuck into the Army," I tactfully explained, "and then get isolated in the Pacific, it can be hard for them, Dr. Wright. They call this a 'picture post,' but that's only for the officers. For the enlisted man, it can get awfully rough and lonely."

"Mr. McDougal, I can't believe my son would destroy himself." His voice was cracking with emotion on the long-distance line. "His last letter said he had found a young woman whom he loved and wished to marry. Bill was finally putting his life together. He was my only child. If there was foul play, I could never rest believing I hadn't done my utmost to uncover the truth. I made him go into the Army. Won't you help me?"

We agreed on my usual fee of $25 a day plus expenses and I promised the old man that before I was finished, the boys in khaki would be sorry they hadn't been more cooperative with him. That was the least I could do for the grieving father.

With President Roosevelt due to arrive on Thursday to review the troops at Schofield Barracks, Major General Briant H. Wells' office was in bedlam. So I was shuffled down the chain of command until I got a "90-day wonder" by the name of Lt. Homer Ridgley, in the office of the Military Police, on the telephone. The next morning I was sitting across from the wonder boy, conjuring up the spirits of my buddies in the Spanish-American War who had been shot down because they took orders from a fool like this. He was a well-educated college brat who in hard times couldn't find a job so ended up in Uncle Sam's Army. He made excuses for his incompetence by assuring me that he had only recently graduated from Fort Bragg's military police training school before being assigned to the "Rock."

"My apologies for being somewhat disorganized, sir," he said, in a military clip. "I only arrived at Schofield last week. The officer in charge before me was quite inefficient in his filing system."

"That's all right."

"An open-and-shut case of suicide, wasn't it?" he said, with nervous authority while turning over papers on his desk.

"So the Army told his father. Do you think I can see that file, Lieutenant, sometime today? After all, his father is paying my salary on a daily wage."

"Of course, sir. I thought it was somewhere on my desk. Sergeant, have you seen the Wright file?"

He spoke to a sharp young Sergeant Kuhn with permanently starched pleats who, in turn, barked orders to a humorless Hawaiian PFC. No one in the Army ever did anything for themselves. The private returned promptly with the file, which I browsed through while Lt. Ridgley returned to their usual incompetence.

Dr. Wright, it seems, had been overly optimistic about his son's new turn towards responsibility. Since his enlistment, Billy had been stationed at several bases, including McCoy, Bragg, Ord and the Presidio. He flunked Officers Candidate School and military police training, was booted out of the horse cavalry and had been put in the stockade twice for being drunk while on duty and once for striking his sergeant. It was a long list of failures for Billy Wright that led him to take a big leap off a little cot in the stockade.

According to the report by a Sgt. Holmes who found the body, Wright had been on leave in Honolulu that day. When he returned to Schofield Barracks, it was about 11 p.m. The sentries at McComb Gate noticed

Wright nearly fell out of the taxi that had dropped him off. He was dirty drunk and, even though he hadn't done anything wrong, they turned him over to the MP's, who threw him into the stockade to sleep it off. They figured being in jail would give him a scare to sober him up. Only it must have frightened him. One more disgrace must have been too much, so he killed himself. At any rate, that was the Army's version of the suicide.

With Lt. Ridgley's permission, the Hawaiian Pvt. Abraham Hanohano escorted me over to the stockade, where Sgt. Holmes was on duty. I had heard stories about the Schofield stockade that made the Black Hole of Calcutta seem like a Waikiki resort. It was a brutal-looking little compound laced in barbed wire, with a cadre of guards who looked more gorilla than human. Rumor had it that the bank robber John Dillinger himself had once spent time in the Schofield Barracks stockade. No doubt the place turned him into the criminal he had become.

Holmes was a thick-necked bully with 15 years' duty at the stockade. His uniform clung to his massive muscles as if the material were made from elastic. The stench from human waste was overpowering, as the sergeant led me to the darkened cell where Pvt. Wright had hanged himself. It was empty now, except for a cot, stool and toilet bucket. Hanging from the ceiling was a single light bulb on a short cord. Evidently Wright had stood on the edge of his cot, tied the cord to his belt buckle, tightened the belt around his neck and then jumped off the cot. His feet would have dangled only a few inches from the floor.

"Tell me, Sergeant, isn't it customary to remove the prisoner's belt before locking him up?" I spoke as nicely as I could so as not to upset the Neanderthal.

"Yeah. Only, this one was just going to sleep off too much booze. Who would have known he was going to do himself in?"

I was escorted by Pvt. Hanohano, who showed me Wright's barracks. As we passed the review grounds, a detail was busy putting up the review bleachers for the thousands of civilians who were expected to join FDR in what the papers were calling the largest peacetime military review in the history of the U.S. Army. Big deal, I said to myself as I asked Hanohano if he had known Wright.

"One *haole* like every other *haole*," he said with an edge of hate.

"You got something against white folks?" I asked.

"They pay my salary, right? This is where Wright stayed."

Some enlisted men were cleaning up the barracks, making it spick-and-span for Roosevelt. When I asked if any of them knew Wright, they went on with their business as if I didn't exist. Khaki boys, I remembered, resented men in civvies. Finally I got a rise out of a fellow named Rosen. All he said was that Wright hadn't been at Schofield too long and was a hard man to know.

When I asked if he had a girl in town, Rosen shrugged he didn't know and went back to his business.

Before leaving Schofield, I made one more stop at Lt. Ridgley's office to examine the autopsy report. The greenhorn was fluttering from desk to phone, busy with security details for the President's visit. The well-pleated Sergeant Kuhn assisted me by digging out the doctor's death certificate and some photos of the body.

"Death by self-inflicted strangulation" was typed in the space reading "Cause of Death."

It was all as neat as a Christmas package, except for one small detail. In the autopsy photograph, the corpse had several ugly bruises in the area of the solar plexus. I asked Kuhn point-blank if such bruises weren't more than a little suspicious.

"We did investigate the bruises, sir. The stockade isn't a nursery school. Pvt. Wright was drunk and disorderly and Sergeant Holmes admitted that he applied a little force to quiet him down."

As I exited McComb Gate and was rolling past Kemoo Farms towards Wahiawa, a soldier on the side of the road flagged me down. It was Rosen, who asked me to pull over in the woods near Lake Wilson, where we couldn't be seen. He was fidgety, puffing on his cig like it was a pacifier.

"Bill Wright and I were buddies from Fort Ord. I couldn't tell you in front of the other men, but he was up to his neck in debt to a tough corporal in our unit named Arnie Meyers, who runs a weekly crap game. I

The notorious Black Cat Cafe, a favorite hangout of the Schofield Barracks soldiers. *(Ray Jerome Baker, Bishop Museum)*

told Bill to cut out the gambling, but he said he need-ed the money to get married. He didn't want his old man to stake him out because he had caused him so much grief already. He wanted to stand on his own two feet now that he was getting his life together. I just can't believe he would have killed himself."

When I asked who Wright was going to marry, Rosen told me she was a nice-looking local dish by the name of Leilani Bryant, who was a waitress at the Black Cat Cafe. Every Wednesday night Meyers staged a big crap game in one of the backrooms. That's where Wright lost his shirt, but found his bride.

"I can't be sure of it," Rosen advised me, "but if Billy was murdered, Meyers had something to do with it."

As much as I like bars, I despise the Black Cat. Located directly across from the YMCA at Alakea and Hotel Streets, all the soldier boys make it their first watering hole the moment they get off the buses. The cops are always breaking up fights between the khaki and locals. If the constant fighting doesn't bother you, then the stench of the place will knock you out. No matter how many scrubbings they give the Black Cat, when you walk into the place the stench of urine is overwhelming.

On Wednesday night the Black Cat wasn't as busy as usual. Most of the men were back at Schofield putting on the last-minute touches for the President's visit. I found a comfortable stool at the bar, ordered a gin tonic from an unfriendly local mixologist. Ever since FDR repealed Prohibition, the juice flowed openly in Honolulu. As I swilled my gin, I tried to guess which waitress was Leilani.

It wasn't hard to pick the woman a man would bet his last wad on. She was a Polynesian beauty in her early twenties, with all the right curves which were well adorned by her tight-fitting sarong. When I offered to buy her a drink in exchange for a few minutes of her time, the bartender gave me a nasty stink eye.

"Don't mind Peewee," she assured me. "He always gets jealous of other men. But he don't own me. You don't look like a soldier boy to me. What can I do for you?"

When I mentioned Billy Wright's name, she almost started to bawl. It didn't take me long to figure out that if Leilani had been his ticket to stability, he was her passport out of the Black Cat. Underneath her street-wise, smart-sister act, Leilani Bryant was just a poor, little Tin Can Alley girl with church upbringing who had wanted out of the poverty and ill-luck of her life. Working in a saloon was dirty, but it did bring home the bread.

I was downing my third gin tonic, when Corporal Meyers and an entourage of khaki thugs pushed their way through the Black Cat into a back room. I don't know why I wasn't surprised when I saw my Neanderthal friend Holmes pulling up the rear. We caught each other's stare in the dim, smoke-filled light of the bar.

"How much was Wright into Meyers for?" I prodded Leilani.

"A few thousand. He tried to win some of it back the night he died. But Meyers took his last penny. So he drank too much whiskey to forget his troubles."

I told her straight that I thought there was maybe a chance that somebody murdered her fiancé. She had to tell me anything that could help.

"Well, Billy had been upset about something other than the money he owed to Meyers. He said he really couldn't tell me, but the more whiskey he drank, the more it bugged him. Finally he jumped up and muttered that 'somebody's a phony.' That was about 9:30 last Wednesday night. He borrowed taxi money, kissed me and rushed back to Schofield."

Forty-five minutes later I was walking back to my office on Merchant Street, when a pair of powerful hands pulled me into a dark alley between the Star-Bulletin and Stangenwald Buildings. The hands didn't say very much but were very busy using my body as a punching bag. I tried to reach for my rod, but the hands had me pinned against the narrow alley wall. I felt my gin tonic come up as a fist drove into my flabby gut. I groaned as I fell to the ground with a boot kicking my back.

"Lay off Wright's death, bastard," said a grunt that sounded like it came from a gorilla. "If you know what is good for you, forget Billy Wright." The boot fell one more time on my head and I snuggled up like a little baby sucking my thumb and fell off to sleep in the alley's gutter.

China was nearly hysterical when she found me bloodied and half-conscious on the floor of our office the next morning. Somehow during the night I had taught myself to walk again and barely made it back to the Inter-Island Steamship Building, where I collapsed on the office floor. She called Doc Riggs over to stitch up a bad cut on my noggin and brought me a bowl of hot saimin from a little Japanese cafe next door.

I spent Thursday and most of Friday laying low in my darkened office, stretched out on a couch, nursing the wounds that Sergeant Holmes had given me with a cheap bottle of gin. Outside on the streets, workmen were busy hanging bunting in anticipation of the Presidential hoopla on Saturday morning. I was still wondering why Dillingham hadn't invited me to FDR's party out at La Pietra, when I took a call from Leilani Bryant.

"Last night, one of Peewee's friends came to the Black Cat," she informed me. "He got really drunk. I heard him tell Peewee that one *haole* paid for Joe, now another one was going to pay. No one was going to push Hawaiians around ever again."

"You think it has something to do with Billy's death?"

"Peewee's friend is in the Army, stationed at Schofield. When I asked him what he meant by 'one *haole* paid for Joe,' he shut up real quick, drank up and left. Peewee told me his friend hated *haoles* because of what had happened to a close buddy of his a couple of years ago. I hope it helps, Mr. McDougal."

"What was the soldier's name?"

"Hanohano. Abe Hanohano."

When I reached Schofield Barracks first thing that morning, I found that the military police office was operating with a skeleton crew. Most of the MP's were in Honolulu escorting the Presidential tour. So I went straightaway to the stockade to have a word with my good friend, Sergeant Holmes. I was toting a thick metal bar with which I was going to rearrange his face. When I finally located him decked out in one of his own cells, I was disappointed to discover I had been a little late for my revenge. The top of his head had been blown away.

After notifying the MP's of Holmes' murder, I searched out Hanohano's quarters. He wasn't there, so I took the liberty of breaking into his footlocker. A steady stream of sweat poured off my brow as I realized that Pvt. Hanohano's locker was a Pandora's box of racial resentment and murder. The sullen, young Hawaiian soldier had saved several news articles about the murder of Joe Kahahawai, the local who had been gunned down two years ago by a Navy officer named Lt. Thomas Massie. From the scribbled margin notes it was obvious that Hanohano had been one of Kahahawai's chums who took the fiasco of the Massie case real personal. After Governor Judd let the murderers of Kahahawai off with a slap on the wrist, Hanohano had been seething with a deadly bitterness.

A torn page from the *Star-Bulletin* then caught my eye. It was FDR's detailed Honolulu itinerary, with his live radio broadcast speech from the steps of Iolani Palace grounds and tree-planting ceremony circled in bold, red ink with a huge exclamation point drawn to the side. By my watch, I figured I had about two hours to save the life of the President of the United States.

I found the skeleton crew of MP's at the stockade, sifting through

FDR delivers his radio address from the steps of Iolani Palace. *(Hawai'i State Archives)*

the brains of Holmes that had been splattered on the wall. Gasping for breath, I tried to explain what I had found.

"There's going to be an assassination attempt on Roosevelt!" I screamed. "Call the President's security right now!"

"Sure, sure. Who you think you're kidding, mister?"

It was impossible to convince them that one of their own boys was about to become an assassin. I showed them what I had found in Hanohano's locker.

"At least call Lt. Ridgley. Tell him to put a guard on Hanohano. That's the least you can do."

They made the call, but Ridgely was on duty. The men in charge were all too busy and smug to listen to the ravings of a private dick.

The road back into Honolulu was jam-packed with country bumpkins, who were meandering into town to get their little glimpse of history. My horn was blaring as I darted in and out of traffic on the Kamehameha Highway. By the time I got to the outskirts of Kalihi, it was already 10 a.m. I turned my car radio on to KGU just in time to hear the President's speech. He was a sitting duck on the stairs of the Palace.

"I leave also with pride in Hawai'i," FDR spoke in his characteristic clip, "pride in your patriotism and in your accomplishments. The problems that you are solving are the problems of the whole nation and your administration in Washington will not forget that you are in very truth, an integral part of the nation."

Hell, if he's shot here, so much for pride in Hawai'i. My horn was blaring like a runaway ambulance.

"And on leaving I want to say a word of congratulation on the efficiency and the fine spirit of the Army and Navy forces of which I am commander-in-chief. They constitute an integral part of our national defense and I stress that word defense. These forces must ever be considered an instrument of continuing peace for our nation's policy seeks peace and does not look to imperialistic aims."

One of those men in your Army, Mr. President, I thought to myself, was about to put a bullet through you. I was pounding on the steering wheel, waiting for the crack of the rifle to shatter the still of the Iolani Palace grounds.

"I shall remember these days— days that were all too short. Your flowers, your scenery, your hospitality, but above all, the

The President plants a kukui nut tree on the Palace grounds, unaware that he is the target of a sinister assassination plot. *(Hawai'i State Archives)*

knowledge that America can well be proud of the Territory of Hawai'i. And so I say to you—Aloha from the bottom of my heart."

The crowd was cheering the President's speech as I drove into a snarl of traffic at King and Bishop Streets. Maybe there was still time as I abandoned my machine and hoofed it to the Palace grounds. The President had re-entered his car as the cavalcade drove slowly through thousands of cheering islanders, while the Royal Hawaiian Band belted out the Presidential march. Motorcycle cops circled the *ewa*-Richards Street side of the Palace grounds, where the tree planting was supposed to take place. The President's open touring car pulled into the grounds.

Lt. Ridgley spotted me first. He was frantically pacing at the MP's command post at the Royal Bandstand, all excited about the call from Schofield which had finally come through only minutes before. I asked if he had put Hanohano under arrest or detention.

"We can't find him, McDougal. He was with us this morning but disappeared after we got here. My God, what's this all about?"

"I'm not sure, but if my guess is right, he's going to take a shot at the President. Have you notified the secret service?"

You could see Ridgley's knees and backbone buckle at the thought of contacting his superiors. I grabbed him hard by his neatly knotted khaki tie and tightened it until I thought his eyes would bulge out.

"Get off your *okole* and start moving or I swear I'll choke you here and now. Savvy?"

I threw him back hard against the bandstand. He muttered something under his breath, then went off to find the secret service. I started scanning the roof of the buildings on Richards Street. If Hanohano was going to shoot the President as he was planting the tree, he was going to need a clear line of fire. And the YWCA directly across the street offered the best sniper position.

The roof and third floor of the YWCA was closed to the public. But with all the pressing flesh and excitement and cops trying to get their own view of the President, it was a breeze passing through their security. This was a bunch of amateurs who were straining their necks to see the President, not watch for an assassin.

I was prowling a deserted third floor with my Colt drawn and cocked. From the commotion and cheering outside, I knew that the President's car had arrived, as I opened the door to a large classroom.

I found Hanohano crouched with his Army skag, a .3006 with telescopic lens, positioned at the window.

"Put it down, Private," I shouted.

As the Royal Hawaiian Band struck up "Hawai'i Ponoi" across the street, Hanohano quickly turned, his rifle aimed at my gut. I fired and he fell back against the wall with a hole in his chest from my smoking Colt. He was still breathing as I pulled his rifle away and Sergeant Kuhn burst into the room, his service revolver drawn.

"What's going on here?"

"He was about to shoot the President. Call an ambulance. He's still alive."

Kuhn strode forward without hesitation, raised his gun and put a bullet between Hanohano's eyes. I was taken totally off guard as a second bullet from his pistol slammed into my side, smashing up a few ribs. The noise outside thunderously droned on as Kuhn picked up Hanohano's rifle. I had never shot a man in the back before, but I wasn't about to let him know that his shot hadn't put me away.

It had been a nasty bloodbath. I was dragging myself out of the room looking for help, when a familiar voice asked me what I had done. It was Lt. Ridgley who was standing over me with an authority in his voice I had never before detected.

"I just stopped an assassination."

"You stupid, meddling fool. I would have never guessed such a dimwitted man could have gotten this far. I totally underestimated you."

A cop came running down the hall towards us just as Ridgley was about to put me out of my misery. When he slipped his gun back in its holster, barking orders about security, I figured it was safe to pass out.

When I woke up at Queen's Hospital the next day, I was looking up at a quiet, well-dressed *haole* without a name.

"You're quite a man, McDougal."

"I do my job. Am I going to live?"

"Maybe. Tell me how much you know."

I told him what I had found out about Hanohano, but admitted I was screwed up as to where Kuhn, Ridgley, Holmes and Wright figured in. He held up the morning paper for me. The headlines said that the Austrian chancellor, Engelbert Dollfuss, had been boldly assassinated that week by members of the Nazi Party. A mad paperhanger named Hitler was about to take full control of the Weimar Republic under the title of Fuhrer.

"What the paper doesn't say, McDougal, is that several similar assassination attempts against western government leaders have been thwarted this week. President Roosevelt is seen by many Nazis as a Jew-loving communist and an obstacle to their world domination. Sergeant Kuhn, we have discovered, had strong connections to the American Nazi Bund. When the President's Hawai'i trip was announced earlier this year, the party selected Kuhn to coordinate FDR's murder.

"To protect himself and the party, Kuhn needed a hit man. So he recruited Hanohano, who was so filled with hatred for American politicians, he could be convinced to shoot the President. After the assassination, Kuhn would simply gun Hanohano down, covering up the involvement of the Nazis."

"But where did Ridgley fit in?"

The nameless man showed me a photograph of a Wilhelm Luckner all decked out in Nazi paraphernalia. The Gestapo didn't trust Kuhn to do the job without help. So one of the inner circle was sent to supervise.

Needing to place him at Schofield Barracks, they killed Lt. Ridgley, who was en route to the islands for his new assignment. The body of the real lieutenant was probably lying on a railroad track somewhere between Fort Bragg and the port of Oakland.

When Luckner showed up at Schofield, poor Billy Wright evidently recognized him as a phony, since he also was at the military police training program at Bragg. When Wright came back to Schofield that last night, he must have confronted Ridgley. So Holmes was paid to turn his back while the conspirators strung Wright up. The murder of Holmes on Saturday morning was just one more loose string to tie up before killing the President.

"Did you catch this Luckner?"

"No, he evidently got lost in the swarm of military police that poured into the third floor of the YWCA when all the gunfire started."

A few months later I learned that the Germans in Samoa had started up a Nazi Party and that a General Luckner was at its head.

"The idea of Nazi terrorists in Hawai'i seems pretty hard to believe," I mused.

"Keep thinking of it that way. As far as the United States government is concerned, no assassination attempt ever took place. The President doesn't want an international incident at this time while thugs are taking over Germany. As far as the police and press are concerned, you shot and killed two men who had murdered Pvt. Wright over gambling debts. Your patriotism would be greatly appreciated in this matter."

"I understand."

Before he left he winked and tossed me a small white envelope. I read the simple message on the inside card over and over again. "Mr. Arthur McDougal. Thank you very much."

It had no signature, but bore the seal of the President of the United States of America. As I tried to go back to sleep, I kept seeing that cocked head, thrusting cigarette holder and jaunty smile that America had come to love and trust. I knew dark days lay ahead for our nation, but that afternoon, somehow, I felt safe and reassured.

[**Editor's Note:** After an exhaustive search at the National Archives, no documentation can be found to authenticate McDougal's contention that he saved the life of the President of the United States during the Hawai'i tour of July 24-28,1934. Under the Freedom of Information Act, any papers from the FBI or military intelligence verifying this story would have long ago surfaced. In Samoa, however, it is a fact that a General Luckner was influential in organizing a Nazi Party in the Pacific Basin. The kukui tree that President Roosevelt planted as a symbol of light, by the way, still stands near the Richards Street entrance to Iolani Palace. However, the small plaque near the tree explaining its importance makes no reference whatsoever to the death-defying bravery of the Honolulu detective who was instrumental in saving the man who would become one of the greatest leaders of the free world.]

CHAPTER ELEVEN

The Wayward Taxi Dancer

He was sitting two stools over at the Green Mill Bar, milking a two-bit Primo for all it was worth and looking like he had lost his best friend in the world. I gave Billy Cummins, Honolulu's best mixologist, the nod and he set the bushy-headed little guy up with another beer. He almost fell off his stool thanking me with his broken English. I don't think a white man had ever done anything for Eddie Cook except maybe bark orders at him.

It's not often I strike up a conversation with a stranger at a bar, but there was something about the kid that drew out Art McDougal's paternal instinct. He didn't stand 5 feet 4 inches tall and his dark, clean-shaven face had that baby look which made him look 10 years younger than his 30 years. From the busty lady, who I assumed wasn't his mother, tattooed on his arm, I figured he had spent a few years in the merchant marines. His wiry body and tight biceps told me the kid also knew how to take care of himself.

Our talk was getting more and more slurred from the beer and whiskey, but I waded through his pidgin English to learn that he had come up to the islands from Tahiti and was washing dishes at the Seaside Hotel in Waikiki. He was living *mauka* of Beretania in the slum we called Blood Town, in a room he shared with two other men from the South Pacific. They were all struggling to make ends meet and at the same time send a few cents home to their families. Eddie even made a few bucks in the ring, once taking on the Filipino champ, Joe Doro. The famed Filipino boxer knocked Eddie flat in the first round.

Eddie Cook in his familiar position, going down for the count. [After extensive research, I cannot verify this is "Eddie Cook." GG] *(Hawai'i State Archives)*

As it always does, the conversation got around to women. I was going through my fourth whiskey straight-up, when he started pouring out his heart.

"Floria no good," he began muttering, sobbing into his beer.

"What's that, kid?" said Cummins, who was wiping the counter top. "You been to Florida?"

"Floria, Floria," Eddie repeated. "My girl. She's no good."

From what I could make out from the blubbering, seems his girlfriend Floria had just dumped him for a young, opium-pushing hood named Joe Mendez.

"Mendez?" I asked Cummins.

"A two-bit bum who's trying to make a name for himself by peddling opium. He drops by now and then." Cummins was an affable Hawaiian guy who knew everybody in town.

"Floria is real swell," Eddie continued. "Mendez made her no good." His gal was a taxi dancer at the Paradise Ballroom who had come from the Philippines a couple of years ago. She was dividing her time between dancing for money and busing tables at the Seaside. That's where they had met. You know, love at first sight.

"She's pretty, mister. But Mendez take her from me. I get so mad, I... I..."

He finished the sentence in Tahitian.

"So what happened?" asked Cummins.

"I came home today without telling Floria. My boss say no more work, so go home. When I walked in, Floria and Mendez kissing in the bed."

"Hell, Mac, he found his old lady banging someone," Cummins blurted out. We were both getting involved in the kid's story. Toughest thing a guy can face is finding his old lady flagrante delicto.

"What did you do then, kid?" Cummins asked.

"I hit the wall. I was so mad."

He showed me his swollen hand that he had used against the wall instead of Floria's and Mendez's heads. Both hands were bruised and lacerated. Eddie hadn't gone to see a doc to get medical attention.

"Tough break, kid. Have another Primo—this one on me."

"Cummins," I said, "you always are a soft touch. You keep giving drinks to broken hearts and the Green Mill will dry up."

"Get off it, Mac. The kid's taking it hard."

It was getting to be midnight so I paid my check and advised Eddie to get his hand examined at the Emergency Hospital. Cummins tossed me a Green Mill matchbook, upon which I wrote the phone number of the International Detective Agency.

"Look, whatever you do, stay clean. Nothing is worth getting into trouble over. And that includes a broad. If you need to get drunk, give me a call."

I had never given anyone my number like that before. And I'll never do it again.

The next day, it was work as usual. The investigation I was working on had become bogged down. The agency had been hired to trace the whereabouts of some minor bank executive named Northridge who had embezzled his employers out of 20 grand. The clock was striking "cocktail hour," when China said I had an urgent call. It was from the Tahitian, Eddie Cook.

"Listen, kid," I said, getting on the horn. "Sorry, but I'm tired tonight. Maybe we can get together next week."

"Mister McDougal. Please *kokua*. I'm in jail."

A quick call to Sgt. Chillingworth gave me the low-down on Eddie's arrest. The naked body of Floria Alcantara, the taxi dancer, had been found bludgeoned to death in her bed that morning by her best friend, another dancer name Maria Sanches. From the autopsy, Dr. Liu said that the victim had been mercilessly beaten on the face and torso. The murder weapon, he conjectured, was a pair of very nasty fists. Although he couldn't be absolutely sure, the murder took place some time past 1 o'clock that morning.

When they interrogated Eddie Cook, they found his hand badly swollen. He then naively confessed to the cops that he found Floria and her lover earlier that day in each other's arms. The detectives took his statement as a confession. Plus he had no alibi. The Green Mill had closed up about 12:30 a.m. and, according to Eddie, he was just walking about town, sobering himself up. The detectives, Chillingworth told me, figured the kid left the Green Mill in a drunken rage, went over to Floria's and took a Polynesian revenge.

I saw Eddie an hour later in an interrogation room at the Merchant Street Police Station. A slick Portuguese lawyer named Soares had been appointed by the court to serve as Eddie's defense attorney. He was chain-smoking Camels over my shoulder as I listened to the kid's story. After the Green Mill closed up, the kid told me he was too drunk to go to the Emergency Hospital to get his hand looked at. And he didn't feel like going back to his flop house. So he walked around town until he finally got tired by Iolani Palace, where he fell asleep under the banyan tree. In the morning he went back to Blood Town, cleaned up and changed his clothes and hightailed it to the Seaside Hotel, where he was arrested that afternoon.

Sitting nervously in the interrogation room, Eddie looked like a scrawny chicken about to have its neck chopped on a Chinatown meat block. Black bruises on his forehead told me that the cops had laid it on real good getting him to "confess." He held on to the little matchbook with my name and number on it as if I was his savior.

"He can get off with maybe 10 to 15 years at Oahu Prison if he opens up, McDougal. The jury's gonna be sympathetic what with his girlfriend cheating on him. All he needs to do is plead guilty."

After 20 years of digging through people's garbage, I knew this type of lawyer real well. If he smells dough, he's the protector of the innocent. If it's poor riffraff like Eddie, then let the court send 'em up the river.

"If the kid says he's innocent," I said in my best threatening tone, "then you better use what legal sense you've got to save 'em, wiseguy, or you better start thinking of a job on the mainland."

"You're a real tough guy, McDougal. And what's in it for a high-priced peeping tom like you?"

I said something about not being that high-priced, as I put my fist into his soft belly, buckling him up like a Japanese fan.

When you take a case for free, you tend to work faster than when the clients pay by the hour. Thanks to Chillingworth, I was allowed to inspect Floria Alcantara's room within the half hour. She had rented a flat next to one of the notorious Honolulu bathhouses, the American Baths, that in actuality was a front for a brothel. Floria had tried to brighten her room up, but it was just a depressing little way station in a life eked out by cleaning up tables and dancing with sweaty-palmed old men. Once in a while she even hooked out of the bathhouse, bouncing in and out of strangers' beds. And all that for what, two bits an hour?

The air reeked with the sweet smell of perfume and stale cigarette smoke, mixed with the scent of unlit candles that sat before a small picture of a protective saint. Floria was a devout Catholic who also had a large portrait of Jesus on one wall. Too bad the prayers hadn't worked. The top of her dresser was covered with little kewpie dolls, two framed photographs of her parents, rosary beads, a silver-plated crucifix and an ashtray overfilled with butts. The blood-stained bedsheets were exactly as the cops had found them.

The police had gone over the room with less than a fine-toothed comb, figuring they already had their man, with the Tahitian locked up. I picked up a few things that didn't mean anything to the cops but could help Eddie Cook. Taped under one of the pull-out drawers was a small glass vial with the residue of black, sticky opium and a small smoking pipe. Mendez had no doubt turned her into a hophead. From the trash can I dug out some crumbled food receipts from Central Market, a note saying "I lov (spelled without the "e") you, J.M.," a used-up matchbook from the Green Mill, and a picture of someone torn into a thousand tiny pieces.

Back at the office, I set China to work on the jigsaw puzzle of the photograph while I decided to ask

Joe Mendez a few questions. A quick call to Binky "The Iceman" Tan put me on Mendez's doorstep—a seedy gambling den in one of the inner courtyards at River and Pauahi. The noise of mah-jongg and crap players mingled with a waft of sweet opium that drifted up from a few darkened dens in the basement. That's where I found Mendez, curled up like a cozy little kitten with a very dangerous-looking oriental tigress.

"It's not smart to smoke the stuff you peddle, Mendez." I've never been known for subtle introductions.

"What's it to you?"

"Nothing, but it means something to a dead kid named Floria."

The tigress' back arched and she snarled. Mendez took a puff of the magic smoke.

"I already wen told the cops everything. I loved her. We were gonna get hitched. I should've killed that Tahitian when I had the chance."

"You got an alibi?"

"Yeah, I was right here, in a big crap game. Enough for Floria and me to go to the mainland, maybe L.A."

The tigress, whose name I found out was Suk Lin Wu, evidently didn't like that idea. Her face, framed by her smartly cropped, shiny black hair, snarled at Mendez as she snatched his pipe away, uncurled her long, well-shaped legs, and pranced off to a lonely crib. There she stretched herself out and took a long draw on dreamland.

"She looks jealous, Mendez."

"Suk Lin's jealous of every man she sleeps around with. She don't mean nothin' to me. Okay, Bull? Now, if you got nothin' else to say, I got work to do."

He got up and laid down next to the tigress, who purred like she was lapping milk from a saucer. The last I saw was one of those long limbs wrapping around Mendez, as he pulled the curtain down across the crib.

I left that pathetic little scene for the music, lights and gaiety of the Paradise Ballroom, a taxi dance club a block away on Maunakea. Floria had been making a few bucks a week dancing here, occasionally taking men back to the American Baths. The Paradise Ballroom was located on the second floor of an old Chinatown building, which also housed the Aloha Ballroom. Each taxi dance joint had a separate entrance at the top of two separate staircases which led to the second floor. A thin wall dividing the dance halls had been cut open for a stage, which extended into both rooms. A Filipino band situated on the stage was playing a continuous string of Spanish tangos, waltzes and slow dances which served both dance halls. In the Paradise Ballroom, young women in tight dresses were being swirled about by mostly older, lonely Filipino gents. In the Aloha Ballroom on the other side, the men were young, hotter and more aggressive.

I bought a string of tickets from a man behind a booth who eyed me suspiciously. They didn't get many *haoles* in the taxi dance halls. I asked around for Maria Sanches, who 5 minutes later ended up in my arms, doing a hot tango that melted my collar.

"How can I help you, sir?" She was about the most sultry woman I had ever met, small-bodied, but nicely shaped. Her face was full-lipped, her eyes hypnotically deep and brown. The rouge on her cheeks heightened her creamy tan, fleshy features that pressed now and then against the stubble of my chin. Her nipples were pressing through the top of her slinky dress, which clung to well-rounded, high breasts. If Floria was anything like Maria, I could see what made a man kill.

"I understand you knew Floria Alcantara." Trying to talk while doing a tango is nearly impossible. The band slowed down the pace and she slipped into my arms.

"Floria was my best friend, sir." She called me "sir" with an air of respect that stemmed from hundreds of years of Spanish colonialism.

"You knew all of her boyfriends?"

"She didn't have good taste in men, sir. They were all no good." Her head rested on my shoulder as a very familiar, sweet perfume made me heady. The year I had spent in the cheap saloons of Corregidor during the Spanish-American War started coming back to me with vivid images of a young recruit getting his first experience with brown-skinned women.

"The little boxer man, he was poor and very jealous. The gambler was a bad man, sir."

"Were there others?"

Pressing her tightly around the waist, I felt her tremble slightly.

"A few. I don't know them, sir."

"Could $5 help you remember?"

"There was one *haole* man she met at the Seaside Hotel. He promised to make her his wife. But he ran away. There was some kind of trouble. Then she started smoking opium with the gambler."

Since we had been dancing for about 10 minutes, I asked her if I could take a break to cool my feet.

"You pay me now, sir, please."

"Sure, here's a ticket."

"Five tickets, please, sir."

"Five? We only danced one dance."

"No, we danced five dances, please, sir."

"What? The music never stopped."

"They play without stopping, sir. They just change songs."

That's the price I pay for not knowing Filipino music, I scolded myself, as I coughed over five tickets. The least they could do is let a guy know when one song was over and another one began.

Maria went off dancing with some old gent who looked like he had spent his whole life cutting cane in the hot Hawaiian fields he was so dried out, shriveled and bent. I went to a phone in the back of the club to call China. I had a hunch that the photograph that was torn up in the trash could be another jilted lover of the wayward taxi dancer. Maybe Maria could tell me something more about Floria's beaus.

I caught China sound asleep at her home.

"Finish the jigsaw puzzle yet?"

"Finally you call, Mac. I finished about three hours ago. And you'll never guess who it was."

"Come on, China. No games. What's up?"

"Mr. Northridge, Mac. Samuel Northridge of First Island Trust."

I almost dropped the phone. The embezzling executive that I had spent one week looking for had also evidently fallen under Floria's charms. He left his rather drab wife and two drabber kids for a life of high-rolling with a tight keg of dynamite. Only the fuse went off too soon.

"Where are you, Mac?" China asked protectively.

"I'm at Floria's dance joint. I got to go, China, but *shishe*," I said, in the one Chinese word I knew.

I was hanging the phone up when I noticed Maria at the other pay phone on the back wall. I sidled up to her, grabbing her around the waist.

"So, who were you calling?"

"A friend. Would you like to dance some more, sir?" Maria asked.

"Sure, why not?"

I tried to pry some more information out of her, but Maria was more interested in having fun and so I let go. After all, I wasn't going to solve the case that night. I don't know how long we danced or how many drinks I swilled, but Art McDougal's world started to spin like a kid's top.

The bed was soft and cozy as the morning light peeked through a bent venetian blind. I was just about to identify my quarters as a sleazy crib in the American Baths, when the door smashed open and three officers in blue and Big John Carney with drawn revolvers pointed their weapons right between my eyes. That's when I felt the moisture on the sheets. Next to me lay Maria Sanches, her naked body spread out like a bearskin rug. A single bullet hole punctured her heart, spilling blood down her upright breasts, filling a pool in her belly button and dripping down her tight stomach to the sheets. My Colt lay on the floor.

My head was still throbbing with whiskey as they threw me into a stinking cell and slammed the bars behind me.

"Mister McDougal! What are you here for?"

Eddie Cook was staring at me open-mouthed from the neighboring cell.

"I don't know, kid. I really don't know."

The cops gave me two phone calls, but I needed only one. China was at the Merchant Street station in 5 minutes with a fresh change of clothes, a thermos of hot kona for my aching head, a copy of the morning *Advertiser* with news of my arrest splashed across the headline and word that the law firm of Beebe and Associates would get me out on bail as soon as I was arraigned before the Grand Jury.

The hardest part of being in jail, besides the embarrassment, was reassuring Eddie Cook to have faith in me. Here he had hoped that I would save his neck, and a day later I was being charged with the same crime.

Soares, the kid's sleazy defense attorney, was taking advantage of my predicament, squeezing the kid to plead guilty to avoid swinging with me from the gallows.

By the looks of the case the D.A.'s office had against me, the hangman was already putting 13 knots in the rope labeled "A. McDougal." I had been seen leaving the Paradise Club with Maria at about 11:30 p.m., headed for the American Baths. The night clerk swore that he saw the two of us go upstairs. I was so stinking drunk that he had to help carry me to the room. He hadn't heard any shot, but during his routine morning room check, he peeked in on Maria's room. He saw the two of us sprawled on the bed and called the police.

Carney enjoyed drilling me on the murder rap. It wasn't every day he got the chance to put the hot lights to the Honolulu detective he despised. Forget the fact that a few years before when he was running for sheriff I had saved his neck from a bribery rap. The fact his old lady and I had rolled in the hay years before was enough to give him a lifetime blood revenge. Carney would have liked to have put the rubber hose to me, but since the establishment of the Police Commission, he wouldn't have laid a finger on me.

"So, why did you kill the Filipina, McDougal?"

"I don't know what you're talking about, flatfoot. I was drunk." There wasn't much more I could say.

The Grand Jury arraigned me on first-degree murder charges and bail was set at $50,000. The Old Man, the head of the International Detective Agency, must have believed my story about being framed. He put up the bail money. But my license was suspended, as well as my permit to carry a gun. The agency gave me an extended leave of absence as Clarence Wong, one of the new boys in the agency, was assigned the job to clear my name.

As long as Eddie Cook was rotting in one of those cells, I wasn't about to sit around my Moiliili cottage getting antsy. Not that I didn't trust Wong. Only, if I was going to be convicted of Murder One, I sure in the hell wasn't going to go without a fight. I packed a neat little .22 I kept for house rats and decided to see a snake named Mendez.

The way I figured it, if he knew his cupcake had latched on to a golden goose like Northridge, he wasn't going to ruin the deal because of love or jealousy. Maybe Floria had been leading Northridge on, getting him to embezzle the $20.000. Or perhaps she was blackmailing him. Either way, Mendez had a lot more to tell me.

I found him and his oriental tigress flashing the dough at Lau Yee Chai's fancy Waikiki restaurant. From the way he almost choked on his dim sum, he seemed surprised to see me.

"Figured you and your boys had me framed all the way to the gallows, Mendez?" I took the liberty of scooping some of the *chow fun* into an empty plate.

"Wait a minute, McDougal. You're not gonna hang your *pilikia* on me."

"I've got nothing to lose, Mendez. Tell me everything you know about Northridge and Floria."

"She was a tramp!" The tigress' fangs were showing.

"Go powder your nose, baby. Listen, McDougal, I'll help you on this one because you may not believe me, but I loved Floria."

The tigress slinked off as she did every time she heard the words "Floria" and "love." Mendez continued, spooning himself a heap of sweet-sour pork.

"She had a heart big enough to love even a mug like me. She had too big a heart. Take that Tahitian kid. They met, she helped him out, he was lonely so...bingo! He thinks she's his girlfriend. Truth was, she had plenty of men, but she never talked about them."

"What about Northridge? You wanted a piece of that action and she wouldn't let you in, so you killed her, right? Then you framed Cook and you..."

He started laughing softly, a quiet, self-confident laugh of a man who knows he is absolutely innocent.

"You're grabbing at straws, McDougal."

"Then who would kill her, Mendez? And then kill Maria because she knew too much?"

"If I knew that, they would be dead. I tell you what, you find who killed Floria and Maria to save your own neck. And when you do, make sure you nail them, okay? For me."

That left Northridge and Eddie Cook as the only possible suspects with a motive. Northridge might as well have been on the moon. After weeks of searching, nothing had turned up. My hunch was he had gotten the taste of the sweet life with Floria. When he embezzled the money to either run off with her or pay off the blackmail, he figured to hightail it out of the islands with the dough. He could always find another Floria south of the border. That left only Eddie as a suspect. I thought back to that night I had met him at the Green Mill, trying to reconstruct every word, looking for a clue that would turn that baby-faced kid into a killer.

The after-work crowd had not yet hit the Green Mill, so it was no problem slipping into the same stool I had used that night. Billy Cummins was on duty and I ordered a scotch whiskey and water, on the rocks. I wanted a clear head.

"Tough luck, Mac. I read about the murder in the *Advertiser*. She must have been some dish."

"Yeah," I said half-heartedly. "Billy, when they shanghai those boys down on Hotel Street, what do they put in their drinks? A Mickey Finn?"

"I don't know, Mac. I guess so, why?"

"Is that what you used in my drink the other night at the Paradise Club?"

"What are you talkin' about?"

"After Maria called you that some gent was asking lots of questions about Floria's boyfriends, you told her to stall me till you got there. I figure you must know all the bartenders in town, right? Did you pay Maria to keep her mouth shut or was the poor girl afraid she'd end up dead like her friend?"

"Gee, Mac, easy on the booze. You're talking wild."

"Am I? So you quietly have my drink spiked and tell Maria to get me over to the brothel. Only instead of knocking me off, like you told her you were going to do, you use my gun to kill the only person that can link you to Floria."

"You better shut up before you say things you'll regret."

"I was trying to connect poor Eddie with the murder, and a matchbook I found in the trash kept coming back to me. Of course, the murderer would have had to have been an idiot to leave the matchbook in the trash. But let's say one of Floria's boyfriends, and she had plenty, had left it there during one of their trysts."

"You're talking about the Green Mill matchbook? Mac, hundreds of guys take these very week."

"Not every guy was standing here a couple of nights ago, listening to a kid spill his guts. She broke your heart, too, didn't she, Billy? Only you couldn't stand it. It must have hurt real bad to hear the kid talk about her, knowing how you felt."

Death Row at Oahu Prison just before the old building was torn down. Prison bars used to separate the windows in the cells. *(Tom Coffman Multimedia)*

The Gallows at Oahu Prison long after capital punishment was abolished in Hawai'i. The steel trapdoors were cemented over in this photograph taken just before the old prison was demolished. *(Tom Coffman Multimedia)*

"She was no good, you hear? Taking up with every guy, even a poor jerk without a dime, for a beer. I wasn't gonna let her get away with it again."

He reached for the shotgun under the bar and got one blast off as I hit the floor. I winged him with my .22 as he headed out the back alley leading into Chaplain Lane. By the time he got to Smith Street I had my pistol aimed on his back.

"Hold it, Billy," I called, hoping he would listen. "We got you dead to rights. You aren't getting away with it. Where can you go? I don't want to shoot you."

The big Hawaiian dropped his shotgun, raised his hands and started bawling.

The cops gave me a good talking to about carrying a weapon while out on bail, the Old Man got his money back and Eddie Cook, thanking me profusely, shoved a $5 bill in my hand before catching the next freighter back to Tahiti. Carney was pretty upset I had slipped through his air-tight murder case.

Cummins was tried and convicted on two counts of murder and was sentenced to hang. With the help of a certain sleazy lawyer, he was able to delay the execution for two years. Then on an early December morning, Billy Cummins walked up the 13 steps to the gallows at Oahu Prison. A black hood was put around his head before the 13-knotted noose was tightened around his neck. The warden read a detailed description of his murders of Floria Alcantara and Maria Sanches. Three officers pushed three electric buttons simultaneously, one of which was connected to a trapdoor under Cummins. The floors fell, sending a loud metallic bang through the prison. As the body fell, it stopped short inches from the floor; the neck snapped and Cummins urinated. He shivered and jerked at the end of the rope for 7 minutes before the prison physician pronounced him dead. Honolulu had lost its best mixologist.

Northridge and the $20,000? We never found a trace of either. Sometimes, though, I fantasize that he is in some steamy tropical bar. A sultry taxi dancer is pressing him to her as the band plays a never-ending tango and I wish him all the luck in the world.

[**Editor's Note:** The Paradise and Aloha Ballrooms on Maunakea Street as described by McDougal were very real establishments providing Honolulu's lonely male population taxi dancing into the 1970's. "Mixologist" was a term referring to "bartenders" and the Green Mill advertised their "mixologist" to be the best in Honolulu. However, nothing else in this story can be verified.]

CHAPTER TWELVE

The Unholy Seance

There isn't a Honolulu poi dog alive who hasn't heard of the ghostly lady in white at Makapuu. Some claim to have seen her—a beautiful young girl in a white muumuu—hitchhiking along the road. When they stop to give her a ride, she disappears. Other times the same lady is seen running along the beach by the Makapuu lighthouse. If you look closely, she leaves no footprints in the sand as she swims out into the sea. I knew a guy once who swore on a stack of Bibles that the ghost of Makapuu rose from the ocean one night while he was fishing and called him by his name! She wanted him to go out into the sea with her to make love. He flattered himself by believing she wanted his body. The lady in white calls your soul.

To a hard-headed private dick, the idea that a ghost is haunting Makapuu Beach is nothing more than hogwash. Only thing is, yeah, I had seen her once. You might even say she saved my life. That was way back in October of 1922, when for a few weeks it seemed that you

Makapuu Lighthouse with the old captain who rescued me standing on the lanai. *(Hawai'i State Archives)*

281

just couldn't keep the dead quiet in Honolulu. Hell, they were even making phone calls.

I had been sick and tired that month of the two-bit adultery cases I was working just to pay my rent, when I was contacted by one of the ritziest dames who had ever sashayed down Bishop Street. Evelyn Kassenburg Pokele was a woman with class, money and the sweetest little dimple in her cheek. When she was simply Miss Evelyn Kassenburg, there wasn't a society page of the *Star-Bulletin* that didn't mention some party the debutante was either throwing or attending, or a charity that she was promoting. Miss Evelyn was one of those young girls who had it all, so she didn't need to flaunt it—a real swell kid with plenty of bread.

That's why the town was buzzing with gossip when she married Jimmy "Shark Bait" Pokele, a spoiled, rich-brat Hawaiian somehow linked to Hawaiian royalty, who made a name for himself racing motorcycles at Moiliili Field. Pokele would have turned any woman's head with his good looks, fair complexion and winning ways, but it always seemed to me he lacked character. Evelyn should have seen right through him. Then again, she never asked me for permission to marry "Shark Bait."

Tragedy always comes to people who are good and innocent at heart. A year after the marriage, while the couple was vacationing in Europe, "Shark Bait" Pokele drowned in a swimming accident off Cannes, France. The island boy was swallowed up by the Mediterranean, which never spit him out.

An appointment with Evelyn Pokele in my office was an occasion for a spring cleaning. I told my secretary, China, to give my office the once-over so I'd make a good impression, and I slipped into my only tailored, double-breasted suit which I kept just for these occasions. The blue tie with the colorful flower lei design matched the suit perfectly. I must have used a whole bottle of witch hazel to slick my hair down. At the stroke of 3 she strode into the Honolulu International Detective Agency, greeted China with a pleasant smile and quietly shut the door behind her as she entered my dressed-up quarters.

There were no airs about this lady. She was dressed elegantly in a white blouse and ankle-length white skirt and white pumps. Her wide-brimmed straw hat was cocked playfully on her head, concealing her silky brown hair, which she had just recently bobbed. Short, boyish hairstyles were the rage among the ladies that year. Her skin was like fresh cream from Woodlawn Dairy, offset by a few girlish freckles on her cheeks and her captivating blue eyes. I couldn't help but notice a solid gold crucifix that nestled securely in her scented cleavage. My collar was getting very wet.

"Mr. McDougal, your reputation in this town for discretion is excellent. My problem may seem a bit unusual, but I assure you I very much need your assistance. And I'll pay well for your time and silence."

My mouth felt as dry as the Ka'u desert. I mumbled something like "thanks" or "okay." Real articulate, McDougal.

"By the way, I love your tie. Where did you purchase it?" Her smile totally disarmed me.

"Thank you, ma'am," I said, blushing. "McInerny."

"It looks very smart on you. May I share my problem with you in complete confidence?"

Taking a cigarette from her purse, she leaned forward across my desk, as I fumbled for some matches. My hand was trembling slightly, as I lit her Lucky Strike. She blew the smoke up and away from me and leaned back into her seat.

"Of course, of course."

"My grand aunt, as you may know, is Freida Kassenburg. She is very dear to me. After my parents died in a train accident, it was Aunty Freida who reared me. And when my husband died last year, it has been my aunt who has helped to lift my spirits. However, I'm afraid someone is trying to drive my aunt insane. She's losing grasp on reality, Mr. McDougal."

I let her pause to wipe a few tears from her eyes. From what I knew about Freida Kassenburg, the ride to the insane asylum wouldn't be very long. When her husband, Otto Kassenburg, died nearly 20 years ago, his widow embarked on a well-publicized campaign to raise him from the grave, or at least to make him tip a table.

Old man Kassenburg had been a German immigrant who used to boast that he had made his fortune panning gold in California during the rush. Truth was he built up his dynasty from peddling women and whiskey to gold-fevered men in San Francisco. From the seedy rackets, he turned to speculating in Hawaiian sugar. Although he was based in Frisco, he had connections with the islands, having once been a chum of Kalakaua. When he died of gluttony at the age of 88, he left an estate of over 20 million smackeroos.

While most of the money was given in trust to his widow, $5 million had been endowed to a small college in San Jose whose board of directors promptly renamed the school Kassenburg College. It was one of those trouble-making schools that trained Bolsheviks and Free Thinkers. For all his wealth, Kassenburg had been a closet socialist who wanted his money to go back to the proletariat—but not, of course, while he was alive.

"My grand aunt claims to be receiving phone calls from the dead, Mr. McDougal. She says that her husband has been calling in the middle of the night, warning her that someone is trying to kill her. She is absolutely beside herself with fear. She won't eat her meals thinking that the food has been poisoned. Getting her out of the house is nearly impossible. She's literally barricaded herself in. With her weak heart, I'm afraid these telephone calls are going to kill her."

She stuffed her half-smoked cigarette out in the ashtray on my desk.

"Do you have something to fortify my nerves?"

"China!" I called outside. "Can Mrs. Pokele have some tea?"

"I was thinking of something stronger," she explained, lowering her voice.

"Oh, sure, sure," I said, pulling a bottle of my best Canadian whiskey out of my bottom drawer. "Forget the tea, China!" I shouted, as I poured us both a shot into glasses I hurriedly wiped clean.

"You are such a gentleman, Mr. McDougal."

"Thank you, Mrs. Pokele. But to be honest with you, it seems to me you need an exorcist, priest or alienist—not a gumshoe." I was trying to tone down my usual flippancy.

"I don't think it's the ghost of Uncle Otto who is making the calls. My grand aunt, Mr. Dougal, is a very wealthy woman who has recently hired a prominent lawyer to rewrite her will. A spiritualist adviser is also living with my aunt. Every night they conduct seances to make clearer contact with Uncle Otto so they can identify who is trying to kill her and to whom she should leave her estate."

Fifteen million bucks was a sweet pot that would have even raised Lazarus.

"Mrs. Pokele, let me assure you that if the phone calls are being made by anyone of flesh and blood, I'll smoke them out of their racket before any more harm is done."

"I knew I could trust you, Mr. McDougal," she said, rising from her chair and looking down at me with her angelic smile. "Tonight my aunt is having another one of her seances. I'd like to invite you and your secretary as my new friends. Please be at our home at about 8:30 p.m. The attire is formal, Mr. McDougal."

She gave my hand an ever-so-light squeeze and sailed out of my office and down the hall. Some school-boy memories of "a phantom of delight" wafted through my addled, sentimental brain.

"China!" I screamed excitedly. "Call McInerny and rent me a tuxedo. And get yourself a fancy evening dress!"

The "Castle" or Puuhonua in Manoa Valley where the strange seances took place. *(Hawai'i State Archives)*

I rushed out to a Pauahi Street barbershop to get a trim and a shave.

Widow Kassenburg had been renting the old estate called the Castle, which sat on a promontory behind Ferdinand Avenue on the *ewa* hill of Manoa Valley. Whatever image you have of a haunted house, I guess that would rightly fit the description of this old Victorian relic with cobwebbed crenelated towers. The Castle family used it as a private residence only a few years before old Mother Castle passed away in 1907. The house was then used as a free Kindergarten and Children's Aid Association orphanage until this year, when Percy Pond Realty was deciding what to do with the property. Until a decision was made, the Widow Kassenburg had obtained a short-term lease on the mansion.

The moon seemed uncommonly full and large that night, as China and I drove along Manoa Road, turning onto the steep road that led to the estate. The lunar light illuminated the tall peaks of Manoa and the hundreds of cottages and taro fields that lay upon the valley floor. I down-geared my machine to make the steep grade up the hill to the Castle as we turned up to the porte-cochere. It was a perfect night for a seance.

China spent the time chewing me out on how good Chinese girls didn't like calling the dead. "You never know who picks up the phone, Mac. Plenty of evil on the other side."

I told her to cool down. It was all a flimflam and I needed her to help me keep an eye on the seance members in case of any tomfoolery. She demanded a $2 bonus, which I chalked up to expenses.

It was 8:30 p.m. when we knocked on the great koa front door. From the outside, the Castle seemed in complete darkness except for a yellowish glow of soft candles from the a first-floor window. A tuxedo-attired Japanese butler opened the door, as a nervous China prattled away in Chinese to no one in particular and I straightened my bow tie. After bowing smartly, the butler ushered us into the parlor which was illuminated by a dozen candles.

The parlor decor was right out of a dime novel, with human skulls decorating the mantles, spirit photographs adorning the heavily draped walls, and tapers burning everywhere. A gramophone played a particularly sobering funeral dirge. The pungent odor of burning incense was stifling. China squeezed my hand so hard she nearly cut the circulation off.

"Auntie, this is Mr. McDougal and his companion, whom I invited to join us tonight. He is very interested in spiritual communication."

"Really? Have you read Mr. Arthur Conan Doyle's new work on the spirit telegraph?"

"Sure," I answered, not sure who this character Doyle was. "I keep up with the literature. Let me introduce my companion. This is..."

"Yi Zwang."

"Yes, she is an oriental fortuneteller who I had brought along to help contact the dead."

China shot me a stink eye that I was certain was a Chinese hex.

"Oh, really, sir?" interrupted a gypsy-looking, white-haired lady in her seventies. "It won't be necessary to receive any Chinese spirit assistance. My spirit guide, Chief Kalama, is one of the most powerful Hawaiian channelers in Summerland. Far more powerful than the Chinese."

"Oh, yes, Mr. McDougal. Baroness Ava is an absolute wonder and Kalama has given us good communication to my dear Otto."

"Chinese invented talking to the dead, lady," added my now-insulted secretary. I squeezed China's arm, calming her national pride.

Widow Kassenburg was one of those Victorian ladies who, in the years after the Great War, seemed to be a vanishing breed. She was wearing a beautiful black taffeta muumuu, with an elegant ivory cameo pinned at her neck. She had taken up the habit of wearing a black-laced shawl over her head as if she was in a perpetual state of mourning for her dear Otto. With these so-called threats on her life, you could read fear and anxiety in her face, although I had to give the old lady a lot of credit for her grace.

The assorted characters joining in the unholy seance had the cadaverous look of vultures waiting to pick over the widow's bones. Baroness Ava, a hammy theatrical phony if I ever saw one, was assisted by her sultry, 20-year-old daughter Editha, who seemed to have trouble keeping all of her anatomy in the confines of her blouse. O.P. Ferreira, one of Honolulu's more dramatic and powerful Portuguese lawyers, known for his lavish style and expensive LaSalle with built-in bar, drew his attention away from Editha just long enough to shoot me a puzzled eye, like "what was a private dick doing impersonating a ghost-seeker?" I flicked my eyebrow in recognition, suggesting he keep his mouth shut.

I didn't know the other four men at the table. One was a bushy-headed and fuzzy-faced egghead with a disapproving manner, who turned out to be Dr. Edgar Knowles, Vice President of Kassenburg College, who had rushed to Honolulu when he heard that Widow Kassenburg was rewriting her will. The dull-witted henchman at his side was a burly muscled bodyguard named Mick, who was hired by the College to protect the old lady. On the opposite end of the table from where I sat was a sassy, pinched-face youngster in his early twenties, who was called "Spunky." He was Evelyn Pokele's cousin.

The good-looking gent I paid the most attention to was wearing a clerical collar. Father Alex Mivelaz was urging Widow Kassenburg to give up her foolishness. He went on and on about demons and evil spirits through necromancy. He could not in good conscience, he finally announced, attend such a polluted activity. From what I could gather, he was a family friend whom Evelyn had asked to persuade her grand aunt out of her supernatural dabbling. Only, he wasn't making any headway, except perhaps with Evelyn. I felt a tiny pang of jealousy when I noticed the way she took his hand when he made his dramatic exit.

"Of all the gall, Evelyn," the final member of the seance quickly added after the priest left. "To invite him here! You never know when to quit, do you? Haven't you caused this family enough embarrassment?"

"Really, Aunt Catherine," Evelyn retorted like a wounded animal. "Your behavior is uncalled for."

From the way she spoke to Evelyn, I took an instant dislike to Widow Kassenburg's daughter, Mrs. Catherine Richardson. Her drab, homely looks were made more sour by her abrasive and arrogant manner. Spunky Richardson, her son, physically cringed whenever his mother spoke.

"Stop it, Mother. Those ugly things were untrue." The disembodied voice from the next room at first seemed to come from the other world. But in a few moments, I could see the very real and pleasing body to which it was connected.

"Mr. McDougal," Evelyn said in relief, knowing she had an ally in the room, "allow me to introduce my cousin, Marianne Richardson."

If Evelyn Pokele had a rival for looks, it was her cousin Marianne. On the slim side like her brother Spunky, she had none of his pinched ugliness. Instead, her face was a captivating oval, with warm, green eyes and a million-dollar smile. She strode right up to me, firmly grasped me with one hand, throwing back her long, strawberry-blond locks with the other.

"So you are interested in the spirit world, also? We are fortunate that Baroness Ava has come to live with Grand Aunty. It allows all of us to commune with the higher beings." The poor, young thing, I thought, has really bought this bunk—hook, line and sinker.

"When I was in Boston last month, I had the opportunity to see a demonstration of Margery's ghostly hand. It literally crawled up my leg and squeezed my thigh. Even Houdini has not been able to prove her a fake."

Hmm, I thought, lucky hand.

"You live in the islands or are only visiting, Miss Richardson?"

"I attend Smith College, Mr. McDougal, where I am studying psychology. Freud, you know? Have you read any of Freud's thoughts on spirit communication and other uncanny phenomena?"

"Sure," I lied.

About that time the Baroness called for the circle to commence and we all sat down at the seance table, upon which was a richly ornate ouija board with a pearl planchette or spirit pointer. We were ordered to hold hands as all the candles were extinguished by the Japanese maid who then beat a frightened retreat.

The next hour was pure hokum. If I had the time or inclination I could have outfoxed the Baroness with her tipping table, flying trumpets, rose-scented breezes and phony automatic writing. It was ludicrous that anyone could mistaken such parlor tricks for a genuine communication with the dead. Knowles interjected his disapproval often enough, until finally Widow Kassenburg asked him to wait in another room. The poor old lady soaked it all in while the rest of us quietly acquiesced. The only fun I had was when Editha, evidently playing footsy under the table with Ferreira, accidentally started rubbing my calf with her naked toes.

"I will now receive a direct message from Otto Kassenburg in the spirit land," announced the Baroness. "Otto, use my hands to write your message." In the dark we could hear the scrawling of a pen on a large pad of sketch paper.

When the lights went out, the automatic message was clear enough—"My beloved Freida. Tonight you join me in the other world. I await with open arms. Otto."

"This is going too far, Baroness." Mrs. Richardson was livid. "My mother cannot tolerate this kind of threat. How dare you!"

"Not I!" protested the Baroness. "I do not control the sentiments of the higher beings. I am but their medium. They have warned her that she was in danger. They have tried to save her life from those who benefit from her death."

"O.P. and I have seen to it that those who may benefit the most," added the Widow, "will benefit the least! Now, really, I am exhausted."

As the elegant old lady made her exit, we were all interrupted by a deep, glottal moan from China. I hadn't paid any attention to her during or after the seance, but she had never moved from her seat. I could see that she was in some kind of trance as her limbs began wildly gyrating across the table. Widow Kassenburg thrust a pencil into her hand and placed the automatic writing pad underneath the point. In a few moments several

Chinese characters were scrawled across several sheets of paper. Then China slumped in her seat and opened her eyes.

"What does it mean, dear?" asked the Widow.

"What?"

"This writing?"

I could see China was genuinely mystified by her own writing. They are in ancient characters, she announced, after studying them.

"I read these characters. I don't know what they say."

Except for the jealous refusal of the Baroness to acknowledge China's performance, the rest of us were quite impressed, even if it made no sense. The Widow and Baroness excused themselves and went up to their rooms, while the rest drifted into the dining room to share a glass of the finest bootleg whiskey I've ever tasted.

"That was a pretty nice act," I whispered to China. "What are you up to?"

"That was no act, Mac," she answered. "I warned you about us Chinese. We invented talking to the dead."

"Yeah, yeah. Listen. If you can pull yourself away from the hocus-pocus, take my machine back to the office. I want you to start checking out a few things tonight. Like any record the Baroness or any other of these animal crackers may have."

"Tonight?"

"You planned on more spirit communications?"

China left in a huff, taking her mystic writing with her. In the meantime I had an opportunity to watch the vultures size each other up. I can't imagine what the Widow's will stated before the rewrite, but from the way she acted, Kassenburg College may be losing a very fat endowment. Ferreira and Knowles got into a little heated argument about Ferreira's legal capabilities. The hooch kept flowing and some half-hearted verbal punches were thrown back and forth and Ferreira traipsed off to a guest room, while Knowles passed out, drunk, on a couch. Sometime at the end of the melee, Editha flashed me a come-on smile, swayed her hips at Ferreira, and went off to the room she shared with her mother.

She was followed soon after by a very bitter Mrs. Richardson, who seemed to enjoy the heat. Spunky and Marianne followed their mother like little ducklings. Mick had already placed himself in a watchman's chair outside the Widow's room. I escorted Evelyn to her door, assured her that her aunt would be all right and then retired to my guest room, which was conveniently located next to the Widow. Propping myself up in a chair against the wall, I listened for what I expected would be a phone call from the dead.

About 3 o'clock in the morning I was aroused from a light sleep by the ringing of the phone in the Widow's room. I nearly fell out of the chair as I dashed for the door. Pushing a snoring Mick aside, I burst into the room to discover Widow Kassenburg hysterically screaming into her telephone, telling her dead husband that she wasn't ready to die. I grabbed the phone out of her hand only to hear the static of a dead line. She was muttering something about her heart as her breathing quickened and her eyes turned white. I was leaning over her, trying to calm her down, when the half-witted Mick grabbed me from behind and slammed me into the wall, pinning my arms. Before I could explain what was happening, I heard that terrible seizure made by the last, dying breath. Widow Kassenburg had died.

When I broke away from the big lug, I dashed downstairs to the hall telephone. If someone inside the house had made the bogus call, then the receiver would still be warm. It was icy cold from the Manoa air. And, according to Knowles, who had come out of his drunken stupor just about the time I first heard the phone ring upstairs, the downstairs phone never rang.

In all the confusion of doctors, ambulance and police that followed, it's only the look of Evelyn Pokele that I remember when she learned her grand aunt had died. She was truly crushed that her beloved protector was gone. There was also a hint of disappointment in her eyes that Arthur McDougal had let her down.

It was about 7 in the morning when I used the downstairs phone to call Sergeant Henry Chillingworth at the sheriff's office. As I picked up the receiver, I heard China on the other end talking away to Evelyn, who was on the upstairs line. I rudely interrupted and asked China if she had just called.

"Yes, Mac. I got some information for you."

I told her I'd be back at the office by 8 and quickly hung up. Turning the telephone over, it took me two seconds to discover how the dead never seemed to disturb anyone but Widow Kassenburg. Someone had turned off the ringer and, in all the excitement, forgot to turn it back on.

An hour later I was reading a police sheet that China had obtained on Baroness Ava, whose real name was Ann O'Delia Diss Debar, a notorious spiritualist fraud. The New Orleans police had sent notices to every major American and European city to be on the lookout for Diss Debar, who had ruined more careers and lives than Svengali. She had escaped New Orleans while out on bail pending swindling charges. Editha was probably some spoiled dove she picked up on the way to Honolulu to use as an apprentice.

"Oh, Mac, one more thing. Those Chinese characters. I asked an old Chinese priest at the Kwan Yin Temple. It says 'Be Cautious of the Undead.'"

"Great," I thought. "Vampires are on my tail."

By the time I got hold of Chillingworth to fill him in on the details of last night's deadly charade, Kassenburg College, under the insistence of Dr. Knowles, had obtained possession of Freida Kassenburg's body. By that afternoon, she had been cremated under the pretension that the cause of death had already been determined by a family doctor. Any chance of conducting a more thorough autopsy just went up in smoke.

The next two days were spent with China, digging into the background of the vulture pack. The only concrete information we turned up in addition to the fake spiritualist was the fact that during the last two years, Kassenburg College had been going deeper and deeper into financial problems. In fact, if they didn't receive a large portion of the Widow's estate by November of 1923, their Free Thinking institute would have to shut its doors. Knowles seemed awfully solicitous towards the Widow, but it may have been a front. With Mick guarding her, it would have been easy to slip her some kind of drug to induce a heart attack.

The Catholic Church on Fort Street. Evelyn Pokele was found murdered in the alleyway to the right of the church. *(Hawaiʻi State Archives)*

There was one other curious item that I had overlooked. It was that hint of scandal suggested by Mrs. Richardson concerning Evelyn and the priest.

Father Mivelaz, I found out from the diocese records, had grown up in the same Manoa Valley neighborhood as Evelyn Pokele. In fact, they had both attended Punahou School and then the same college in California before he turned to the cloth and she ended up in the arms of "Shark Bait." No wonder you could sense something going on between them. I figured it wouldn't hurt to pay the priest a visit.

I found him in the rectory at the old Catholic church on Fort Street. He, of course, denied any sexual involvement with Evelyn. Yes, they had been close and she had grown excessively fond of him during their college days. But he had always had a religious conviction that when he became 21 years old he would enter the priesthood. He took his vows seriously. Although usually I didn't trust a man who wanted to become a self-proclaimed eunuch, I believed him.

As I was about to leave the rectory, I noticed a small Japanese woman, stooped and limping, watching me keenly from the kitchen. She was at a large table, deftly cleaning fish with a serrated, pearl-handled knife. Although she must have been only in her late twenties, she appeared at first like an old woman. It was hard to see her face clearly, since she wore a black silk veil resembling one of Valentino's harem vamps in the silents. But her eyes told me real clear—lay off her man.

The next morning at 7:30, I was having breakfast with Sergeant Chillingworth at the Child's Cafe in the Blaisdell Hotel. I was filling him in on the financial status of Kassenburg College and our fraudulent Baroness, when he informed me that the reading of Widow Kassenburg's will was to take place that morning at 10 in Ferreira's office. I was downing my third cup of kona when a frantic priest came running out of the Catholic church across the street, screaming for help. Chillingworth and I dashed out of the cafe and followed him back to the *makai* side of the church to a dense grove of bushes leading to Union Square. I knew from the creamy color of the stiff leg sticking out of the bushes that I didn't want to look any further.

Evelyn Pokele lay on her back in the shrubs, her eyes open in frozen horror. A serrated, pearl-handled knife was pressed deep into her heart, her white blouse stained crimson. There was, however, no blood on any of the plants. I noted a very thin, long bruise on the right side of her neck. Her crucifix was missing.

Two hours later the sheriff's office sent people to the Pua Lane home of Hiromi Shimakawa, a cook and maid for the rectory. It was her fish knife that had been used to kill Evelyn sometime around 11 o'clock the night before, as determined by the coroner. In addition, they had an eyewitness who saw Shimakawa running from the rectory down Fort Street towards Beretania at around 11:10 p.m. Mrs. Okada, the owner of the Japanese Bazaar located across the street from the church, knew the exact moment because she always closed up her store at precisely that time. In the streetlight she saw the veil and distinctive limp of the crippled woman.

Her motive in killing Evelyn Pokele? Shimakawa was fixated on Father Mivelaz. She had been a real beauty before a tragic fire had left her a cripple with a hideously scarred face. Her husband deserted her, so she found help at the Catholic church, where the young, good-looking priest gave her spiritual solace. She was especially jealous of Evelyn, who often paid visits to Father Mivelaz. Shimakawa couldn't handle their secret trysts, the cops deduced, so she sliced up her rival. The sheriff's office considered it an open-and-shut case.

Only, they couldn't find Shimakawa. She had gone on the lam without leaving a trace.

Just after 10 o'clock, I showed up at Ferreira's office, which was located in the Boston Building on Fort Street. The Kassenburg heirs had just received the details of Evelyn's murder from the sheriff's office and I was giving them the McDougal lie detector test of sincerity. Mrs. Richardson and Spunk were feigning nicely. Marianne was self-composed, subdued. The Baroness was reassuring us that "there is no death," while Knowles was doing a nice job of shaking his head sadly.

"I knew that girl would get in trouble with that priest. Imagine, a man of God. She wore that crucifix like it was a wedding ring."

"Please, Mother. Don't speak ill of Evelyn." Marianne was animated, her face flush. "That evil woman snatched something very precious to Evelyn. You wouldn't understand that, Mother. It's called love. Clean love."

"Really, Marianne, you are such a sentimentalist."

When O.P. Ferreira finally read Widow Kassenburg's will, you could have heard a pin fall. Evelyn Pokele was to receive the entire $15 million estate. Not a penny to the relatives or the school.

"Damn my mother! She always hated me!" Mrs. Richardson's outburst was theatrically loud.

"Wait! There's a codicil," continued Ferreira. "In the case of Evelyn's death within one year of mine, I leave $10 million to Kassenburg College, $2 million to my daughter, $1 million each to her two children, $500,000 to my faithful spiritual adviser, Baroness Ava, and $500,000 to my devoted maid, Yuriko."

So they all took a piece of the pie, while poor Evelyn ends up dead in a sordid little passion triangle. Father Mivelaz had been placed incommunicado by Archbishop Alencastre, paying penance for his involvement in the fiasco. He told the cops that he had been sound asleep in the rectory at 11 p.m. No, he hadn't anticipated seeing Evelyn.

Knowles' alibi was, ironically, Ferreira. The two had been engaged in another tirade at Ferreira's law office. Knowles said he was sure that Ferreira was playing crooked with the rewriting of the will and confronted him that evening.

Mrs. Richardson and her children also had tight alibis the night Evelyn was murdered. The mother, house servants said, was passed out in her room from her overindulgence in bootleg. Spunky was with some friends, shooting pool in a Hotel Street dive. He was there until midnight.

Marianne had gone to a special late-night showing of "Pied Piper Malone" at the Kaimuki Playhouse. Evelyn was supposed to have met her at 9:30 p.m. in the lobby, but never showed. The usher verified that the distinctive beauty waited for her friend until 10 p.m. and then went in alone. Yes, he saw her leave at the end of the performance—about 11:50 p.m.

The pigeon to squeeze, I figured, was O.P. Ferreira. That night I paid a visit to his beachfront home past Waimanalo, towards Makapuu Point. I showed up unannounced, so he greeted me in his garish silk nightgown that still had the smell of very cheap gypsy perfume. O.P. lived real fast. Too fast. He assured me that his legal reputation was impeccable. I told him that he was a fat, pompous fool who was about to take the big fall.

"What did the original will say, O.P.?"

"That is privileged information."

I put my brass knuckles into his groin and he keeled over like the *Titanic*.

"Meet my privilege, O.P."

"I'll get your license for that," he gasped.

"A real sweet kid who trusted me is dead. You can eat my license for all I care. Now tell me what the will said or I'll make sure your little tart in the next room won't have much left to nibble on tonight."

"Kassenburg College was going to get the whole 15 million. But when the phone calls started from Otto, she thought they were trying to kill her. She didn't want them to get her husband's money. That's all I know."

As I was driving back to town on the new government road around Makapuu Point, I noticed a pair of headlights coming up fast. It was a small Stutz Bearcat that closed the distance and rammed my tail. He was running me off the road, just as we narrowed the turn towards the lighthouse.

The fool hit me too hard and I could feel that our bumpers had locked. He was trying to guide me into the cliff on my right, but my Willys-Knight took control and I pulled him with me as I veered through a railing and sailed through the embankment towards the mysterious swirling glare of the lighthouse.

That's when I saw her. Standing on the side of the road in a flowing white dress, arms wide-open, beckoning to me. The roar of smashing steel and glass and the stench of burning rubber wrapped me tight as I leaped toward that beautiful Hawaiian woman with outstretched arms. I think she kissed me. Once.

A toothless, grizzle-faced old man with the breath of stale fish and pipe tobacco was peering into my face when I opened my eyes. The old Army cot I was stretched out on groaned as I pried myself up, only to feel every muscle in my body scream.

"Better take it easy, young fella. You had a pretty bad spill. Good thing you fell out of your car or you'd have ended up like the other driver. I radioed the sheriff's office."

"Where am I?"

"Makapuu Lighthouse. I tend this grand lady. Captain Carter's me name. Willy, my assistant, and I heard the crash and went down to see what the fuss was. Found you all banged up not far from the wreckage."

"Thanks to your daughter I had enough sense to jump before we hit the rocks below." I went on to describe the beautiful woman in white that lured me to her.

"That ain't me daughter, boy. You must've seen Malei. She's the ghostly lady of Makapuu. Guess she took a fancy to you."

I asked him about the driver of the other car.

"Poor devil is dead. The windshield exploded in his face."

"It looks like hamburger meat," added the boy named Willy.

An hour later the cops, with Sergeant Chillingworth, had driven out through the "badlands" and was sifting through the wreckage. My Willys-Knight was twisted metal junk. The Stutz Bearcat was no better. The driver's face had been destroyed beyond recognition. In the trunk we found some bloodstains that probably belonged to Evelyn Pokele. And in the dead driver's pocket the cops found the crucifix that had once had the privilege of embracing her neck.

"Whoever he is, Chillingworth, he killed Evelyn. That was her crucifix."

"What are you talking about?"

"She was wearing that crucifix when she was murdered. It was snatched from her neck, causing that little thin bruise."

"I wished you'd have let us in on that sooner, Mac."

I explained that in all the confusion the morning we found Evelyn, I had just assumed the cops would figure it out. What concerned me now was identifying the faceless roadster who had tried to kill me and flush out any of his confederates.

The plan seemed hokey, but effective. Baroness Ava, who had not yet had her hand exposed by the cops, was enticed to conduct a seance with China, my personal oriental medium. Everyone who had been at Widow Kassenburg's castle the night of her death was invited to help create the spiritual energy needed to bring the spirit of the faceless driver back from the dead. He would identify himself and those who helped him kill Evelyn.

Despite a lot of grumbling from the nonbeliever Knowles, they were all present that evening in the Widow's "seance room." No one had the nerve not to be there and thereby implicate him or herself as having something to hide. Just to cover all bases, I asked Widow Kassenburg's Japanese maid, who had inherited a cool half a million to join us.

The circle joined hands in the darkened room as the Baroness called the spirit of the driver of the Stutz Bearcat to identify himself. About a half-hour went by with no sign from the dead, when China suddenly began to mutter some crazy Chinese chant and suddenly a disembodied voice filled the room.

"Greetings from the other world."

The Baroness and her "daughter" stirred as the voice descended from the ether.

"Are you the man who tried to kill me?" I asked the disembodied voice. "If so, what was your name?"

"Forgive me. In my human life I was filled with greed and hate. My name was Jimmy Pokele."

The outbursts from the circle broke the mood. I tried to quiet them down so China could continue, but it was impossible. I watched them closely—Knowles, the college vice president and his hired thug Mick, along with Mrs. Richardson and her children, seemed genuinely surprised. So were the Baroness and her sexy daughter. The Widow's maid seemed nonplused. O.P. Ferreira was perspiring so bad his starched collar melted.

It was something about the "shark bait" color and gangling height of the unidentified driver that told me the drowned husband had come back very much alive to Hawai'i to kill his wife. Ferreira's reaction told me that my hunch was on the mark.

As the group was breaking up, China started her automatic writing routine, letting out supernatural moans and scribbling Chinese characters across pages and pages of paper. We all watched in amazement until she fell back, exhausted. The characters were in simple, modern Chinese so that China could easily translate them.

"Death Visits the Circle."

After our little dramatic debut, I treated China and Chillingworth to hot saimin at a little stand near Waikiki Park. Chillingworth had been the disembodied spirit, speaking through a simple-speaking tube that we had rigged up that afternoon in the next room. I told China that automatic writing bit at the end may have been overdone.

"Mac, I wasn't faking. I don't know how I did that."

I stayed near my office phone late that evening, expecting a nervous call from a rich-living lawyer who had stepped over the legal line. When Ferreira finally rang me up, he was close by in his office at the Boston Building.

Ten minutes later I was listening to his confession. Two months ago "Shark Bait" Pokele had shown up at his Waimanalo bungalow with a simple, sweet offer. He and Evelyn had faked the drowning the year before so that she could nuzzle up to her grand aunt and he could maneuver easily behind the scenes. The lady was old and superstitious so they devised the phone calls from the dead to force her to rewrite her will. Evelyn would get the money instead of the Bolshevik college and the two of them would disappear to the Orient.

Ferreira was promised that he'd be set up real pretty. All he needed to do was bring a phony spiritualist into the little drama to help continue the messages from dead Otto. Ferreira knew about the Baroness' background and paid her off to deliver the right spirit communications as given to him by Pokele. Editha was just the icing on Ferreira's tasty cake.

"Did Evelyn ever contact you directly about this scheme?"

"No. And Pokele told me never to talk to her about it. She was going to stay real clean."

After the will was rewritten to give the money to Evelyn, Ferreira said Pokele brought up the idea of the codicil. It would make the old lady feel more comfortable in case something unfortunate happened to Evelyn. Only, when he suggested making a provision for Evelyn's early death to the Widow, she insisted on leaving some of her money to her medium and faithful Japanese maid.

I asked him if he was the one who had turned off the ringer on the downstairs phone when Pokele impersonated the dead Otto. He denied any knowledge of it. He figured Evelyn was handling the inside job.

"When she was murdered by that woman at the Catholic church, I was as surprised as everyone else. I didn't know she was fooling around with the priest. Of course, she was a great-looking broad."

I would have smacked the weasel for that remark an hour earlier, but somehow my memories of Evelyn Pokele had been a bit tarnished. Still, there were a few things that didn't add up.

I convinced Ferreira that his best bet was to spill his guts to the cops. He'd probably be disbarred for being involved in the conspiracy, but it was better than taking the rap for murder.

We had just turned the corner at King and Bethel and were walking towards the police station on Merchant, when a large sedan rolled towards us on the dark street and a shotgun sent two blasts our way. I pushed Ferreira hard towards the sidewalk, but not before his arm was nearly ripped to shreds. The other blast shattered a store window and sent a shower of deadly glass down Bethel.

I hit the sidewalk, peeling off four rounds from my Colt. I don't think I hit the gunman, but one shell ripped into the engine. The automobile veered down Bethel, nearly slamming into the front door of the post office, when it hit one of the old cannons that had been put into the sidewalk as hitching posts 50 years before. The cannons stopped the sedan cold and fire engulfed the interior. The gas tank must have lit because a blast like dynamite shook downtown, as the sedan became an inferno.

Spunky Richardson was baked alive. The firemen found only some charred bones and a skull. Fortunately, his dental records matched the teeth in the grisly burnt skull. Ferreira was rushed to Queen's Emergency Hospital, where he lost his arm.

Pokele's accomplice, they reasoned, wasn't Evelyn as he had told Ferreira, but Spunky. First they needed to get the Widow to turn over her money to Evelyn. Then they'd use the scandalous rumors to make it look like the crippled cook Shimakawa had killed Evelyn out of jealousy. Spunky, who was small and skinny, had probably worn a wig, dress and veil the night of the murder, knowing that the owner of the Japanese Bazaar would close up at around 11 o'clock. Shimakawa, the cops figured, was buried somewhere in a plantation field.

The conditions of the codicil would give Spunky, who had been dismissed by his grand aunt as a nonentity, $1 million. When the heat was off and the will out of escrow, he and Pokele would quietly leave town together. The cops deduced that they were lovers.

The newspapers played up the seedy side of the story real big. Kassenburg College announced that it would seek full control over the Widow's estate. Then, in a "conciliatory gesture" to avoid lengthy litigation with Mrs. Richardson, announced that they would be content with only $10 million, leaving $5 million to Mrs. Richardson and her daughter. Everyone seemed happy.

Everyone but Art McDougal. With Pokele's reputation for womanizing, I couldn't buy it that he and the ugly, pinch-faced Spunky were lovers. And the police seemed to overlook Spunky's alibi the night of the murder that he had been at a pool hall on Hotel Street. "You can't believe the punks and hoodlums that hang out there," they told me.

A few weeks later I read in the society pages that Mrs. Richardson was holding a shipboard reception at Pier 7 in honor of her daughter, who was returning to the mainland to resume her psychology studies at Smith College. I figured I'd bust the party, since after all I was nearly a member of the family.

I received the telegraph message that I had been waiting for and ambled over to Pier 7, where the Matson liner *Malolo* was docked. Mrs. Richardson's party was in full swing. I found a slightly tipsy Marianne the center of attraction in a cloister of sheiky-head, suited dandies. I slipped my arm around Marianne's waist and led her to the second-deck promenade. Her long, blond hair smelled great as she rested her head against me.

"I'll miss you, McDougal," she said tenderly. "We never got enough time alone. You're quite a man."

"I'll visit you, Marianne."

She looked up at me with a wry, puzzled smile.

"You care for me that much? You'd come that far?"

"It's not that far to Oahu Prison," I assured her.

"What are you talking about?"

I showed her the telegraph message from Smith College. She hadn't been a student there in a year.

"I never paid much attention to going to school, but it struck me funny that you were here in October. Seems you just dropped out one day. I figure it was the day Jimmy Pokele came back into your life.

"Spunky wasn't his lover. You were. The night she was murdered, Evelyn was supposed to meet you at the Kaimuki Playhouse. That's where Pokele grabbed her, stuck the fish knife into her heart and stuffed her body into the trunk of his car. You, of course, made sure that the usher noticed you before you left by a back exit.

"You then sped downtown, dumped her body in the bushes near the church and did a nice job impersonating the jealous cook for the Japanese Bazaar owner. Then Pokele took you back to the Playhouse to complete your alibi."

She didn't flinch, but gave me a lovely, romantic smile. "There's no crime dropping out of school, Mr. McDougal."

I showed her the crucifix that Chillingworth had given me when the case was "closed." I was talking fast and hard, trying to smash through her cool facade.

"When I showed up at Ferreira's office for the reading of the will, you mentioned something about the 'evil woman taking Evelyn's crucifix.' I didn't think of it at the time, figuring maybe the police had told you. But the police didn't know she had been wearing the crucifix. Not until I told them a few days later."

She dropped her glass of champagne and backed away. I'd cracked her and I went full-steam ahead.

"You were smart. Don't be greedy, you told yourself. Take only a million and don't cast any suspicion on yourself as a suspect. But you were too anxious with the clever clues you planted. Where's the poor cook buried, Marianne? Did you kill her or did Pokele?"

"Shut up!"

"Then, when your lover boy ends up dead trying to rub me out, you got nervous, didn't you? If Ferreira spilled the beans, then maybe your inheritance would be given to the college. So you let your weak-minded brother in on the deal. After all, he was used to rubbing shoulders with the wrong crowd. If he wanted to keep his million, you convinced him, he'd better knock the lawyer off. You must have been pretty desperate."

She gave me a passionate kiss that nearly buckled my knees. The offer she made in my ear with her moist lips was real juicy.

"Sorry, sister. Four people are dead because you like money. It's too easy to be your fifth victim some night when you get tired of me."

With only a small pang of regret, I turned my chance for fortune over to the cops.

Ferreira was disbarred and spent a year in prison for conspiracy. The Baroness was extradited to New Orleans, while her phony daughter slipped out of sight. Father Mivelaz was sent off to South America to avoid further scandals and his poor cook's body was never found. And Dr. Knowles? He was arrested two years later on charges of embezzling the college out of $300,000. So much for anti-capitalists.

Marianne Richardson was found guilt of first-degree murder and conspiracy after a trial that was a sordid sensation. As far as I know, she spent the rest of her life shriveling up in a mainland penitentiary.

The case was all wrapped up except for one last detail. I brought China along figuring that her little stunt of automatic writing had been the only true evidence of spirit contact during the whole fiasco. We parked at the spot where my Willys-Knight had gone over the edge. At the place on the sand where I had seen the lady in white standing, beckoning me to her, I carefully draped a beautiful *maile* leaf lei.

I don't know if she was real or my imagination. In either case, I wanted the Lady of Makapuu to know that Art McDougal was real grateful that during the unholy seance, the dead had been on his side.

[*Editor's Note:* *The details of the case involving the death of Freida Kassenburg sound suspiciously like Art McDougal has plagiarized heavily from the controversy surrounding the death of Mrs. Jane Lathrop Stanford at the Moana Hotel on February 28, 1905. High Sheriff William Henry announced after examination of Mrs. Stanford's bicarbonate of soda that the benefactress of Stanford University possibly had been murdered. One of the suspects was her "secretary/medium," a young woman who was alleged to have helped Mrs. Stanford contact her deceased husband, California railroad magnate Leland Stanford. Curiously, Stanford University's distinguished president, David Starr Jordan, concluded Mrs. Stanford had died of heart disease exacerbated by indigestion even before he had arrived in Honolulu to retrieve the corpse.*

Returning to California with the body of Mrs. Stanford, San Francisco detectives looking into the case stated that Mrs. Stanford had died of natural causes. Case closed. One year later, Sheriff Henry intimated that one of his leading suspects in the case was David Starr Jordan himself. The true nature of the death of

Mrs. Stanford remains, however, speculation, as all biographies state simply that she died in Honolulu of natural causes.

Whether Mrs. Kassenburg was renting the Castle home called Puuhonua is also unlikely. While the orphanage in the old Manoa mansion had been closed in 1922, there is no evidence that Percy Pond rented the home out to any visiting dignitaries. The structure was used by the Pan-Pacific Union until its demolition in 1941.

The final mystery connected with this story is the presence of the "lady in white" at Makapuu. The spirit of a woman is indeed said to haunt that beach as described by McDougal. The true nature of her identity and the characteristics of her haunting, however, must await a future investigation in the Obake series.]

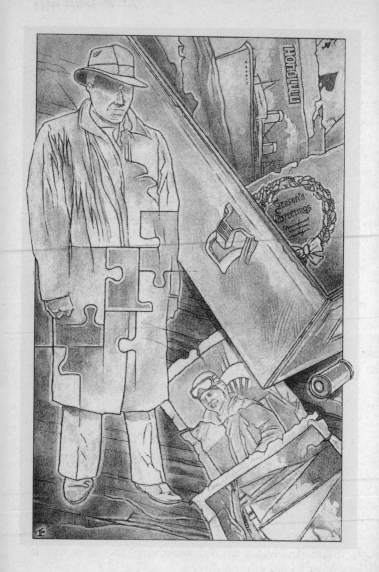

An Enigma Named McDougal

When the manuscript for *Honolulu Mysteries* was finally finished and all Ross Yamanaka's paintings given their final touches, I took the package we had worked on so long to the bedside of Art McDougal. I knew that it had been a few weeks since his last coherent emergence from a coma, but I was hoping that perhaps this day I would be lucky. Perhaps he would open his eyes and bark out his usual command, "Grant, where in the hell is my whiskey?" Then we'd share a shot of the Canadian poison he had always kept in his bottom drawer. I figured it could only kill him, and what difference would that make now?

In one of his lucid moments last month, he had ordered me to pull one of the drawers out of his dresser and get the key he had taped to the bottom a few years earlier. He instructed me that on the day he dies, the key was to be used to open an old metal box that he had kept on the closet shelf.

"Now wait till I'm dead, Grant," he would admonish me like a son. "I wouldn't want to look you in the eye again if you saw the contents of the box before I passed on."

I suppose it was wrong to open the box, considering his strong feelings against it before his death. He could linger for another year, his physician had told me. Maybe the box contained something I should include in the manuscript, I convinced myself. The puzzle of a dying human life could perhaps be explained by what the cherished box contained.

When I opened it, there was a letter addressed to me. It was in his shaky, fragile handwriting.

"Grant: Since you're reading this, I'm dead. What value does a man's life have really except to himself? You asked once if I was dirty. Maybe I was. I don't know. Can you walk in the filth without getting crap on your shoes? I like to think I was a clean cop, but that's for you to decide. The little things in this box taken together equal Art McDougal. You figure them out. Aloha, Mac."

Always the detective, he left me this final conundrum, which I have looked over a thousand times to no avail. An envelope with a little lock of jet black hair. A deck of playing cards, the ace of spades marked with a burned bullet hole. A pin from the Royal Insurance Company for Salesman of the Month. A Christmas postcard to "Little Arthur" dated December 11, 1892, from an aunt in New Jersey. A clipping from the newspaper discussing the murder of his partner Onishi in 1924. A ticket stub from an ocean liner to Tokyo. A picture of Amelia Earhart. A scrawled thank-you note signed by "FDR." A brief farewell note from a woman named Jay Ann. A faded photograph of a sailing boat. A business card from the Honolulu International Detective Agency with the home number of Arthur McDuffie written on the back. And an empty shell casing from a .38 caliber pistol.

I wondered how many of the items in the box were genuinely collected from this gumshoe's life, and how many, if any, were forgeries. He was my own personal relic of a bygone era and, like his mysterious friend in San Francisco, I wanted to keep him alive forever. I felt perhaps safer if he was still around, ready to take on the next thug that shattered our peaceful world. His breath gently became heavy as we waited for the Big Sleep. I fingered the small items collected from a man's life, feeling puny and helpless to face the mysteries this noble, flawed spirit now waited to embrace.

GLOSSARY

a'a • lava

akamai • smart, clever, expert

aumakua • family or personal god

bolo head • baldheaded

furo • Japanese hot bath, bathhouse

haole • white person, American, Englishman, Caucasian

hapai • pregnant

haupia • pudding formerly made of arrowroot and coconut cream

hui • club, association, society, corporation, firm, partnership

imu • underground oven

kahuna • priest, minister, sorcerer, expert in any profession

kama'aina • native-born, one born in a place, host

kanaka • human being, man, Hawaiian

kolohe • mischievous, naughty, rascal, mischief-maker

kukae • excreta

kuleana • right, title, property, responsibility, jurisdiction

lepo • dirt, earth, ground, filth, excrement

lo'i • irrigated terrace, especially for taro

lolo • paralyzed, numb; feeble-minded

lua • toilet, outhouse

luna • foreman, boss, overseer

mahu • homosexual of either sex

make • die; dead

malihini • stranger, newcomer, guest

malo • male's loincloth

manapua • Chinese dumpling

mano • shark, general name

mauka • inland

okole • buttocks

okolehao • liquor distilled from ti root in a still of the same name; later a gin as made of rice or pineapple juices

o'o • digging stick

pake • China; Chinese

paniolo • cowboy

pau • finished, ended, completed, over, all done

pau hana • finished work

pilau • rot, stench, rottenness; to stink; putrid, soiled, rotten

pilikia • trouble of any kind, great or small; tragedy, nuisance, bother, distress

pipikaula • beef salted and dried in the sun, broiled before eaten

pule anaana • black magic, evil sorcery; to practice this

rot gut • raw, inferior liquor (slang)

sukoshi • a little big (Japanese)

tutukane • grandfather

wahine • woman, lady, wife

wikiwiki • fast, hurry

About the Author

Glen Grant is widely known as Hawai'i's foremost storyteller, a raconteur of ghost stories and historical tales drawn from our rich multicultural island heritage. Through his popular walking tours and theater programs offered by Honolulu TimeWalks, he has introduced thousands of islanders and visitors to the men and women from Hawai'i's past whose colorful and sometimes controversial lives have helped shape our community's unique identity.

In OBAKE: *Ghost Stories in Hawai'i*, Grant created in 1994 a best-selling collection of supernatural tales that captured the imagination and interest of thousands of island residents. With *Honolulu Mysteries*, he moves in new directions with the detective genre, introducing the mysterious Arthur McDougal, a private gumshoe from the era of Charlie Chan's Honolulu. Drawn from actual historical cases, mixed with supernatural overtones and linked to characters both real and fictional, *Honolulu Mysteries* creates a truly original portrait of a town that Grant has come to know and love through archives, history books and regularly "beating its pavement."

Born into the Los Angeles of Raymond Chandler's Philip Marlowe, Grant moved to Hawai'i in 1970 where he studied and taught at the University of Hawai'i in the American Studies Department. After receiving his doctorate in American Studies, he worked with the Mission Houses Museum and Kapiolani Community College, pioneering "living history" presentations and tours in Hawai'i and helping to initiate the Interpret Hawai'i statewide visitor industry cultural training programs. Since 1992 he has taught at Tokai International College while working with Honolulu TimeWalks. He is also the author of *From the Skies of Paradise: Oahu*; *From the Skies of Paradise: The Big Island of Hawai'i*; *Hawai'i, The Big Island: A Visit to a Realm of Beauty, History and Fire*; and is co-author of *Ellison S. Onizuka: A Remembrance*. Other than his involvement with Arthur McDougal, he stresses, he has no other affiliation with the world of law enforcement or private investigation.